T0387238

Resource Accounting for Sustainability Assessment

The demands placed on land, water, energy and other natural resources are exacerbated as the world population continues to increase together with the expectations of economic growth. This, combined with concerns over environmental change, presents a set of scientific, policy and management issues that are critical for sustainability.

Resource Accounting for Sustainability Assessment: The nexus between energy, food, water and land use offers an approach for multi-scale, integrated assessment of this nexus. It presents a comprehensive and original method of resource accounting for integrated sustainability assessments. The approach is illustrated with three detailed case studies: the islands of Mauritius, the Indian state of Punjab, and the energy economy of South Africa. The relationship between flows of goods, services and materials in these case studies offer valuable insights. The book provides a much needed quality control on the information used in deliberative processes about policy and planning activities.

This innovative book will be of interest to researchers, students and practitioners in the fields of sustainability science, international development, industrial ecology, sustainable resource management, geography and ecological economics.

Mario Giampietro is ICREA Research Professor at the Institute of Environmental Science and Technology (ICTA), Autonomous University of Barcelona, Spain.

Richard J. Aspinall is Honorary Research Fellow at the James Hutton Institute and Honorary Professor, School of Geosciences, University of Aberdeen, UK.

Jesus Ramos-Martin is Assistant Professor at the Department of Economics and Economic History, Autonomous University of Barcelona, Spain.

Sandra G.F. Bukkens is a Research Assistant at the Institute of Environmental Science and Technology (ICTA), Autonomous University of Barcelona, Spain.

This is a cohesive book taking on different facets of a unified issue. And what an issue it is; huge, daunting, and something we all knew must be done. But nobody else had the vision and courage to take it on. It is metabolism applied to ecology and society; it is post-normal science in action. Anyone wishing to address metabolism of biology, ecology and society simply must get on top of this work, or just be left behind in the muddle that was heretofore mistaken as acceptable. There are no excuses now.

Timothy F. H. Allen, *University of Madison, USA*

In order to widen horizons and make firm steps towards a new paradigm for resource analysis, a biophysically based approach to prospective studies is fundamental to expose myths constructed under the dominant chrematistic framework. This book is not only oriented to foster debate within academia but especially to guide decision making in public policy truthfully committed and concerned with the future of our civilization. For these reasons I fully recommend the reader to immerse in the contents of this book.

Andrés Arauz, *Vice Minister of Planning and Development for Well Living, Ecuador*

This book shows the need for a non-reductionist approach to biophysical sustainability, and how to accomplish this through a multi-scale characterization. It crosses numerous disciplines and accomplishes a rigorous and comprehensive analysis of sustainability. The result is a *tour de force*.

Joseph A. Tainter, *Utah State University, USA*

Understanding the relationships between water, land use, energy and food is a core sustainability challenge. These relationships depend on geography, population, and economic and social conditions. Extended case studies from South Africa, Mauritius and Punjab show how decisions must vary among locations and demonstrate an approach for understanding sustainable futures. This book provides students, researchers and policy makers with a framework and guide for considering sustainable development choices.

Valerie Thomas, *Georgia Institute of Technology, USA*

Routledge Explorations in Sustainability and Governance

Resource Accounting for Sustainability Assessment
The nexus between energy, food, water and land use
Edited by Mario Giampietro, Richard J. Aspinall, Jesus Ramos-Martin, and Sandra G.F. Bukkens

Resource Accounting for Sustainability Assessment

The nexus between energy, food, water and land use

Edited by Mario Giampietro, Richard J. Aspinall, Jesus Ramos-Martin, and Sandra G.F. Bukkens

LONDON AND NEW YORK

First published 2014
by Routledge
2 Park Square, Milton Park, Abingdon, Oxon, OX14 4RN

and by Routledge
711 Third Avenue, New York, NY 10017

Routledge is an imprint of the Taylor & Francis Group, an informa business

British Library Cataloguing in Publication Data
A catalogue record for this book is available from the British Library

Library of Congress Cataloging-in-Publication Data
Resource accounting for sustainability assessment : the nexus between energy, food, water and land use / edited by Mario Giampietro, Richard J. Aspinall, Jesus Ramos-Martin, and Sandra G.F. Bukkens.
pages cm — (Routledge explorations in sustainability and governance)
Includes bibliographical references and index.
1. Natural resources—Accounting. 2. Sustainable development.
I. Giampietro, M. (Mario), editor of compilation.
HF5686.N3R46 2014
333.7—dc23
2013045367

ISBN13: 978-0-415-72059-5 (hbk)
ISBN13: 978-1-315-86689-5 (ebk)

Typeset in Times New Roman by
Swales & Willis Ltd, Exeter, Devon, UK

To Olga, Sofia, Nadia, Zoe, Ariadna, Genevieve and Léonard

Hoping that when they have grown up science will have finally come to terms with the fact that we are guests of nature

Contents

Illustrations

Figures

Tables

Contributors

Richard J. Aspinall is Honorary Research Fellow at the James Hutton Institute and Honorary Professor, School of Geosciences, University of Aberdeen, UK. Previously he was Chief Executive and Director of the Macaulay Land Use Research Institute, Aberdeen, UK. His research is in land systems, sustainability science, environmental change, and the use of interdisciplinary approaches for analysis of coupled human–environment systems. His methodological expertise is in GIS, remote sensing, and spatial statistics and analysis. He has held posts in both the UK and the USA, and was also involved in the scientific direction and management of the Global Land Project from 2005 to 2011. He is Editor of the *Journal of Land Use Science*.

Sandra G.F. Bukkens is an agricultural engineer specialized in human nutrition and food systems. Her research interests cover human metabolism and the characterization of sustainability and performance of food systems in relation to different dimensions of analysis. She is a Research Assistant at the Institute of Environmental Science and Technology (ICTA) of the Autonomous University of Barcelona (UAB), Spain.

Juan José Cadillo-Benalcazar is a biologist with a research interest in the role of water and food in the socio-economic development of society. He is presently working on the application of Multi-Scale Integrated Analysis of Societal and Ecosystem Metabolism (MuSIASEM) to water use in Lima Metropolitana, Peru. He holds an M.Sc. in Soil and Water Management and is presently a Ph.D. candidate at the Institute of Environmental Science and Technology (ICTA) of the Autonomous University of Barcelona (UAB), Spain.

François Diaz-Maurin is a Post-Doctoral Researcher at the Institute of Environmental Science and Technology (ICTA) of the Autonomous University of Barcelona (UAB), Spain, and works on the application of Multi-Scale Integrated Analysis of Societal and Ecosystem Metabolism (MuSIASEM) to energy supply issues. He joined the Integrated Assessment research group of ICTA-UAB with four years of prior experience as an engineer in the French and US nuclear industries. He serves as Review Editor of the journal *Frontiers in Energy Research* (Nature Publishing Group).

Mario Giampietro is ICREA Research Professor at the Institute of Environmental Science and Technology (ICTA) of the Autonomous University of Barcelona (UAB), Spain. He is an expert in energy analysis and integrated assessment of sustainability issues, and the 'father' of the innovative scientific approach Multi-Scale Integrated Analysis of Societal and Ecosystem Metabolism (MuSIASEM). He has more than 150 scientific publications and is the author of several books.

Tiziano Gomiero is a Post-Doctoral Researcher at the Institute of Environmental Science and Technology (ICTA) of the Autonomous University of Barcelona (UAB), Spain. His main interests are integrated farming and food system analysis, rural development, organic farming, and biodiversity and environmental conservation. On these topics, he has worked in various international projects in both Europe and Asia. He holds an M.Sc. in Nature Science form the Università di Padova, Italy, an M.Sc. in Ecological Economics and Environmental Management and a Ph.D. in Environmental Science from the UAB.

Zora Kovacic is a Ph.D. candidate at the Institute of Environmental Science and Technology (ICTA) of the Autonomous University of Barcelona (UAB), Spain. Her research focuses on the analysis of the process of production and use of scientific knowledge for governance in the context of high uncertainty and the existence of a plurality of legitimate worldviews. Her research interests also include the analysis of the relationship between socio-economic variables and the biophysical characterization of human systems. Her background is in Economics and Development Studies, and Environmental Science.

Pedro L. Lomas is a Researcher at the Institute of Environmental Science and Technology (ICTA) of the Autonomous University of Barcelona (UAB), Spain. He is an environmental natural scientist whose work is mainly focused on the study of coupled human–nature systems through the integrated assessment of social and ecosystem metabolism for sustainability from a biophysical point of view, by applying concepts from thermodynamics, energetics, systems ecology and complex systems theory.

Cristina Madrid-Lopez is a Ph.D. candidate at the Institute of Environmental Science and Technology (ICTA) of the Autonomous University of Barcelona (UAB), Spain. Her research deals with the water-related interaction between human and natural systems, including the nexus between water and other resources, with the aim of building a methodological framework for integrated water resources management. She has been a Visiting Researcher at King's College London and the Water Footprint Network, and has led the development of Multi-Scale Integrated Analysis of Societal and Ecosystem Metabolism (MuSIASEM) for Water.

Jesus Ramos-Martin (Economist, Ph.D. Environmental Sciences) is an ecological economist with expertise in the field of economic development and evolution of human systems from a biophysical point of view, by applying concepts from energy analysis, thermodynamics and complex systems theory. He is Assistant Professor at the Department of Economics and Economic History, and researcher at the Institute for Environmental Science and Technology (ICTA) at the Autonomous University of Barcelona (UAB), Spain.

Tarik Serrano-Tovar is a Ph.D. candidate at the Institute of Environmental Science and Technology (ICTA) of the Autonomous University of Barcelona (UAB), Spain. His research interest is in the integration of geographic information systems (GIS) and multi-scaling properties into the scientific representation proposed by Multi-Scale Integrated Analysis of Societal and Ecosystem Metabolism (MuSIASEM), and in the application of integrated analytical approaches to rural systems and energy networks. He has experience working on rural systems, with cases in South India, Laos and Guatemala, and has been working at the Pennsylvania State University on an analysis of US energy consumption patterns.

Acknowledgements

Mario Giampietro gratefully acknowledges the financial support provided by the Catalan Institute of Research and Advanced Studies (ICREA), and by the Government of Catalonia (AGAUR: SGR2009–594) for his research group 'Integrated Assessment: Sociology, Technology and the Environment' (IASTE) at the Universitat Autònoma de Barcelona.

We also acknowledge the financial support by the Deutsche Gesellschaft für Internationale Zusammenarbeit (GIZ) to the scientific organization LIPHE4 for an exploratory project on the application of MuSIASEM to the analysis of the nexus.

We are thankful to Oliver Dubois for encouraging the idea of integrating the analyses of the metabolic patterns of energy, food and water into a nexus assessment. Additional thanks are due to Kozo Mayumi, Alevgul Sorman, Raul Velasco, Alessandro Flammini and Emilio Vanni.

Abbreviations

AG	agricultural (and fishing) sector
BEP	bioeconomic pressure
BM	building and manufacturing sector
BP	British Petroleum
CAP	Common Agricultural Policy
CL	capacity load
CSP	concentrated solar power
CWR	crop water requirement
DEM	digital elevation model
EC	energy carrier
EI	energy intensity
EIA	Energy Information Administration
ELP	economic labour productivity
EM	energy and mining sector
EMR	exosomatic metabolic rate
EPL	exosomatic power level
EROI	energy return on investment
ET	energy throughput
EU	European Union
EvT	evapotranspiration
EWR	ecosystem water recharge
FAO	Food and Agriculture Organization of the United Nations
FISIM	financial intermediation services indirectly measured
GDP	gross domestic product
GDSP	gross domestic state product
GER	gross energy requirement
GHG	greenhouse gas
GIS	geographic information system
GoI	Government of India
GoP	Government of Punjab
GPP	gross primary productivity
GPS	global positioning system
GSEC	gross supply of energy carriers

GVA	gross value added
GW	ground water
GWR	gross water requirement
GWU	gross water use
HA	human activity
HEIA	high-external-input agriculture
HH	household sector
HLW	high-level (radioactive) waste
IEA	International Energy Agency
ILO	International Labour Organization
IPC	intensity of power capacity
LCLUC	Land-Cover/Land-Use Change (NASA programme)
LEIA	low-external-input agriculture
LU	land use
LUCC	Land Use and Cover Change (IGBP/IHDP programme)
MEA	Millennium Ecosystem Assessment
ML	managed land
MSP	minimum support price
MuSIASEM	Multi-Scale Integrated Analysis of Societal and Ecosystem Metabolism
NFS	net food supply
NPP	net primary production
NSEC	net supply(/consumption) of energy carriers
NWU	net water use
OL	operation load
PAWF	plant active water flow
PC	power capacity
PECM	physical energy content method
PES	primary energy source
PF	primary flows sector
PS	(primary and secondary) production sector(s)
PSM	partial substitution method
PW	paid work sector
REU	requirement of end use
REUD	requirement of end use in the dissipative compartment
SA	societal average
SAS	societal appropriation of soil
SAW	societal appropriation of water
SB	standing biomass
SEH	strength of the exosomatic hypercycle
SES	socio-ecological system
SG	service and government sector
SI	international system of units
SSA	Statistics South Africa
SW	surface water
TET	total energy throughput

TFT	total food throughput
THA	total human activity
TML	total managed land
TPC	total power capacity
TPES	total primary energy supply
TR	transport sector
UF	utilization factor
WB	World Bank
WMD	water metabolic density
WMR	water metabolic rate
WS	society as a whole

Units

EJ	exajoule (10^{18} joule)
GJ	gigajoule (10^{9} joule)
GW	gigawatt (10^{9} watt)
h	hour
ha	hectare
hm^3	cubic hectometre
hp	horsepower
J	joule
kg	kilogram
kt	kilotonne (10^{3} tonne)
kW	kilowatt (10^{3} watt)
MJ	megajoule (10^{6} joule)
m/s	metres/second
MT	megatonne (10^{6} tonne)
Mtoe	megatonne of oil equivalent (10^{6} toe)
MW	megawatt (10^{6} watt)
PJ	petajoule (10^{15} joule)
tce	tonne of coal equivalent
TJ	terajoule (10^{12} joule)
toe	tonne of oil equivalent
W	watt
Wh	watt-hour
W/m^2	watt per square metre
yr	year

1 Addressing the complexity of integrated resource assessment

Mario Giampietro, Richard J. Aspinall, Jesus Ramos-Martin and Sandra G.F. Bukkens

Summary

This chapter introduces the nexus of food, water and energy security, and links this with: land use and environmental quality; population growth and demographics; economies and wealth; and socio-economic and environmental systems. The chapter also outlines the structure of the book, emphasizing the different elements of a multi-scale assessment of the nexus of land, water, food, energy, population and economies considered as a series of interdependent metabolic systems.

1.1 Introduction: the food, water, energy, land and population nexus

International and national concerns over food, water and energy security, and the growing demands placed on land and other natural resources by global population increase and climate and other environmental changes present a nexus of issues (Beddington 2010) that are attracting an increasing level of scientific enquiry (Godfray *et al.* 2010) and attention from policy makers (Pretty *et al.* 2010; Foresight, 2011).[1] Provision of food and food security against a background of increasing demands for energy, increasing demands for water (Hanjra and Qureshi 2010), multiple uses of land (Foley *et al.* 2005), and declining quality and function of natural resources (Millennium Ecosystem Assessment 2005) remains a critical international priority. Many food, water and energy security issues are associated with inequalities in resource distribution and access (Ingram *et al.* 2010), but other fundamental reasons are related to the total amount of food, water and energy available, to drivers of land change, and to the management of resources.

Each of the component systems of the food–water–energy–land nexus presents a range of scientific challenges and has been subject to considerable research. However, the *systems-level interactions* of food, water, energy and land systems demand additional and focused insights based on novel scientific approaches. These approaches must be able to address the integrative, adaptive, hierarchical, complex and multi-scale nature of interdependencies between the different elements of the nexus, and the dynamics of their interactions encapsulated in their interacting requirements and metabolisms; such an assessment remains a grand challenge for research and an urgent priority need for policy and decision making.

This book brings food, water, energy and land systems together with environment, economics and wealth, and population growth and demographics, within a multi-scale accounting framework.

The goals of this integration and accounting framework are to develop:

- an inter- and trans-disciplinary, scientific understanding and knowledge base of systems-level interactions and interrelationships of food, water, energy and land systems at multiple scales;
- a suite of procedures for integrated assessment and diagnostic analysis of food, water, energy and land systems and resources that is capable of operation and application at multiple spatial, temporal and organizational scales;
- a set of tools that helps to elucidate and communicate the results of diagnostic analysis and assessment at multiple scales and for particular geographic locations; and
- a set of protocols and tools for simulation and experimentation that contributes to an integrated understanding and analysis of food, water, energy and land systems, and that informs debate and progress in sustainability science, resource management, and policy making.

The methods presented cross eight boundaries:

1. between food, water, energy, and land and environment systems;
2. between spatial, temporal and organizational scales;
3. between environmental, economic and social systems;
4. between scientific disciplines and epistemologies;
5. between science and policy;
6. between scientific understanding and governance;
7. between scientists and other communities; and
8. between the challenges presented by real-world, real-time, local–national–global scale problems and the limitations of reductionist approaches to science.

1.2 The food, water, energy, land and population nexus as a complex systems problem in sustainability science

Over the last few years there has been an increase in academic interest in the nexus between food, energy, water, land use and population. This interest is not only because of the individual growing importance of each of the elements, but also a result of recognition, from those working in sustainability science, that it is impossible to analyse the different elements of the nexus one at the time, as if they were independent from each other. Indeed, the very idea and description of the interface of food, energy, water, land and population as a 'nexus' emphasizes the need for integrated analysis and understanding. Addressing the nexus within sustainability science requires forms of integrated analysis that are capable of individuating and quantifying relations across different dimensions of sustainability and the interrelated systems that support sustainability of life. The nexus, as a topic for sustainability science, thus inherently presents itself as a complex system problem, with associated qualities of emergence, irreducible hierarchical continuity, contingence, and non-linear interactions and relations among inputs and outputs.

The unavoidable character of the nexus, with many different dimensions, scales and interactions relevant to sustainability, is forcing those engaged in quantitative analysis in new directions. The paradigm of reductionism, which was so effective in shaping research strategies in quantitative science in the past, is simply not suited to the task of addressing the nexus. Many generating quantitative analyses are still using tools and approaches developed within the framework of reductionism, which address one scale and one dimension at a time. In marked contrast, sustainability science requires that different dimensions of analysis and different scales are handled simultaneously, something which is out of the reach of reductionist approaches. New narratives which make new conceptualizations possible are required in order to develop more useful perceptions and representations of the sustainability predicament. This is where the issue of complexity enters: after decades of segregation of research in centres that study complexity, and theoretical discussions about the definition of the term 'complexity', the challenges of addressing science and policy related to the nexus of food, energy, water, land use and environment demand application of the new generation of theoretical concepts developed within complexity science to analyse and address the practical applications and implications of food, water, energy and environmental security, global changes and population growth. These concepts, briefly discussed in Part I of the book, include: *complex adaptive systems* (Holland 1995; Cilliers 1998); *autopoietic systems* (Maturana and Varela 1980, 1998); *metabolic networks self-organized through informed autocatalytic loops* (H.T. Odum 1971, 1996); *ecosystems' dynamics and resilience* (Holling 1973); *ascendancy* and the distinction between the *hypercyclic and dissipative part* of a system (Ulanowicz 1986, 1997); *ecosystem health and integrity* (Kay *et al.* 1999; Kay and Regier 2000; Ulanowicz 1995); *reflexivity of self-organizing systems* (Rosen 1985); *holarchies* (Koestler 1969); the *modelling relation* (Rosen 1985, 2000); *punctuated equilibrium* (Eldredge and Gould 1972; Gould 1992); and *hierarchy theory* (Simon 1962; Whyte *et al.* 1969; Allen and Starr 1982; Allen and Hoekstra 1992; Ahl and Allen 1996). A more detailed discussion of the relation between these concepts and the development of a conceptual framework for multi-level and multi-dimensional analysis of sustainability is available in Giampietro *et al.* (2012, 2013).

1.3 This book

This book presents an innovative approach to quantitative analysis capable of generating results based on insights derived from complexity science. The work presented is a considerable expansion of previous work on multi-scale and multi-dimensional analysis that was aimed at integrating quantitative characterizations of socio-economic, biophysical and ecological processes (Giampietro and

Mayumi 2000a, 2000b; Giampietro 2004; Giampietro *et al.* 2009). For discussions of the benefits of complexity science compared with more traditional reductionist approaches readers are referred to works by Kauffman, Allen, Ulanowicz and others (Ulanowicz 1979, 2004; Kauffman 1993; Allen *et al.* 2003).

Applying multi-scale, multi-dimensional integrated analysis to the challenges associated with the nexus requires developing the theory and toolkit to the diverse and non-equivalent domains of quantitative accounts and metabolic flows for food, energy and water. Additionally, this has to be done in relation both to land systems (representing both land use and concepts and issues of natural capital) and to key relevant socio-economic characteristics (demographics, economic structure, imports and exports). Three case studies provide a test of the approach, using available datasets and real-world systems.

Part of the work for this book was originally carried out in an exploratory project developed with the Energy Group of the Climate, Energy and Tenure Division (NRC) of the UN Food and Agriculture Organization (FAO) and sponsored by the Deutsche Gesellschaft für Internationale Zusammenarbeit (GIZ). In that project we were asked to illustrate the possibility of applying the approach, known as MuSIASEM, originally developed for food (Giampietro 2004) and energy (Giampietro *et al.* 2009, 2012, 2013; Ramos-Martin *et al.* 2009), and subsequently expanded to water (Madrid *et al.* 2013), to the integrated analysis of different flows simultaneously, to explore the nexus. For this reason, the book does not present actual 'scientific results' as quantitative analysis and scenarios to be used for decision making. Rather, it focuses on illustrating the basic concepts and the practical tools through which our innovative accounting method can be applied. The book shares our practical solutions developed and applied to achieve an integrated accounting of food, energy and water in land and socio-economic systems.

1.4 The structure of the book

The book is organized in three parts (after this chapter) (see Figure 1.1).

Part I: Theory

Chapter 2 presents an overview of the MuSIASEM approach, describing what it is about and how it works. The chapter shows that both the conceptualization of the nexus (based on the concept of metabolic patterns) and the formalization of the quantitative analysis (based on multi-level grammars) are based on innovative concepts interfacing semantic framing with flexible methods of formalization that can be tailored across scales and dimensions.

Chapter 3 presents the basic theoretical concepts behind the chosen scientific narrative of metabolic patterns. This chapter emphasizes that the concept of metabolism, nowadays very popular in sustainability science, is not just another buzz-word. Rather it is a very robust scientific narrative that is needed for conceptualizing the nature and the functioning of complex self-organizing systems.

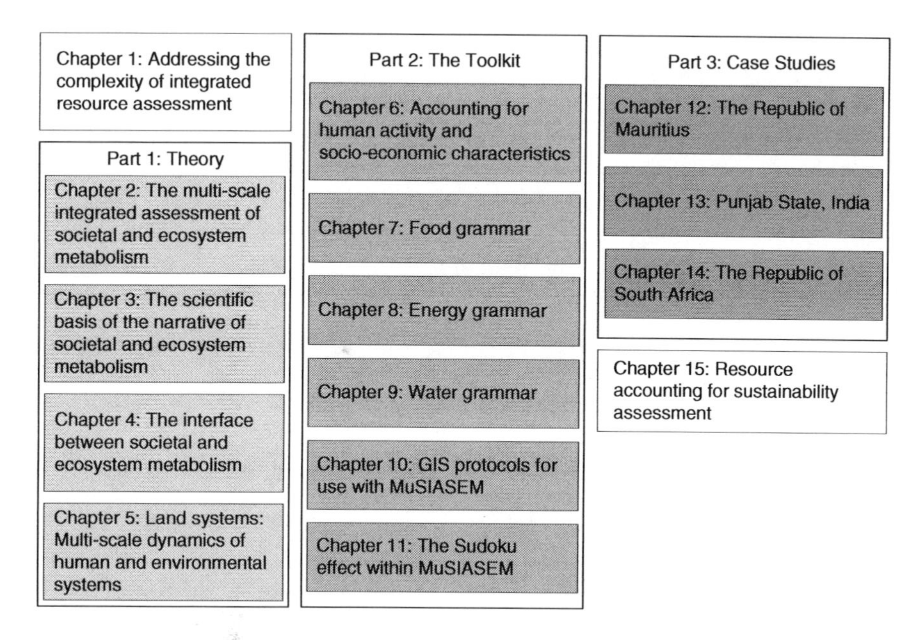

Figure 1.1 Schematic illustration of the structure of the book

Chapter 4 presents the basic theoretical concepts behind the chosen accounting method. The flow–fund model, proposed by Georgescu-Roegen for biophysical analysis of the economic process, is the approach used for handling quantitative information referring to different dimensions and different scales. The chapter presents the basic approach and its applications to the analysis of the interface between societal and ecosystem metabolism.

Chapter 5 provides a general overview of the nature and functioning of land systems in the context of a multi-scale representation and analysis of coupled human–environment systems. Links to resource accounting and the operation of the multi-scale integrated assessment procedure are through a variety of mechanisms, including natural capital as a dimension of land systems.

Part II: The toolkit

Chapter 6 presents an overview of the grammar used to interface demographic and socio-economic characteristics (determining the profile of allocation of the fund human activity) and monetary flows across the various compartments of the society. This grammar is essential in order to contextualize the biophysical information provided by the other grammars, which describe the metabolic flows food, energy and water. Quantitative examples from the case studies presented in Part III are used to illustrate the grammar.

Chapter 7 presents an overview of the grammar used to analyse the metabolic pattern of food. This combines an external view (the supply of a given mix of food products) and an internal view (the requirement for a given mix of nutrients). This grammar addresses the non-linearity between the food energy input (contained in the gross production of food products) and food energy output (nutrient intake in the diet) owing to an internal autocatalytic loop of food energy (feed, eggs, seeds) used to generate food energy. The grammar provides several categories for quantitative accounting that can be used to study the feasibility (compatibility with external constraints), viability (compatibility with internal constraints) and desirability (compatibility with human expectations). Quantitative examples from the case studies in Part III are used to illustrate the grammar.

Chapter 8 presents an overview of the grammar used to analyse the metabolic pattern of energy. This includes an external view (the supply of a given mix of primary energy sources) and an internal view (the requirement of a given mix of energy carriers). This grammar addresses the non-linearity between the primary energy input (contained in the gross supply of primary energy sources) and secondary energy output (energy carriers consumed in end uses) owing to an internal autocatalytic loop of energy (e.g. oil, coal, nuclear, wind) used to generate electricity accounted for usually within the energy sector. The grammar provides several categories for quantitative accounting that can be used to study the feasibility (compatibility with external constraints), viability (compatibility with internal constraints) and desirability (compatibility with human expectations). Quantitative examples from the case studies in Part III are used to illustrate the grammar.

Chapter 9 presents an overview of the grammar used to analyse the metabolic pattern of water. This combines an external view (the supply of a given mix of water funds – soil water, ground water, surface water) and an internal view (the requirement of a given mix of water end uses that are guaranteed by different typologies of water supply, e.g. underground, surface, soil water). This grammar makes it possible to carry out the feasibility check (compatibility with external constraints) in spatial terms, moving across different scales of analysis. Quantitative examples from the case studies are used to illustrate the grammar.

Chapter 10 presents a set of protocols for the use of GIS as part of MuSIASEM. One focus of the use of GIS is the quantitative analysis based in MuSIASEM's multi-level tables; GIS can provide input to these tables. GIS can also provide other data and insights that complement MuSIASEM, not least communication via maps. Quantitative examples from the case studies are used to illustrate the protocols.

Chapter 11 presents key features of the MuSIASEM quantitative approach in the multi-scale, multi-dimensional integration of food, energy, water, land and environment, population and economy. The quantitative information generated by the various grammars is combined within multi-level tables, and it is then possible to generate a 'Sudoku effect' that registers and respects the multi-scale interdependencies between food, energy and water metabolisms, land, population and economy. The accounting tables are used in two ways: in diagnostic mode and in simulation mode.

Use of the MuSIASEM tables in diagnostic mode represents the characteristics of an existing metabolic pattern. The MuSIASEM tables reveal the metabolic characteristics of the system at multiple scales. This includes quantitative characteristics at lower-level elements, observable only at the local scale, through scaling up to describe whole compartments, and then, through further scaling up, to characterize the whole society. With this multi-scale structure, the complex information space defined by the multi-level tables is richly informative of internal system relationships and interactions.

Following this diagnostic use of MuSIASEM, the approach can be used in simulation mode. Values of the various elements of the multi-level table are subject to a 'Sudoku effect' that defines the congruence of interactions between food, energy, water, land and human activity, simultaneously at multiple scales. That is, when we consider scenarios, the numbers placed in the multi-level tables have to go through a series of congruence checks that conform to interactions of the flows and funds of the different system components, defined through the grammars. The expected characteristics at the local scale must give results that are congruent with the expected characteristics at the large scale, obtained by applying the production rules determined by the grammars (Chapters 6–9) and by the organization of the multi-level tables.

Part III: Case studies

Three exemplar analyses are presented. Although these are based on data for the respective study areas, they should not be used for policy analysis. We recommend that MuSIASEM is used within a participatory approach (e.g. sustainable livelihoods, ecosystem approach, participatory GIS), with relevant communities and institutions involved as appropriate. The case studies give worked examples, based on the theory (Part I) and using the toolkit (Part II), and give concrete examples of the implementation and application of the integrated accounting system.

Chapter 12 presents examples of the results obtained in the Mauritius case study. This case study has been chosen to provide a detailed example of an application of the MuSIASEM toolkit, in which the analysis of the flows is also carried out in GIS, both in the diagnostic mode (to characterize the actual metabolic pattern of the island across scales and dimensions in relation to the nexus) and in the simulation mode (to check the feasibility, viability and desirability of possible scenarios).

Chapter 13 presents examples of the results obtained in the Punjab case study. This case study has been chosen to provide an example of an application of the MuSIASEM approach to the analysis of the link between socio-economic characteristics of the context of agricultural production (observed at different levels – international markets, India, Punjab and the rural households) and the indicators of environmental loading associated with agricultural production in rural areas (overdrafting of water for irrigation). This analysis shows the crucial role that cheap electricity (due to subsidies) plays in this situation.

Chapter 14 presents examples of the results obtained in the South Africa case study. This case study has been chosen to provide an example of an application of the MuSIASEM approach to the assessment of the feasibility and viability of alternative energy sources. More specifically the characteristics of two potential alternative primary energy sources (concentrated solar power and electricity from biomass residues) are assessed in relation to the actual characteristics of the energy sector of South Africa.

Conclusion

Chapter 15, 'Resource accounting for sustainability assessment', revisits the themes of the book in the context of the series, of which this text is the first. The development of this multi-scale, multi-dimensional accounting framework for analysis of the nexus of food, energy and water uses theory and lessons from complexity science to address a globally significant challenge for analysis in sustainability. Making the approach operational represents the birth of a quantitative post-Cartesian science that can directly address some of the most complex issues of sustainability and change that are currently faced.

Note

1 A detailed list of initiatives under the Nexus framework can be found at the Water, Energy and Food Security Resource Platform NEXUS, http://www.water-energy-food.org/.

Part I

Theory

2 The Multi-Scale Integrated Analysis of Societal and Ecosystem Metabolism

Mario Giampietro and Sandra G.F. Bukkens

Summary

This chapter presents Multi-Scale Integrated Analysis of Societal and Ecosystem Metabolism (MuSIASEM) as a tool to analyse the nexus between energy, food, water, land use, and socio-economic characteristics. MuSIASEM can be used for diagnostic and simulation purposes by checking the viability, desirability and feasibility of current and proposed metabolic patterns of society. Its application involves several steps: definition of what the system *is* in terms of fund elements (human activity, managed land, power capacity) and what it *does* in terms of flow elements (energy, food, water, monetary flows); construction of a multi-scale, multi-dimensional representation of the metabolic pattern; and checking viability and desirability in relation to internal constraints, and feasibility in relation to external constraints.

2.1 MuSIASEM as a tool to analyse the nexus between energy, food, water, land use, and socio-economic characteristics

The MuSIASEM is an innovative approach to accounting that integrates quantitative information generated by distinct types of conventional models based on different dimensions and scales of analysis. It builds on several innovative concepts derived from bioeconomics and complex systems theory, such as the flow-fund model, multi-purpose grammars and impredicative loop analysis. The application of these concepts allows the *simultaneous* use of technical, economic, social, demographic and ecological variables in the analysis of the metabolic pattern of modern societies, even if these variables are defined within different dimensions of analysis and non-equivalent descriptive domains and refer to different hierarchical levels and scales. Given this special feature, MuSIASEM allows us to effectively analyse the nexus between energy, food and water, considering heterogeneous factors such as population dynamics, greenhouse gas (GHG) emissions and land use changes at the national or sub-national level. The accounting system is able to integrate data from national statistics and/or other readily available datasets (e.g. FAO Food Balance Sheets, ILO labour statistics, BP energy statistics) with data from geographic information systems (GIS).

MuSIASEM is the result of years of research and has benefited from the ideas and contributions of many people. A detailed overview of the theoretical basis of the approach and its possible applications is available in Giampietro (2004) and Giampietro *et al.* (2012, 2013).

2.1.1 MuSIASEM as a diagnostic–simulation tool

MuSIASEM can be employed for diagnostic as well as for simulation purposes.

As a diagnostic tool, the MuSIASEM accounting system is used to characterize the existing metabolic pattern of the socio-economic system under analysis by providing integrated information on:

1 Population, work force, technological capital, managed land, and total available land (defined as *fund elements*);
2 Flows of food, energy, water and money (defined as *flow elements*). For each of these flows we define the total requirement, the fraction for internal consumption, the losses, the degree of self-sufficiency (internal supply), and imports and exports.
3 A series of flow/fund ratios characterizing the rate (per hour of human activity) and density (per hectare of managed land) of the above flows across different scales (including the whole society and each one of the lower-level compartments defined in the accounting scheme, such as the various economic sectors). These ratios are then compared against reference values (benchmarks) describing known 'types' of socio-economic systems.

As a simulation tool, MuSIASEM provides a feasibility, viability and desirability check of proposed scenarios. The approach allows us to:

1 Check the *feasibility* of proposed scenarios by looking at the compatibility of the system with the boundary conditions. These so-called *external constraints* are checked by comparing the required societal flows to both the supply and the sink side of the local interface with the environment. This analysis is obtained by characterizing the required flows (dictated by the internal characteristics of the socio-economic system) with GIS data. The MuSIASEM methodology makes it possible to generate an environmental impact matrix for this purpose.
2 Check the *viability* of proposed scenarios by looking at the internal congruence between the requirement and the supply of flows across different compartments of society. This check can be done at different scales after characterizing the rate (per hour) and the density (per hectare) of the various flows in the chosen scenarios. For example, data on consumption aggregated at the level of the whole society must give a result that is congruent with the technical coefficients (e.g. yields, productivity of production factors, requirement of specific processes) describing the supply at local scales. The

MuSIASEM methodology uses a multi-level, multi-dimensional representation for this task that generates a so-called *Sudoku effect* on the dataset. This Sudoku effect can be used to check the congruence of values across the different scales and dimensions of analysis.

3 Check the *desirability* of viable scenarios by comparing the resulting metabolic pattern (a set of flow/fund ratios) at the level of end uses (the expression of specific functions at the local scale, such as sugarcane production or public transportation) to benchmark values of the same set of flow/fund ratios (expected features of the functions to be expressed) characteristic of given types of socio-economic systems.

2.2 The basic steps of MuSIASEM

In practical terms, the MuSIASEM approach involves the following six steps:

- *Step 1: definition of the socio-economic system as a nested hierarchy of functional compartments guaranteeing survival, reproduction and adaptability*

This first step involves the definition of the nested hierarchical structure of functional compartments of society. We first define the overall system at level *n* (the identity of the system, a pre-analytical choice establishing the boundaries of the system), and then define within this 'whole' a set of lower-level functional compartments at level ($n - 1$) (e.g. household sector, paid work sector) on the basis of the functions expressed in society (e.g. reproducing human labour, generation of income).These lower-level compartments can then be further subdivided (levels $n - 2$, $n - 3$, etc.), depending on the aim of the study. The basic nested hierarchical structure used in our case studies is illustrated in Figure 2.1.

As shown in Figure 2.1, the functional compartments can be aggregated into two macro-compartments, a *hypercyclic* and a *dissipative* compartment, expressing emergent properties observable only at a larger scale. The terms *hypercyclic* and *dissipative* are derived from theoretical ecology (Ulanowicz 1986, 1997). The hypercycle is that part of a complex system (e.g. society) that drives the functioning of the entire system by generating the required flows (food, energy, water), technology and infrastructures for itself as well as for the rest of the system. The dissipative part, on the other hand, consumes the surplus of resources provided by the hypercycle and is responsible for the reproduction and adaptability of human activity, thus holding together the entire system. This distinction allows us to analyse the viability of the dynamic equilibrium of the various flows (energy, food, water) in an impredicative loop analysis (see step 5). The concept of hypercycle is explained in more detail in Chapter 8.

The selection of compartments must be practical for data collection: the data required to define both the size and the characteristics of individual compartments must be amenable to subdivisions expressed in available statistics.

The importance of selection of sub-compartments (below the $n - 1$ level) should be emphasized, as it not only allows us to single out certain aspects of

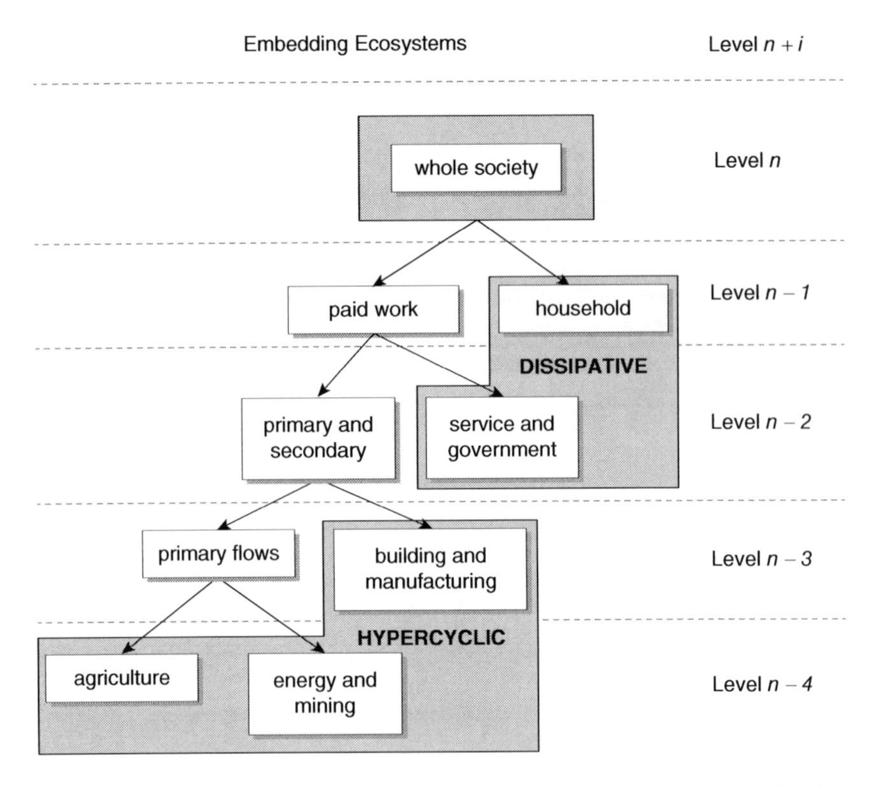

Figure 2.1 The basic nested hierarchical structure of functional compartments of society

societal functioning but also permits us to confront large-scale assessments (i.e. top-down assessments based on aggregated statistics) with local-scale assessments (i.e. bottom-up assessments based on technical coefficients observed at the local level). This double check guarantees the robustness of scenario analysis of metabolic patterns given that at all times the characteristics of the whole and the main compartments observed at the larger scale must be compatible with those of the sub-compartments and lower-level elements observed at the local scale.

Given that the functional compartments are made of structural elements (fund elements, such as human activity, managed land and power capacity) that can be observed and measured at the local scale, their size can be quantified. For example, total human activity (the total hours of human activity per year associated with a given population size, defined as population × 8,760) provides a quantitative assessment of the size of society in relation to the socio-economic perspective. Total managed land (the hectares of managed land associated with the activities of the population) provides a quantitative assessment of the size of society in relation to the ecological perspective. The definition of the compartment sizes (expressed either in hours of human activity or in hectares of managed land) must provide closure at all levels. Thus, at any one level, the set of compartments must be collectively exhaustive and mutually exclusive. In simpler terms this means that the sum of the sizes of the lower-level parts (level $i-1$) must equal the size of its immediate upper-level compartment (i) for any level i.

- *Step 2: definition and quantification of the profile of investment of fund elements over the functional compartments of the system (defining dendrograms of fund elements)*

This step involves the selection of relevant fund elements and their allocation to the various functional compartments of the system. In the case studies (Chapters 12–14), we consider three fund elements, human activity (human time), managed land, and power capacity (technical capital). Human activity is our key fund element for socio-economic analysis, on which we base the definition and the size of functional compartments (see Chapter 6).

Step 2 typically results in the generation of *dendrograms* in which the total amounts of fund elements (referring to the whole society on a year basis) are repeatedly split up as we move further down the nested hierarchical structure. An example of fund dendrograms is shown on the right-hand side of Figure 2.2. This series of splits is used to characterize the relative sizes of the different lower-level compartments in terms of the three fund elements of human activity (HA), managed land (ML) and power capacity (PC). Note that the first bifurcation (α) for human activity depends on a demographic variable (the dependency ratio) and socio-economic variables (work load, length of education, retirement age, absence, unemployment), while the branching within the paid work sectors (β, γ, δ) depends on the characteristics of the economy. Clearly the depth of the dendrogram depends on the goal of the study and the availability of data for the fund element in question.

- *Step 3: quantitative definition of the flows required for expressing the functions (defining dendrograms of flow elements)*

This step involves the definition and quantification of the various flows (food, energy, water, money) used by the selected fund elements (human activity, managed land, power capacity) associated with the functional compartments at different levels of analysis. Examples of flow dendrograms are shown on the left side of Figure 2.2. The bifurcations of the various flows shown are derived from 'grammars'. Within our approach, a grammar can be seen as a formal system of rules for accounting for metabolic flows. We have developed specific grammars for food, energy, water, and monetary flows. These grammars identify and characterize the respective flows across the various compartments of society in terms of both quantity and quality. They are presented in detail in Part II of this book (see, for example, Figures 7.2, 8.1 and 9.1).

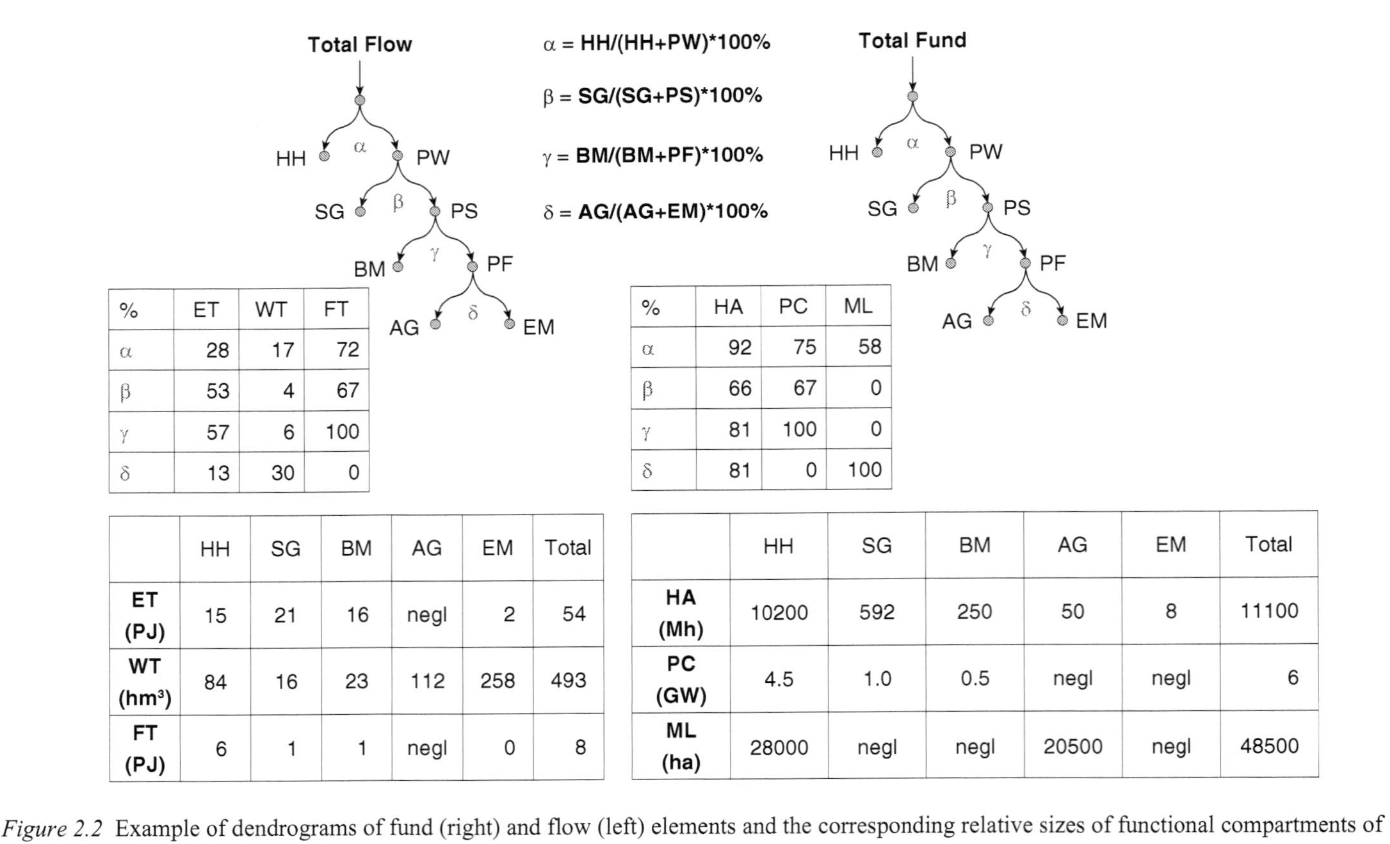

%	ET	WT	FT
α	28	17	72
β	53	4	67
γ	57	6	100
δ	13	30	0

%	HA	PC	ML
α	92	75	58
β	66	67	0
γ	81	100	0
δ	81	0	100

	HH	SG	BM	AG	EM	Total
ET (PJ)	15	21	16	negl	2	54
WT (hm^3)	84	16	23	112	258	493
FT (PJ)	6	1	1	negl	0	8

	HH	SG	BM	AG	EM	Total
HA (Mh)	10200	592	250	50	8	11100
PC (GW)	4.5	1.0	0.5	negl	negl	6
ML (ha)	28000	negl	negl	20500	negl	48500

Figure 2.2 Example of dendrograms of fund (right) and flow (left) elements and the corresponding relative sizes of functional compartments of society

Note: Fund elements include human activity (HA), power capacity (PC) and managed land (ML); flow elements include energy (ET = energy throughput), food (FT = food throughput) and water (WT = water throughput).

Four pieces of information referring to two non-equivalent views of the metabolic pattern are essential to the construction of these grammars:

i *Gross supply or required flows from the context:* This is the overall flow that must be produced locally or made available through imports. It refers to the *external perception* of the societal throughput flow, for example requirements for primary agricultural products (e.g. beef, grains, vegetables), requirements for primary energy sources (e.g. coal, uranium, wind), and requirements for water funds (e.g. rivers, aquifers) from which the needed supply of water can be extracted. This flow is assessed with an accounting method that allows for a check on external constraints.
ii *Flows for internal end uses:* This is the set of flows going through the various functional compartments to guarantee final uses. It refers to the *internal view* of the throughput flow, for example requirements for nutrient carriers (e.g. proteins, carbohydrates, fats), requirements for energy carriers (e.g. electricity, fuels and process heat), and requirements for water supply by categories of end use (e.g. drinkable, for irrigation, for cooling). The characteristics of these end uses are defined by the grammars in both quantity and quality.
iii *Losses determining the difference between gross and net supply for internal end uses:* This is the fraction of the gross supply flow that does not make it to final consumption because it is lost in the network. It is assessed from the internal point of view.
iv *Internal autocatalytic investment determining the disposable supply for the dissipative compartment:* This is the share of the flows that must be invested in their own production. This assessment can be carried out only from the internal viewpoint. This information specifically concerns the metabolic pattern of energy and food, where a fraction of the net supply is consumed internally by the compartment producing the flow. Indeed, energy carriers are used in the energy sector to produce energy carriers, and food products (seeds, eggs and crops used as feed) are used in the agricultural sector to produce food products. This internal investment in an autocatalytic loop implies that, by default, a certain fraction of the net supply (not considering the losses) is unavailable for end uses in the dissipative compartment.

- *Step 4: generation of the multi-level, multi-dimensional representation of the metabolic pattern*

Having defined and quantified the funds and flows, MuSIASEM makes use of a multi-level, multi-dimensional representation of flow and fund elements to combine the various descriptions given by the dendrograms (step 2) and the grammars (step 3) (see Table 12.7). In this way, we obtain an integrated characterization combining non-equivalent quantitative descriptions of the metabolic pattern across different hierarchical levels and scales (e.g. the whole, its compartments and their subsectors) and different dimensions of analysis (e.g. demographic, economic, biophysical dimensions). Indeed, combining the distribution profiles of the flow elements (energy, food, water, money) with the fund elements (human activity, managed land, power capacity) across the different functional compartments (HH, SG, BM, AG and EM), we obtain a set of *flow/fund ratios* that effectively describe (diagnose) the characteristics of the metabolic pattern of society at different scales. A simplified example of such assessment referring to the economic labour productivity (ELP) obtained from the dendrograms of human activity (fund) and value added (flow) is shown in Figure 6.3.

More in general we can say that:

i The specific flow/fund ratios calculated at the different levels of analysis (n, $n - 1$, $n - 2$) describe how the various compartments perform at their own scale of operation. These ratios are *intensive variables* (rates, densities, intensities) characterizing qualitative aspects of the fund element per unit (e.g. the specific energy flow per hour of human activity in agriculture, the specific water flow per hectare of managed land in a given category of land use). Therefore, together, they describe characteristics of the system across different levels (and scales). For example, the energy throughput per hour of human activity can be calculated at different levels, for the whole agricultural sector or for a given crop system; the GDP per hour of human activity can be calculated for the whole paid work sector or in a specific industrial plant; the water throughput per hectare can be calculated for the whole agricultural sector or in a given plot. Further, these assessments can be aggregated (scaling up) or disaggregated (scaling down).

ii The relative sizes of lower-level fund elements compared to society as a whole provide information on the structural relation between the functional parts and the whole. This information is based on *extensive variables* ('How large are the fund elements?') and is useful to 'classify' socio-economic systems. For example, in high-income countries the percentage of the total work force in agriculture is typically less than 5 per cent of the total, while that in the service sector is more than 65 per cent. In post-industrial societies the longer life expectancy implies that less than 40 per cent of the population is included in the work force. In relation to the fund element managed land, this type of large-scale picture also provides useful information on the degree of seriousness of environmental constraints. For instance: What is the fraction of total managed land allocated to agriculture? (Is there still room for expansion?) What is the share of total agricultural land put to high-external-input agriculture? What is the available renewable supply of water for the agricultural sector? With suitable definitions of land system type and quality, land area can give a measure of the natural capital of the system.

iii The share of total flow consumption that is imported, rather than internally generated, provides information on the degree of openness of the system.

It is important to keep in mind that the characteristics of the various fund and flow elements affect each other at different scales and in relation to different dimensions. This reflects the typical impredicative relation of causality found in autopoietic systems (i.e. systems making themselves) such as human society. For instance, we can say that the gross domestic product (GDP) per capita and gross value added (GVA) of the various economic (sub)sectors impose constraints on society in relation to the distribution of human activity (labour time), level of capitalization (e.g. power capacity) and land uses across the set of economic sectors. However, we can also say that the GDP and GVA are determined by these factors.

- *Step 5: checking the viability and desirability domain for the metabolic pattern – definition of internal constraints to sustainability*

A metabolic pattern is *viable* if, given the structural constraints (the size and characteristics of fund elements), it is capable of generating an adequate internal supply of the various flows it consumes (food, energy, manufactured goods, infrastructures, services). Viability is checked by cross-verifying the stability of the dynamic budgets of the individual flows (food, energy, water, money) in relation to internal constraints. For example, the total flow of food consumed by society must be provided by the agricultural sector or by imports. When checking against the internal constraints, this food supply has to be secured with only a limited share of the fund elements (human labour, power capacity, managed land) used within the society either for producing food or for paying for the imports of food (= producing and selling other products of an equivalent economic value). In the same way, the total flow of energy carriers consumed by society must be supplied by the energy and mining sector or by imports, while using only a limited share of the fund elements. The same rationale applies to money, water and other flows. As the sum of the production factors, made up both of fund elements (human labour, managed land, power capacity) and of flow elements (food, energy, water), must equal society's total endowment (in this method of accounting), we obtain an integrated set of forced relations across the dynamic budgets. This is what we call the *Sudoku* effect.

At the macro level of analysis, the *desirability* of the metabolic pattern refers to the internal pressure experienced within socio-economic systems to allocate a relatively large share of the available fund elements (human activity, power capacity) and consumed flows (energy, food and water) to the household sector, the service and government sector and the transportation sector (together these sectors make up the so-called 'dissipative compartment'). In fact, the larger this share, the better is the material standard of living. The question of whether a given society can afford a large 'societal overhead' on human labour in the primary and secondary sectors can be answered only by assessing the surplus generated by the hypercyclic compartment.

Desirability in a metabolic pattern can be checked by looking at the value of the *bioeconomic pressure (BEP)*, defined as the ratio of the amount of fund and flow elements allocated to the dissipative compartment to the total amount of fund and flow elements. It has been shown that in modern societies the larger is this ratio, the better are the conventional indicators of development (Giampietro *et al.* 2012).

- *Step 6: checking the feasibility of the metabolic pattern in terms of resource requirement (supply side) and environmental loading (sink side) – definition of external constraints to sustainability*

By looking at the aggregate *gross requirement* of biophysical flows/natural resources (either directly used or embodied in imports) on the supply side and the corresponding *flow of wastes* on the sink side we can assess the environmental loading of a given metabolic pattern. It is important to realize that the *gross requirement* (and the resulting flow of *wastes*) describes the interaction of society with its natural environment and hence does not equal the *net requirement* of biophysical flows consumed by the various compartments within society. For example, in the assessment of the resource requirement and sink capacity for agriculture, we consider not only the food consumed by the population (the net requirement), but also the feed crops involved in animal products (the internal autocatalytic loop in the agricultural sector) and the post-harvest losses in the food system. The same applies to the resource requirement (primary energy sources) and sink capacity (CO_2 emission) for the energy sector: we include not only the final consumption of energy carriers (electricity, fuels and heat) inside society (net requirement), but also 1) the fossil energy consumed in the double conversion of thermal energy into electricity; 2) the losses in conversion and distribution; and 3) the effect of changes in land uses on atmospheric CO_2 (even though this assessment has not been carried out for the cases in this book). The quantitative analysis of the interaction of society with its context (the embedding ecosystems) is articulated in spatial terms across scales, using GIS data. Indeed, levels of environmental loading, defined as the difference between the flow densities of natural land cover and those of managed land uses, have to be assessed simultaneously at different hierarchical levels and scales (e.g. soil, crop field, watershed, national scale, global scale) – this is discussed in Chapters 4 and 5. The scaling of this quantitative information can be handled only by employing GIS (Chapter 10).

2.3 The conceptual tools underlying the MuSIASEM toolkit

The application of MuSIASEM is based on the integrated use of four conceptual tools derived from complexity theory:

1 Multi-level, multi-dimensional representations are employed, in the form of dendrograms, tables or matrices/vectors, to check congruence over datasets in relation to the feasibility (external constraints), viability (internal constraints) and desirability (compatibility with social values and institutions) of a given metabolic pattern. The adjective 'multi-level' refers to the various hierarchical levels of analysis (n, $n - 1$, $n - 2$, etc.) considered, while 'multi-dimensional' relates to the distinct types of variables (biophysical, economic) included in the analysis.

2 Multi-level grammars are employed for the accounting of flows (food, energy, water, monetary flows). These grammars are general accounting schemes (defined in semantic terms) that encompass both the outside (supply side) and the inside perspective (requirement side) on the system. The grammars deal with the existence of internal autocatalytic loops (in the case of food and

energy security) and define the proper identity of flows at the local scale to assess losses and final consumption. Grammars for food, energy, water and monetary flows are detailed in Part II of this book.

3 Impredicative loop analysis is used to handle the chicken–egg paradox typical of autopoietic systems such as human society. It effectively deals with the fact that the characteristics of the whole (society) impose constraints on the characteristics of the parts (sectors) and vice versa. This is a well-known phenomenon and has been studied extensively in the field of ecology, the most eloquent example being undoubtedly the predator–prey relation. Indeed, the number of predators determines the number of prey when observing the system at one scale, whereas it is the number of prey that determines the number of predators when observing the system at a smaller scale (Carpenter and Kitchell 1987).
4 The 'Sudoku effect' is employed in scenario analysis of the metabolic pattern (simulation tool) so as to simultaneously consider different types of constraints defined at different levels of analysis. This conceptual tool derives its name from the popular Sudoku game, and its application is detailed in Chapter 11.

Practical applications of the different conceptual tools will be presented in detail in the following chapters. Chapter 3 provides a short introduction to theoretical concepts behind their use.

3 The scientific basis of the narrative of societal and ecosystem metabolism

Mario Giampietro

Summary

This chapter challenges the idea that the term 'metabolism' can only be applied in a metaphorical sense to the analysis of society and the ecosystem. Supporting arguments are presented from the theory of non-equilibrium thermodynamics, complex systems, ecology and bioeconomics, and from the established use of this term in social science. The application of the concept of metabolism in its literal sense has two important implications: 1) the need simultaneously to use two non-equivalent but complementary views of the metabolic pattern – from inside the system (to check internal viability) and from outside the system (to check external feasibility); and 2) the need to distinguish between exosomatic and endosomatic metabolism. Potential sources of confusion are clarified: 1) that the metabolic pattern of society and the ecosystem can only be observed at different scales; 2) that an analysis of material and energy flows must be based on the specific characteristics of the structural (fund) elements of the metabolic pattern; and 3) that the feasibility of the metabolic pattern of society depends on processes beyond human control.

3.1 Introduction

The application of the concept of metabolism to the study of the nexus between land, water, food, energy, wealth and population represents a radical departure from the traditional reductionist approach to resource accounting that is based on the adoption of a single scale and dimension of analysis at a time. It also represents an extremely useful approach to assessing the sustainability of the interaction between human socio-economic systems and their embedding ecosystems.

The metabolism of complex self-organizing systems, including socio-economic systems and ecosystems, operates across various spatial, temporal and organizational scales. In fact, as we shall see in this chapter, the very concept of metabolism implies that metabolic patterns are established by connecting processes that take place on different scales. This makes the concept extremely suitable to establish a bridge between the non-equivalent representations of human society and the ecosystem and to explore the nexus among land, water, food, energy, wealth and population in relation to the issue of sustainability.

In this chapter I intend to clarify the existing confusion around the concept of metabolism by providing the theoretical foundations for its application to socio-economic systems interpreted in the broadest sense.

3.2 The concept of metabolism is not merely a metaphor!

Recently, the scientific literature on sustainability has shown a boom in the use of the term 'metabolism'. Many papers proposing quantitative analysis of the interactions of human societies and embedding ecosystems have titles that include expressions such as 'metabolic studies', 'urban metabolism', 'social metabolism' and 'water metabolism'. However, in spite of the generous use of the term 'metabolism', most of these papers fail to provide a clear definition of what they mean by the label, let alone a theoretical discussion of the basic epistemological conundrum that the use of this concept entails for quantitative analysis. This casual use of the label 'metabolism' has generated confusion around the term, and it is being transformed into a buzz-word, rather than being used in a well-defined scientific narrative. With good reasons, several authors have scrutinized and criticized its indiscriminate use in the scientific literature (Lifset 2004; Castán Broto *et al.* 2012; Golubiewski 2012).

As a matter of fact, the use of the concept of metabolism to describe both ecosystems and socio-economic systems is backed up by robust theoretical work in the field of non-equilibrium thermodynamics, complex systems theory, theoretical discussions about the foundations of life, theoretical ecology, bioeconomics (*à la* Georgescu-Roegen), and a long tradition in social sciences. This means that, if one wants to adopt the concept of metabolism to develop the quantitative analysis of sustainability, one has to use the knowledge accumulated in these scientific fields and, consequently, address the main epistemological challenges inherent in the study of complex self-organizing systems:

1 They are by definition open systems, and this makes it difficult to define a clear and unique boundary for their analysis.
2 They are organized over several hierarchical levels; therefore they must be observed at different scales and represented combining, simultaneously, non-equivalent descriptions.
3 They are all special. They have a history that determines their expected identity (the type to which they belong), but they also exhibit unexpected features owing to past stochastic events.

These tough challenges probably explain – but do not justify – why the term 'metabolism' is mostly used loosely, in a metaphorical sense, leaving behind its theoretical baggage.

The general interpretation that the term 'metabolism' should be reserved only for 'the set of life-sustaining chemical transformations within the cells of living organisms' (http://en.wikipedia.org/wiki/Metabolism) should be considered a form of excessive reductionism. In fact, the network of biochemical transformations taking place in a given set of organic molecules – the conventional way of defining metabolism – is just one possible instance of a more general pattern, and it is my firm belief that the term 'metabolism' can be applied to any integrated set of functions expressed by a complex self-organizing system capable of gathering energy and material inputs and dumping wastes into the environment in order to reproduce itself according to information stored in the system. Interpreted in this broad sense, the concept of metabolism can be applied to the study of expected characteristics of ecosystems, the interface between societal and ecosystem metabolism (Chapter 4) and more in general to socio-economic systems, including the interface between economic, demographic and biophysical processes (the rest of this book).

3.3 Theory relevant to the application of the concept of metabolism

The application of the concept of metabolism to human societies and ecosystems, which are *dissipative systems*, logically builds on the theory of non-equilibrium thermodynamics (Prigogine 1961, 1978; Glansdorff and Prigogine 1971; Nicolis and Prigogine 1977; Prigogine and Stengers 1984). A given dissipative system represents an observable pattern, distinct from its environment, which can be expressed and maintained as long as the gradients required for its existence remain favourable. Given this definition, simple dissipative systems, such as tornadoes or water flows, are 'improbable' because according to the law of classic thermodynamics the gradients generating dissipative systems tend to be destroyed as a result of their very existence! Therefore, for a dissipative system to preserve its identity in time, it must be able to maintain the expected set of gradients with its environment that determine its identity. This can be achieved only by learning how to take advantage of favourable boundary conditions for reproducing itself.

In relation to this narrative, the concept of metabolism has been explicitly used by Schrödinger in his seminal book *What Is Life?*, in which he attempts to identify the basic features of living systems. According to him, the question to be answered is: 'How does the living organism avoid decay?' "The obvious answer is: by eating, drinking, breathing and (in the case of plants) assimilating. The technical term is metabolism. The Greek word . . . meaning change or exchange" (Schrödinger 1967, p. 71). Rather than associating the concept of metabolism with a special set of expected relations over biochemical reactions within organisms (the reductionist interpretation of the term), Schrödinger uses the concept in a very generic way: to explain life itself.

The concept of metabolism was introduced by Lotka (1922) to describe the functioning of biological systems. In his view, the greater is the ability of biological systems (i.e. individual organisms, species and ecosystems) to gather energy input and to convert this input into growth, reproduction and maintenance, the higher will be their survival rate. In his words, "in the struggle for existence, the advantage must go to those organisms whose energy capturing devices are most efficient in directing available energies into channels favourable to the preservation of the species" (Lotka 1922, p. 147). Later, Lotka also suggested extending the concept of metabolism to human societies, making a distinction between 'endosomatic' and 'exosomatic' metabolism (see also section 3.4.2). In terms of the emergence of an exosomatic metabolism (indicating a stabilized set of flows of energy and material inputs transformed under human control within the socio-economic process outside the human body), "it has in a most real way bound men together into one body: so very real and material is the bond that society might aptly be described as one huge multiple Siamese twin" (Lotka 1956, p. 369). A detailed discussion of the evolution of the concept of metabolism in sustainability science and its theoretical implications has been provided elsewhere (Giampietro and Mayumi 2009; Giampietro *et al.* 2012).

Following the work of Schrödinger and Lotka, different lines of research on the foundations of life, complexity and self-organization converged on the need to introduce a more general class of systems to accommodate all complex systems capable of self-organization and adaptation, including biological, ecological and socio-economic systems. Several names have been proposed for such a class, including *complex adaptive systems* (Cilliers 1998; Holland 2006), *autopoietic systems* (literally meaning 'systems that are making themselves') (Maturana and Varela 1980, 1998), and *metabolic networks self-organizing through informed autocatalytic loops* (H.T. Odum 1971, 1996). They have in common that the proposed class of systems can reproduce themselves only by: 1) interacting with their context (gathering inputs of energy and matter and releasing wastes); 2) using information accumulated during their history; 3) operating simultaneously across different levels of organization; and 4) carrying out activities that provide a return larger than their cost in biophysical terms.

Padovan (2000) and Fischer-Kowalski (1997) have provided a good overview of the development of the concept of metabolism in social science. In the context of this book the work of the following scientists is particularly relevant: August Comte, who framed the notion of 'life' using a narrative similar to that of Schrödinger (life is the result of a fairly harmonious cooperation between two inseparable elements: the organism and the environment); Herbert Spencer, who worked on the analysis of societal metabolism in its internal components; and Albert Schäffle, who identified the 'base' of the metabolic pattern of human society in the labour power obtained by mixing together human activity and other agents boosting it (what is described in our approach as the exosomatic metabolic pattern determined by profiles of allocation of human activity). Padovan (2000, p. 7) describes the analysis provided by Schäffle as follows:

> All effective work consumed part of this 'base' of energy and made renewal of the base necessary. In the same way the social body too requires an exchange of materials, which simultaneously penetrates every part of the social body: production, circulation, distribution, intermediary exchanges, use and elimination of the materials necessary for maintaining both the person and institutions of the social unit.

This description is perfectly consistent with the logic of accounting of MuSIASEM.

Thus, the term 'metabolism' has been firmly established in theoretical terms and applied in quantitative analysis also outside the disciplines of biochemistry and physiology, in particular in the following partially overlapping disciplinary fields:

1 Theoretical ecology (which will be discussed in Chapter 4).
2 Bioeconomics. Pioneers in this field include: Jevons ([1865] 1906), Ostwald (1907, 1911), Lotka (1922, 1956), Soddy (1926), Zipf (1941, 1949), White (1943, 1949) and Cottrell (1955). An overview has been provided by Martinez-Alier (1987). Georgescu-Roegen developed a theoretical framework (the flow-fund model to develop quantitative methods for the analysis of the metabolic patterns of modern society is discussed in Chapter 4).
3 Non-equilibrium thermodynamics applied to the study of sustainability. Among the authors who played a pioneering role in the development of this field are: H.T. Odum 1971, 1983, 1996; Hall *et al.* 1986; Tsuchida and Murota 1987; Allen and Hoekstra 1992; Kay and Schneider 1992; Schneider and Kay 1994; Giampietro and Mayumi 2000a, 2000b; Kay 2000; Allen *et al.* 2003.

3.4 Implications of the theory on metabolism for quantitative analysis

The main expected features of complex self-organizing systems can be used to define typologies of metabolic patterns expressed by these systems. These key features can then be used to study the sustainability of observed metabolic patterns or to check the compatibility of proposed changes in relation to internal and external constraints. To this purpose we need simultaneously to consider the internal and external view on the metabolic system.

The narrative proposed by Herman Daly (1994, p. 28) neatly explains the difference between external and internal constraints:

> The world is moving from an era in which man-made capital was the limiting factor into an era in which remaining natural capital is the limiting factor. The production of caught fish is currently limited by remaining fish populations, not by the number of fishing boats; timber production is limited by remaining forests, not by sawmills.

In this example, a shortage of fishing boats (the technological capital available to the metabolic system) limiting the catch would represent an internal constraint, whereas a low fish population limiting the catch represents an external constraint (what is feasible given the characteristics of the context, i.e. the fish population in the sea).

3.4.1 The inside and the outside view on metabolic systems

When we look from inside the system (internal view) at the dynamic equilibrium between the supply and requirement of flows we can define the *viability domain* of the societal metabolism.

The viability domain provides combinations of extensive variables (sizes of societal compartments) and intensive variables (metabolic characteristics of compartments) describing the functioning of society that generate a stable internal supply of required inputs (energy and material). The internal view focuses on the activities of the hypercyclic part of society (the part producing surplus for the entire system), or what has been called by North (1990) 'the set of transformation supply activities'. In modern economies these activities are carried out by the sectors of agriculture, energy and mining, and building and manufacturing.

The desirability of the societal metabolic pattern regards the purely dissipative part of society. It focuses on the use of the surplus made available by the hypercyclic part to express additional functions, such as the reproduction of institutions, the storage of information and the development of resilience and adaptability. North (1990) calls the activities of this dissipative part 'transaction activities' (in the service and government sector) and 'final consumption activities' (in the household sector).

When looking from outside the system (external view) at the flows on the supply and sink side of societal metabolism, we are studying the stability of boundary conditions. In fact, external constraints determine the *feasibility* of the overall metabolic pattern in relation to the characteristics of the context. We can assess the feasibility domain of societal metabolism by checking the congruence between the overall throughput of the society (what is required as supply and what is disposed of as waste) and the available resources and sink capacity determined by natural processes that take place in the context and that are beyond human control.

3.4.2 Endosomatic and exosomatic metabolism

As noted earlier, the distinction between endosomatic and exosomatic metabolism was first introduced by Lotka (1956) in relation to societal metabolism. This distinction refers to the nature of the power capacity used by society to transform flows of energy input into flows of useful energy (applied power) under human control. Lotka felt the need for this distinction after observing the tremendous gain in importance of the exosomatic metabolism of society in human affairs following the industrial revolution. The impressive accumulation of technological capital (easing the internal constraints) and the abundant supply of fossil energy (easing the external constraints) implied a dramatic increase in the power capacity available and used to boost the productivity of human activity (Cottrell 1955; Hall *et al.* 1986). Following the industrial revolution, human activity became important in terms of providing control over the delivery of machine power, rather than in terms of muscular power delivered. The distinction between exosomatic and endosomatic energy conversions was proposed, later on, by Georgescu-Roegen (1975) as a working concept for the energetic analyses of bioeconomics and sustainability. We provide here the following definitions, based on the work of both Lotka and Georgescu-Roegen:

- *Endosomatic metabolism* refers to physiological conversions of different types of energy inputs (various food items consumed) into end uses (applied human muscle power) that take place *inside* the human body. In the endosomatic metabolism, human activity provides at the same time: 1) control on the applied power; and 2) power capacity (human muscles) for the generation of applied power. The stability of the endosomatic metabolism of society is closely related to the concept of food security: humans produce, control and apply power, but they require food inputs for doing so.

- *Exosomatic metabolism* refers to the energy converted *outside* the human body with the goal of amplifying the output of useful work associated with human activity (e.g. the use of tractors, the melting of metals, air transportation). For exosomatic metabolism to take place, we need: 1) energy input (energy carriers such as petrol, biofuel); 2) power capacity (exosomatic devices or technological capital, such as cars); and 3) human activity (labour) to guide and control the generation and use of exosomatic applied power in order to effectively fulfil tasks (guarantee the end use). The stability of the exosomatic metabolism of society is closely related to the concept of energy security.

In this distinction, animal power should be considered as a form of exosomatic metabolism used by humans to amplify their capability of interacting with their external world. In terms of this distinction, the animal feed used for power generation should be considered as an energy input to the exosomatic metabolism, whereas animal feed used to produce animal products consumed in the diet should be considered as an indirect consumption associated with the endosomatic metabolism (see also Chapter 7).

The theory outlined above provides a solid base for the application of the concept of metabolism to the analysis of the sustainability of socio-economic systems. In the following, I address some specific aspects of sustainability assessments that have become muddled owing to the abuse of the term 'metabolism' in sustainability science.

3.5 Socio-ecological systems do not necessarily have a defined metabolic pattern

In this section I point out that, whereas societies and ecosystems do express metabolic patterns, socio-ecological systems may *not* have a specific metabolic pattern.

The term 'socio-ecological systems' has been proposed (e.g. Young *et al.* 2006) exactly to address the obvious fact that the characteristics of human-controlled biophysical processes do affect and are affected by the characteristics of ecosystem-controlled biophysical processes. Hence it is essential to consider the interaction of humans with their embedding ecosystems in a holistic way. The success and rapid diffusion of this term in social science can be explained by the isolation of this scientific discipline (typical of modern science). Many social scientists and economists working on the issue of sustainability simply are not aware of the work done in the field of bioeconomics and human ecology.

The concept of societal and ecosystem metabolism can certainly be used to study the interface between the pattern of activities (material and energy flows) controlled by a society and the pattern of activities expressed by ecosystems. However, as will be repeatedly shown in this book, at the moment of accounting for the relative flows (and funds) of society and the ecosystem, we find a consistent mismatch of scale. The space–time scale at which we can detect relevant characteristics of the metabolic pattern of human societies (how the socio-economic process uses food, energy, water, materials and land to reproduce and improve itself) is different from the scale at which we can detect relevant characteristics of ecosystems and ecological communities (how ecological processes use solar energy, water and materials to reproduce and improve themselves). Relevant processes under human control are typically described by flow rates per hour or flow densities per hectare, with values averaged on a year basis, whereas relevant characteristics of natural processes beyond human control (resilience of ecosystems, stability of ecological communities) can be described only on a much larger space–time scale (eventually including the entire biosphere).

Thus, we can talk of an expected metabolic pattern of a given typology of society, observed and represented at a given scale, and of an expected metabolic pattern of a given typology of ecosystem, observed and represented at a given, larger scale. But we *cannot* observe and represent in quantitative terms, using a single scale, the metabolic pattern of a given socio-ecological complex. Whatever space–time scale we would adopt, we would see the metabolic pattern of one system or another, but not both.

3.6 Material and energy flow accounting is not the same as studying metabolic patterns

Another source of confusion around the term 'metabolism' derives from the fact that many scientists use this term to refer to the accounting of material and energy flows in socio-economic systems in general (e.g. Fischer-Kowalski and Haberl 2007). The idea that any accounting of biophysical quantities related to socio-economic systems can be associated with the concept of metabolism is simply mistaken. The fact that we can measure the flow of water (and relative kinetic energy) passing through a tap does not mean we are analysing the metabolism of the tap. Taps do not belong to the class of complex self-organizing systems. Their identity does not depend on the throughput of water, and therefore they do not express an expected metabolic pattern. The concept of metabolism is based on the existence of a specific set of relations between the identity of the system reproducing itself (e.g. a lion or New York City) and the identity of the network of flows (energy and material inputs) required for this purpose (e.g. an antelope is a metabolic input for the lion, whereas fossil energy is a metabolic input for New York City).

In metabolic systems the identity of the flow is strictly related to the identity of the fund element processing it. Therefore, when dealing with metabolic systems, we cannot talk in general terms of quantities of 'energy' or 'matter' but only of quantities of 'required flows of energy' or 'required flows of material' whose expected characteristics depend on the characteristics of the fund elements using them. The implications of this point for the analyst are profound. It demands that, when carrying out an assessment of energy inputs for a complex self-organizing system, we must know beforehand the identity of the structural and functional elements that are responsible, at the local scale, for the specific metabolic activities we want to measure. For instance, we must know that cars require petrol as an energy input, refrigerators electricity, sailing boats wind, and human beings food. Thus, when dealing with the quantitative analysis of an integrated set of energy transformations belonging to a given metabolic pattern, it is impossible to use a generic criterion of accounting such as 'energy input'. Such a criterion refers to many different things that have to be measured in different ways and at different scales! Examples of this point are illustrated in Chapters 7, 8 and 9, presenting the different grammars needed to assess the metabolic pattern of food, energy and water respectively.

When dealing with the quantitative analysis of the metabolic pattern of a complex self-organizing system operating across different levels of organization, we have to be able to generate a multi-scale characterization of material and energy flows, which must be tailored to the identities of the various fund elements using these flows within the metabolic pattern. For instance, 1MJ of 'energy' consumed by New York City cannot be accounted for in the same category as 1MJ of 'energy' consumed by an air conditioner. If the accounting of energy and material flows is not tailored to the specific identity of the fund metabolizing them, then the analysis cannot be used to detect 'expected characteristics' of a metabolic pattern. Put in another way, an integrated analysis of the energy and material flows required for the reproduction of a society can be done only after giving a pre-analytical definition of what type of society we are talking about, which includes the pre-analytical choice of a set of categories of accounting relevant for the metabolic pattern considered (Giampietro *et al.* 2013).

3.7 The concept of metabolic pattern requires the proper handling of scales

> If it is very easy to substitute other factors for natural resources, then there is in principle no 'problem'. The world can, in effect, get along without natural resources, so exhaustion is just an event, not a catastrophe.
>
> (Solow 1974)

If only Robert Solow had been familiar with the concept of metabolism, he would not have made this bold statement. Socio-economic systems are dissipative systems. Hence, they are open systems that must gather a continuous flow of inputs from their context and discharge the resulting flow of wastes in order to reproduce their identity in time (be sustainable). Unfortunately, the stability of favourable boundary conditions sustaining this process depends entirely on processes beyond human control!

The substitution that Solow refers to takes place inside the system and regards only processes under human control. Provided the result of the substitution falls within the viability domain of the metabolic pattern, there is indeed some room for adjustments to the internal characteristics of the metabolic pattern. However, the feasibility domain, referring to the stability of boundary conditions, cannot be enlarged by internal changes. Human societies may be able to adjust and operate without a certain input or learn how to reduce a certain output, but they cannot increase the amount of favourable natural gradients available. This unpleasant fact is mandated by the second law of thermodynamics: energy cannot be created, only transformed!

This confusion in the analysis of the sustainability of socio-ecological systems is common and boils down to the issue of scale. To check the viability of the societal metabolic pattern we must study the ability to reproduce (and develop) an adequate set of structural and functional elements (parts) capable of expressing an integrated set of actions guaranteeing the reproduction of the whole. For this task, we have to adopt a scale that is suitable to study processes under human control that take place inside the system. To check the feasibility of the societal metabolic pattern we must analyse the natural processes beyond human control capable of stabilizing the input flows (supply side) and absorbing the waste flows (sink side) that are associated with the processes taking place inside the system. For this task, we have to adopt a scale that is suitable for studying natural processes outside the system. This double requirement of compatibility (viability on the inside and feasibility on the outside) translates into the need to explicitly address the issue of scale.

As we will see in the grammars of food, energy and water presented in this book the issue of scale leads to a bifurcation in the categorization of flow accounting on the interface between the inside and the outside view. For example, the joules measuring the consumption of electricity of a refrigerator (inside view) do not map on to the joules of primary energy required to make that electricity (outside).

Addressing the issue of scale is also essential for the correct categorization of flow types within the system so as to understand the compatibility between the characteristics of the metabolic pattern of a part of the system observed at the local scale and the characteristics of the metabolic pattern of the whole observed at the large scale. For example, if we describe the metabolic pattern of food in China on the large scale we will find that the same material flow type (e.g. human faeces) should be accounted for as a useful input in a given part of the whole (at the local scale) and as a harmful waste in another part (still at the local scale). For example, in the metabolic pattern of rural Chinese villages (a local scale in relation to the country as a whole) the density of the flow of human faeces is compatible with the capacity for recycling it into a useful input for agricultural production. On the contrary, in the metabolic pattern of Beijing (also a local scale) the flow of human faeces is too dense to result usefully as an input for another process. In this part of the system, this flow represents a waste disposal problem.

The same scale-related problem is found in the categorization of flow types when accounting for energy inputs. Remaining in China, we find that, in rural villages, rice straw is a useful energy carrier (used for cooking). On the other hand, in Beijing, rice straw is not a suitable energy carrier to run household activities and should not be accounted for among the energy carriers.

In conclusion, the analysis of the metabolic pattern of complex societies requires us to address the issue of multiple scales in the pre-analytical step:

1. At the local scale, we define what or who is using inputs of energy, food, water and land. At this scale, we can observe the characteristics of energy converters (the power capacity provided by structural elements).
2. At the meso scale, we define for what purpose these inputs are used. At this scale we can identify the functions expressed (in relation to the emergent property of the whole) by the structural or functional elements converting energy into applied power.
3. At the large scale, we define the factors determining the feasibility of the emergent property associated with the reproduction of the society as a whole, that is, the existence of favourable boundary conditions determined by processes outside human control.

Only after having defined the characteristics of the metabolic pattern across these different scales does it become possible to discuss and select an integrated system of accounting. The scaling problem is also discussed in Chapter 4 in relation to the implementation of the concept of metabolism for quantitative analysis.

4 The interface between societal and ecosystem metabolism

Mario Giampietro and Pedro L. Lomas

Summary

This chapter presents the theoretical basis of the quantitative approach used in MuSIASEM to characterize the interface between societal and ecosystem metabolism. We show that the main epistemological complications of implementing the concept of societal metabolism – that is, the multi-scale hierarchical organization of metabolic systems and the impredicativity in the definition of the whole and the parts – can be handled by Georgescu-Roegen's flow-fund model. This model also provides a means to operationalize the notion of sustainability of socio-ecological systems. The concept of ecosystem metabolism as defined by H.T. Odum lies at the basis of our approach to quantifying the ecosystem alteration caused by societal metabolism. This approach is illustrated for low- and high-external-input agriculture. To analyse the metabolic flows on the interface between society and ecosystems it is useful to single out rural (as opposed to urban) metabolism within MuSIASEM. Templates to assess the metabolic pattern of rural areas (land systems) are provided.

4.1 Implementing the concept of metabolism for quantitative analysis

4.1.1 Metabolic systems are complex self-organizing systems

Complex self-organizing systems, such as socio-economic systems and ecosystems, are invariably hierarchically organized, and to represent them in a meaningful way we must characterize their metabolic pattern over different levels of organization. It follows that a quantitative analysis of the metabolic pattern of complex self-organizing systems is incompatible with conventional reductionist approaches for the following reasons:

- *Complex self-organizing systems require a multi-scale characterization.* The coexistence of several levels of organization implies that we have to simultaneously consider: 1) the small scale, where we can observe and describe the operation of the individual parts; 2) the medium scale, where we can observe and describe the interaction among the parts within the system boundaries that results in the expression of emergent properties of the whole; and 3) the large scale, where we can observe and describe the processes influencing the boundary conditions that determine the survival of the system as a whole. The need to simultaneously describe processes at three distinct space–time scales (small, medium and large) forces us to adopt non-equivalent descriptive domains (Giampietro 2004; Giampietro *et al.* 2006, 2007). Adopting a single scale at a time, as done in conventional quantitative analysis, one simply cannot process all the information needed to study the sustainability of a complex self-organizing system such as human society.

- *The identity of a complex self-organizing system rests on an impredicative definition.* For the metabolic process of complex self-organizing systems to be sustainable there must be congruence between the internal processes capable of dissipating energy inputs (inside the system) and the external processes capable of providing the required inputs and absorbing the resulting wastes (outside the system). This is where reductionism gets into trouble. When representing and quantifying the relevant characteristics of these two sets of processes it is necessary to use simultaneously two non-equivalent perceptions of events. Looking top down (the large-scale view) we see that the organization (identity) of the whole determines and guarantees the proper functioning and reproduction of the parts. But when looking bottom up (from the small scale) we see that it is the identity of the parts that determines, through their interaction, the reproduction of the identity of the whole (emergent property). In the specific case of human societies, looking from inside the system we can see processes under human control determining the *viability* of the metabolic pattern, whereas from the outside we see processes beyond human control determining the *feasibility* of the metabolic pattern. Thus, we inevitably end up with a set of systemic impredicative relations in the resulting quantitative analysis: the identities of the parts determine the identity of the whole and vice versa. This feature challenges the application of conventional analytical approaches to causality when dealing with complex self-organizing systems.

4.1.2 Metabolic systems are open systems

Metabolic systems are by definition open. They are made up of the input flows they gather from their environment and continuously leak part of their structural components in the form of wastes into the environment. This starting point presents us with an epistemological problem at the moment of defining boundaries for our accounting scheme. When and how does an input become part of the system, and when and how does a part of the system become waste?

From inside the system, we perceive metabolic flows, and define their relevant characteristics, in relation to the nature of the system's parts using those flows as input. For example, 1MJ of petrol will result in an energy input for a car but not for a cow. In the outside view, however, we perceive flows in relation to the nature of the processes supplying the inputs and sink capacity for the system. In this perception, the definition of relevant characteristics of the supply of inputs and sink capacity will refer to processes taking place in the system's context (embedding ecosystems).

The flow-fund model suggested by Georgescu-Roegen (1971) does provide a working solution for this epistemological problem of working with an open system defined on multiple scales. In fact, the flow-fund model makes it possible to frame the analysis of metabolic flows across contiguous hierarchical levels:

- On the interface between the small and medium scale we have the inputs and the outputs going into and out of individual compartments (parts of the system).
- On the interface between the medium and large scale we have the inputs and the outputs going into and out of the whole system (system as part of its context).

As we will see in the next section, in this way it becomes possible to develop a coherent method of accounting for the various metabolic flows. The flow-fund model allows us to establish a set of semantic criteria for defining 'what the system is' and 'what the system does' in the representation of a metabolic pattern, and this definition can be implemented across different levels of organization (subparts, parts and the whole).

4.2 Implementing the concept of societal metabolism: Georgescu-Roegen's bioeconomics

The work of Nicholas Georgescu-Roegen lends itself extremely well to the implementation of the concept of metabolic pattern of socio-economic systems. Georgescu-Roegen proposed the concept of bioeconomics to deal with what he perceived as a systemic epistemological flaw of neo-classical economic analysis, that is, the neglect of the issue of scale (Georgescu-Roegen 1971, 1975; Mayumi 2001). According to Georgescu-Roegen, the ultimate goal of the economy is *not* to produce and to consume goods and services, *but rather to reproduce and improve the set of processes required to produce and to consume goods and services*. This view is consistent with the idea that the economy is a complex self-organizing system reproducing itself through informed autocatalytic loops, and not a system merely producing outputs. This notion has profound implications for those interested in the quantitative analysis of sustainability. Indeed, the concept of bioeconomics moves the focus away from an input/output analysis of *flow elements*, in which the various flows of goods and services consumed (input) and produced (output) are measured in monetary values or prices (Aristotle's *chrematistics*), to an analysis of *fund elements* focusing on the reproduction of production factors, including human beings and institutions (Aristotle's *oikonomia*). In Georgescu-Roegen's view, the various flows are used and transformed by fund elements within a larger pattern of production and consumption. The economy can reproduce the economic process by reproducing the fund elements under the conditions of feasibility (external constraints), viability (internal constraints) and desirability (normative values). As will be illustrated in the following chapters, this change in perception of 'what an economy is' and 'what it does' represents a revolution in the analysis of the societal metabolic pattern.

The analytical approach proposed by Georgescu-Roegen makes a distinction between *flow elements*, represented by inputs (e.g. food, energy and mineral inputs) and wastes (e.g. rubbish, GHG and other pollutants), and *fund elements*, represented by the structural elements (e.g. human beings, land, technical capital) that constitute the functional compartments (e.g. economic sectors) of the system. This distinction makes it possible to explicitly address the issue of scale. In fact, *fund elements* have to be preserved (reproduced) in the medium term and improved in the long term for the system to survive. This means that their identity has to remain the same over the time scale of the analysis (e.g. hours, days, years or decades). On the contrary, *flow elements* represent inputs and outputs required to reproduce these fund elements, such as energy, material, water and monetary flows. By definition flows have to either appear (outputs) or disappear (inputs) over the duration of the analysis.

The distinction between flows and funds forces the analyst to declare the choice of levels of analysis in a pre-analytical step so as to be able to monitor metabolic characteristics across scales. At the small scale we can observe and measure local metabolic characteristics (flow/fund ratios, i.e. process rates, densities or intensities), which are typically expressed per hour or per square metre (e.g. local labour productivity). At the medium scale we can assess compartment sizes by aggregating the values of the various constituting fund elements. For example, we can calculate the size of the labour force engaged with the agricultural sector and the corresponding total hectares in production. Given their metabolic characteristics (flows per hour and per hectare), the relative sizes of fund elements will determine the corresponding flow sizes of compartments. For instance, multiplying the typical or observed flow (weighted average) – kilograms of corn per hour of work in agriculture – by the aggregate hours of agricultural work in corn production, we find the overall flow of corn production in the agricultural sector. Therefore, the allocation of a given fund (e.g. land) with known metabolic characteristics (e.g. a given flow per hectare) to a compartment of the socio-economic system (e.g. hectares of corn in agriculture) defines the total flow of that compartment (e.g. total flow of corn production in agriculture).

By focusing on the characteristics and relative sizes of the functional compartments of the economy, bioeconomics makes it possible to study at the same time the effects of structural changes within the economy (analysis of internal constraints) and the effects of changes in boundary conditions (analysis of external constraints). Bioeconomics thus allows us to link: 1) the inside and outside perception of the system, which is essential for addressing complex issues such as demographic changes, globalization, peak oil and climate change; and 2) monetary flows to corresponding biophysical flows (energy, water, materials) at the various levels of analyses and scales, which is essential to understanding the issue of economic viability. Monetary flows and biophysical flows can be analysed in relation to the profile of allocation of fund elements (labour, capital and land) required for the reproduction of the various functions of the economy. In this way, we obtain a characterization of economic and biophysical productivities of the various fund elements defined across different compartments and scales.

4.3 The interface between societal and ecosystem metabolism

All metabolic systems are open systems reproduced by a continuous exchange of flows of energy and matter with their context. This is true both for societies and for ecosystems. The flow-fund conceptual model proposed by Georgescu-Roegen (1971) allows us to recognize and to describe the metabolic patterns both of societies and of ecosystems. This makes it an extremely useful tool in disentangling and interpreting the complex set of interactions presented by the resource flows exchanged across different socio-economic systems (externalization by trade) and between socio-economic and ecological systems (using the concept of impact assessment; see section 4.4). In particular, a flow-fund analysis of the metabolic pattern of societies elucidates the nature of the processes generating flows and helps to individuate the factors determining the sustainability of a given pattern of ecosystem exploitation.

4.3.1 Sustainability in the flow-fund model

The flow-fund model helps clear a great deal of the confusion prevailing in the field of sustainability analysis. Following the pioneering work of, among others, Boulding (1966) and Daly (1973), sustainability science has been based on the narrative of steady-state economics. This school proposes the use of only two accounting categories to define the elements making up the socio-economic pattern:

- *stocks* (of people and artefacts), which should remain constant in time (steady-state);
- *flows* (energy and material), representing the throughput of the metabolic pattern.

Georgescu-Roegen's flow-fund analysis of the metabolic pattern of society proposes a more sophisticated definition, proposing three categories of accounting rather than two, to also include the nature of the processes generating flows:

1. *Flow* elements – referring to quantities disappearing or appearing during the time duration of the analysis. Examples are food, electricity, process heat, petrol, and irrigation water.
2. *Fund* elements – referring to quantities measuring the structural size of functional elements remaining 'the same' during the time duration of the analysis (agents that are reproduced and maintained in the representation). Examples include human beings, land uses in various typologies, and machinery.
3. *Stock* elements – referring to reservoirs or buffers of flows, which change their identity (they are depleted or filled) during the time duration of the analysis,

because of the flows. Examples include underground water reservoirs with an extraction rate exceeding the recharge rate, oil and gas reservoirs, coal, and copper ores.

As regards *the nature of metabolic flows*, the flow-fund model makes a distinction between:

1 *Stock-flows* – flows obtained from a stock (or disposed of from storage) inside the boundaries of the system, the use of which causes a change in the identity of the stock (or storage), for example beer tapped from a barrel or non-biodegradable rubbish dumped into a landfill.
2 *Fund-flows* – flows obtained from (or absorbed by) a fund inside the boundaries of the system, the extraction (or recycling) of which does not cause a change in the identity of the fund element, for example the proper milking of a cow or the home composting of organic waste.
3 *Imported/exported flows* – flows derived from (or sent) outside the borders of the system. They can be either stock-flows or fund-flows. The import or export of flows presumes favourable biophysical and economic boundary conditions (the feasibility and viability of the act of importing and exporting).

Thus, in regard to the concept of sustainability, flows metabolized by human society (food, water and energy) can be obtained through either stock depletion or fund exploitation. The former represent *non-renewable resources*, such as petrol produced from the depletion of fossil energy stocks or irrigation water obtained from the overdraft of underground water reservoirs. Flows obtained through fund-flow exploitation represent *renewable resources* as long as their extraction does not damage the ecological funds from which they are derived. Examples are grain produced in low-external-input agriculture, irrigation water from sustainable withdrawal from aquifers, or electricity generated from wind.

4.3.2 Externalization

Given the openness of virtually all modern socio-economic systems, imports and exports of flows across the boundaries of socio-ecological systems are a fact and a sure complication for the analyst. Hence when analysing a specific country it is essential to assess the level of openness of the metabolic pattern. Favourable terms of trade often make it possible for societies to externalize the depletion of resource stocks and/or exploitation of fund capacity, unavailable within national borders, to other socio-ecological systems. But if such imported flows are generated in a non-sustainable way elsewhere it should not be considered a sustainable solution by the importing society. However, the saying 'Out of sight, out of mind' still seems to drive those supporting the idea of perpetual growth, as exemplified by the sterile debates over dematerialization, where dematerialization boils down to being mainly externalization of resource-intensive activities to other countries.

4.3.3 On fund-flows and scale

The distinction between stock-flows and fund-flows, regardless of their origin, specifically points at the distinct effects of their metabolism on ecological systems. Stock-flows are by definition unsustainable; fund-flows are sustainable only if the process of fund exploitation does not interfere with the reproduction or quality of the ecological fund. Depending on the nature of the ecological fund, the assessment of whether or not its exploitation is sustainable does require the adoption of different scales:

- The reproduction of the fund biomass, as represented by terrestrial ecosystems and their constitutive elements, depends on solar energy, genetic information, water, and nutrient cycles, and can be assessed only at a large space–time scale.
- The reproduction of the fund soil is a long-term process, the characteristics of which can be observed only at a small spatial scale.
- The reproduction of water bodies, such as rivers, lakes and underground aquifers, depends on long-term processes providing external inputs (rain, inflows), and on local spatial constraints to water flows.
- The reproduction of the ecosphere, a term referring to the complex whole of fund elements determining the stability of metabolic processes on this planet, depends on very long-term processes (biogeochemical cycles) and refers to global characteristics such as atmospheric composition, climate, oceanic conditions and biodiversity.

All these fund elements may be negatively affected by human exploitation through excessive flow withdrawal and/or flow release (e.g. GHG emission), active destruction of specific components, or specific harm through localized pollution. This stress may cause both quantitative and qualitative alterations in ecological funds. For this reason MuSIASEM opts for a general framework that interfaces the analysis of the metabolic pattern of socio-economic systems (and their components) with that of ecological systems (and their components) across different scales. An example of such analysis is given in Chapter 9 in relation to the water grammar.

4.4 Assessment of the alteration of the metabolic pattern of ecosystems

4.4.1 Expected metabolic patterns of ecosystem types

In the 1960s and 1970s, the brothers E.P. and H.T. Odum successfully developed a general theoretical framework for the physical accounting of flows of nutrients and energy within ecosystems (e.g. E.P. Odum 1968) and subsequently showed the existence of systemic properties of ecosystems (E.P. Odum 1969, 1971). On the basis of this information, they developed a meta-narrative to study ecosystems, in which the concept of ecosystem metabolism is interpreted as the association of a set of expected structural and functional characteristics of both the whole and the parts to a known ecosystem type.

Other concepts that closely resemble the original idea of the Odum brothers have been proposed, such as *ecosystem integrity* and *ecosystem health*. These concepts also assume the possibility of defining an expected set of characteristics for known types of ecosystems, and propose the development of indicators describing how the actual characteristics of human-altered ecosystems differ from the state of ecological integrity of the corresponding undisturbed ecosystems (e.g. Kay and Schneider 1992; Karr 1999; Waltner-Toews *et al.* 2008).

In this approach, known *types* of ecosystems with integrity provide a set of reference values (benchmarks) to assess the level of stress on altered ecosystems, where an ecosystem type is interpreted as a set of expected relations among the characteristics of the flow and fund elements making up its metabolic pattern and described simultaneously across different levels of organization and scales. The definition of a typology of metabolic patterns of ecosystems with integrity builds on the work of many other theoretical ecologists (e.g. Margalef 1968; Ulanowicz 1986, 1995).

Thus, by applying this rationale we can compare an empirical dataset describing the characteristics of an altered ecosystem to a set of expected quantitative values, so-called reference or benchmark values (e.g. an undisturbed tropical forest or chaparral), to obtain a quantitative indication about the degree of alteration induced by human intervention. This rationale is at the basis of a broad family of indicators, including among others *ascendancy* (Ulanowicz 1986), the *ecological integrity index* (Andreasen *et al.* 2001; Zampella *et al.* 2006; Reza and Abdullah 2011), the *nature index* (Certain *et al.* 2011) and the *environmental loading ratio* (the latter implemented within the approach of emergy synthesis proposed by H.T. Odum 1996). However, the usefulness and validity of these indicators depend on the pertinence of their formalization.

Below we propose to implement this same rationale within the accounting system of MuSIASEM.

4.4.2 Impact indicators of terrestrial ecosystem stress in MuSIASEM

MuSIASEM uses a family of impact indicators of terrestrial ecosystem stress based on a comparison of the evapotranspiration of water (a sort of 'thermodynamic cost' requiring dissipated energy) per unit of standing biomass of terrestrial ecosystems. The difference in value of this index between an observed altered ecosystem (agro-ecosystem) and its corresponding unaltered ecosystem type reflects the degree of disturbance of the natural process of self-organization (Giampietro and Pimentel 1991; Giampietro *et al.* 1992). Undisturbed ecosystems maximize their level of energy dissipation by sustaining as large an amount of standing biomass (SB) as possible at the lowest possible thermodynamic cost (Mayumi and Giampietro 2004). This approach is illustrated in Figure 4.1 for the alteration of tropical ecosystems by crop cultivation.

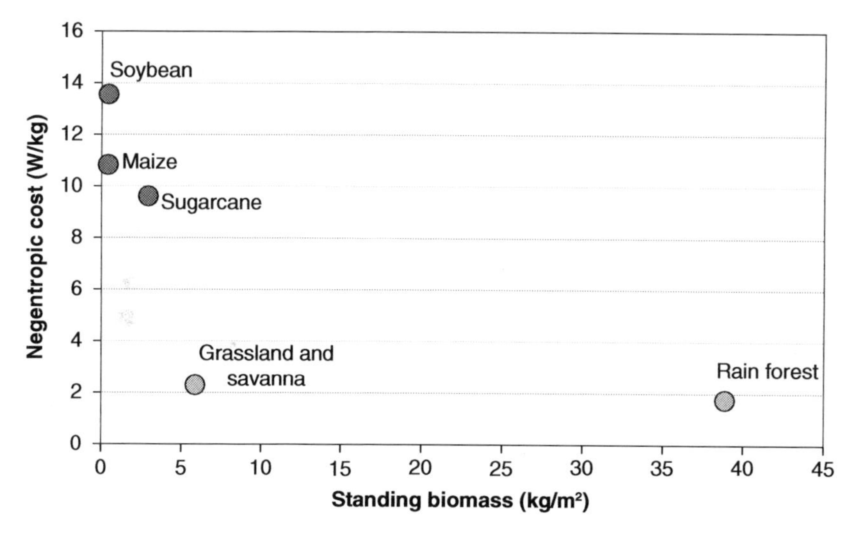

Figure 4.1 Flow/fund ratio (negentropic cost) (vertical axis) and fund size (standing biomass) (horizontal axis) for tropical ecosystem types and selected tropical crop monocultures

Data sources: See Table 4.1.

Note: Negentropic cost is calculated as: PAWF/SB, where PAWF = plant active water flow, SB = standing biomass.

In line with the philosophy of MuSIASEM, standing biomass is defined as a fund element that determines the size of the terrestrial ecosystem, whereas the energy needed to guarantee the water evapotranspiration is a flow element. The resulting flow/fund ratio (negentropic cost) represents a specific metabolic characteristic of the system.

Thus, as shown in Figure 4.1 and Table 4.1, the human alteration of ecosystems expresses itself in a decrease in standing biomass (reduction of fund) and an increase in the flow of energy metabolized (thermodynamic or negentropic cost) per unit of standing biomass on a year basis (flow/fund ratio). The negentropic cost can be calculated from the flow of gross primary productivity (GPP), that is, the chemical energy produced in the form of biomass, which is directly related to the required flow of evapotranspirated water (plant active water flow, PAWF, needed to move the nutrients from the roots to the leaves) and the corresponding quantity of 'solar radiation' consumed in this process.

4.4.3 The alteration of terrestrial ecosystems by agricultural production

Being a form of ecosystem exploitation, agriculture necessarily takes place on the interface between societal and ecosystem metabolism. In Figure 4.2, we frame the impact of traditional or 'low-external-input' agriculture (LEIA) (top graph) and intensive or 'high-external-input' agriculture (HEIA) (bottom graph) on

Table 4.1 Ecological indices for unaltered tropical ecosystem types and selected tropical crop monocultures

	Sugarcane	*Soybean*	*Maize*	*Tropical grassland and savanna*	*Rainforest*
NPP (kg/m^2*yr)[a]	2.8	0.4	0.3	1.1	2.5
SB (kg/m^2)[a]	2.8	0.4	0.3	5.8	38.8
RR[b]	0.35	0.54	0.43	0.49	0.76
GPP (g/m^2*yr)[b]	4,289	777	594	2,104	10,563
PAWF (kg/m^2*yr)[c]	346	63	48	170	852
GPP (W/m^2)[d]	2.4	0.4	0.3	1.2	5.9
PAWF (W/m^2)[d]	26.8	4.8	3.7	13.1	66.0
NEC (W/kg)[e]	9.6	13.6	10.9	2.3	1.7

Notes:

a Net primary productivity (NPP) and standing biomass (SB) of ecosystems from Saugier *et al.* (2001); yield (NPP) of monocultures from FAOSTAT for 1991. SB of monoculture crops assumed equal to NPP. Coefficients to obtain final NPP of crops (i.e. dry matter content and harvest index) from Goudriaan *et al.* (2001) for 1991.

b Respiration rate (RR) = Ra/GPP, where Ra = autotrophic respiration and GPP = gross primary productivity. RR from Amthor (1989) and Amthor and Baldocchi (2001); GPP estimated as NPP/(1−RR).

c PAWF = 80.7 kg of water per kg of primary productivity.

d 1 kg/m^2*yr of primary production (dry matter) = 4,250 $kcal/m^2$*yr = 0.56 W/m^2 (Giampietro *et al.* 1992). 1 kg of evaporated water = 2.44 MJ at 25°C (Lide 2009).

e NEC (negentropic cost) = PAWF/SB.

ecosystem metabolism. The difference between these two forms of ecosystem exploitation lies in the level of openness of the nutrient cycles.

As shown in Figure 4.2 (bottom graph), HEIA is characterized by high productivity obtained through a combination of: 1) complete alteration of the original ecosystem (crop fields are ploughed and the natural vegetation is replaced by monoculture; pesticides are used to prevent other species from devouring a share of the NPP); 2) total linearization of nutrient flows (timed fertilization of crop fields in concentrated mineral form, often applied in excess). The resulting agro-ecosystem represents a radical departure from the original metabolic pattern, and this 'unnatural' state is reflected by a discrepancy between the metabolic characteristics of the altered ecosystem and the reference values for the corresponding original ecosystem type (see Figure 4.1 and Table 4.1). Monocultures (a form of HEIA) in particular have an extremely large GPP in spite of their small SB (averaged over the year). This large GPP is due not to abundance of unaltered ecological funds (HEIA is *not* a form of fund-flow exploitation) but to the massive use of external inputs. As a result, monocultures exhibit a much larger flow/fund ratio than undisturbed ecosystems. In this mode of production, the flow of NPP represents an input flow for the socio-economic system taken away from the fields; it does not contribute to the reproduction of ecological funds.

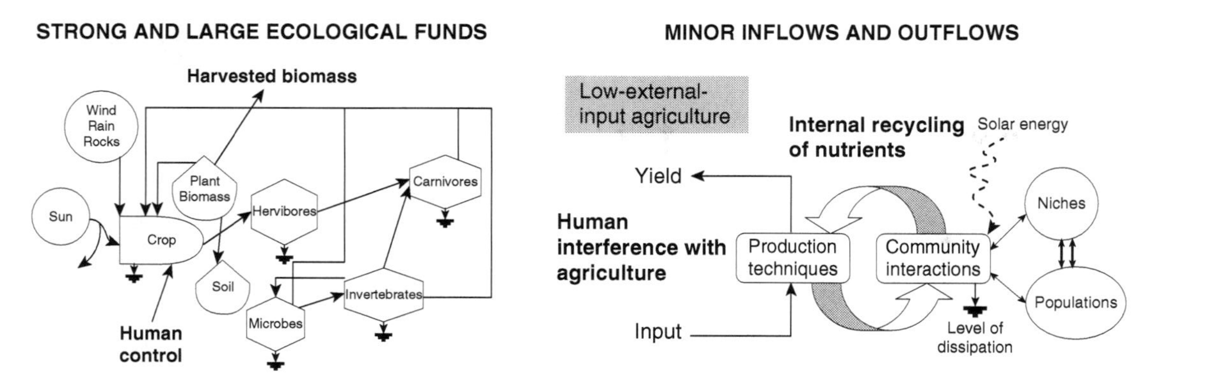

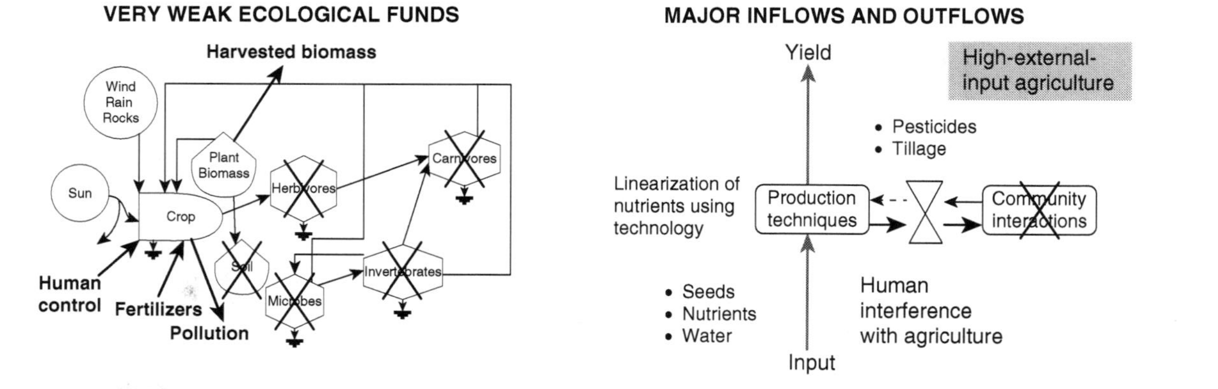

Figure 4.2 Schematic representation of the effects of low-external-input agriculture (LEIA) (upper graph) and high-external-input agriculture (HEIA) (lower graph) on ecosystem metabolism

4.5 Singling out the rural metabolic pattern

One of the major problems encountered in interfacing the analysis of societal and ecosystem metabolism is that modern economies based on international trade, credit/debt leverage, and fossil energy use have lost their direct connection with the land (Mayumi 1991). They are open economies, in space and time. The result is that their biophysical resource requirement – both the aggregate and per capita – is masked at the national scale. Indeed, a significant part of the demand for biophysical production factors (flows, funds and stocks), such as fossil energy, land, water and labour, is met *indirectly*, the production factors being embodied in imported products and services. In this way, domestic biophysical limits to the supply and sink capacity are overcome, and 'the consequences' of over-exploitation are externalized to other countries (see also section 4.3.2).

Trade and specialization also affect the concentration of flows *within* modern economies. In developed countries, usually more than 95 per cent of the GDP is generated in urban areas occupying less than 3 per cent of the land (Giampietro *et al.* 2012). Rural economies (e.g. agriculture) may occupy as much as 90 per cent of the total managed land, consume more than 75 per cent of the water resources, but hardly contribute to the national GDP (less than 2 per cent in most developed countries) (Giampietro *et al.* 2012). Thus the majority of the biophysical interaction between modern economies and ecological processes takes place in a sector (agriculture) that is practically invisible in economic analysis. Indeed, because of these large asymmetries in the share of land use and value added produced, the density of monetary flows (per hectare) is more than 1,000 times larger in urban than in rural areas. This situation demands the use of non-equivalent descriptive domains for describing and analysing biophysical and economic processes taking place in urban and rural areas. MuSIASEM, with its flexible definition of hierarchical levels, dimensions and categories of accounting crossing different scales, has been purposely designed to handle the integration of distinct quantitative representations of the metabolic pattern derived from non-equivalent descriptive domains.

We can single out the rural part of the socio-economic system by employing a flow accounting system based on the fund element land use rather than human activity (see also Chapter 6) so as to focus on the feasibility of the societal metabolic pattern in relation to natural resources. In rural areas we can easily establish a relation between categories of human activities, defining specific sub-compartments (such as cultivation of corn) and the density of flows (such as yield and energy inputs per hectare of corn) in the corresponding land uses. For this reason, we can better describe rural systems as land systems, as a subcategory of socio-ecological systems (see Chapter 5). To get back to the level of the whole socio-ecological system we have to integrate the representation of the metabolism of the rural part with the representation of the metabolism of the urban part. In this way, we can categorize the total amount of managed land in a set of defined land uses with expected or typical metabolic characteristics.

Thus, when dealing with the analysis of the metabolic pattern of rural areas, we have to describe:

- the interface between the rural metabolism and the local ecosystem metabolism by looking at the exchange of biophysical flows;
- the interdependence between the rural and urban metabolism of society by analysing the exchange of biophysical flows and functional services;
- the openness of the rural metabolic pattern by assessing the relative contribution of imports and exports in the overall rural metabolic pattern.

This multi-level approach deals with the problematic boundary definition for a quantitative analysis of the interaction between the metabolic pattern of a given society and its ecosystems and allows us to confront economic variables (mainly determined by the characteristics of urban processes) with environmental variables (requiring an effective analysis of processes taking place in rural areas). We illustrate this approach to environmental accounting for two distinct rural production systems, LEIA and HEIA. The ecosystem view on these systems has been described earlier, in Figure 4.2. In the next two subsections we present a template for such an analysis based on the flow-fund model and on recent work of Serrano-Tovar and Giampietro (2014).

4.5.1 The metabolic pattern of rural societies practising LEIA

In Figure 4.3 we propose a template for the analysis of the metabolic pattern of rural communities practising the most extreme form of LEIA, that is, subsistence agriculture.

The two pie charts in the middle of Figure 4.3 show the pattern of allocation of the two main fund elements, human activity (left) and managed land (right), to different categories. Total human activity (in h/yr), defined at level *n*, is divided into three categories: physiological overhead (HA_{PO}), farm work (HA_{W}), and social activities, leisure and education (HA_{SLE}). The total managed land (in ha/yr), defined at level *n*, is allocated to six different land uses: forestry and pasture (LU_{FP}) and five categories of crop cultivation.

The template further identifies three crucial factors for the analysis of the feasibility, viability and desirability of the metabolic pattern:

1. *Openness of the socio-ecological system*: At the top of Figure 4.3 we see that the interaction of the rural community with the 'outside' (import/export) is non-existent. Indeed, pre-industrial subsistence societies are basically closed systems.
2. *Dependence on urban areas*: The left of Figure 4.3 shows the interface of the rural community with the urban part of society. Reflecting the internal organization of pre-industrial society, the integration with urban activities is limited for LEIA.
3. *Dependence on ecosystem funds*: The bottom part of Figure 4.3 shows that the interaction between LEIA rural metabolism and ecosystem metabolism generally represents a plus for human societies (free supply of environmental funds required for the stabilization of required inputs) and a minus for the ecosystems (ecosystem stress in the form of environmental loading), at least

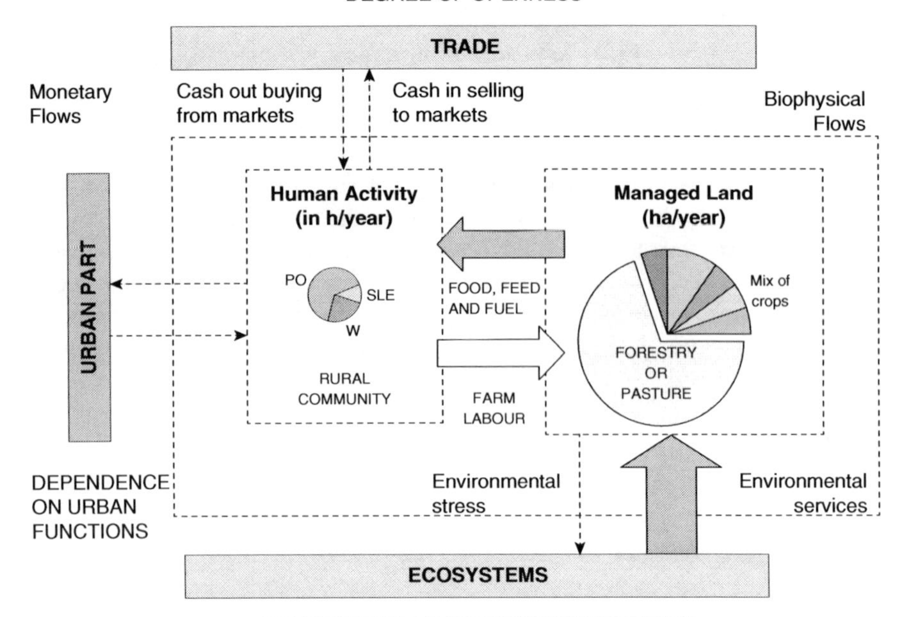

Figure 4.3 Template representing the metabolic pattern of rural communities practising low-external-input agriculture (LEIA)

Source: Adapted from Serrano-Tovar and Giampietro (2014).

Note: PO = physiological overhead; SLE = social, leisure and education; W = work.

in the medium-short term. However, if human activity results in an excessive alteration of the original metabolic pattern of ecosystems, the reproduction of ecosystem funds may be compromised and with that the ecosystem services. History provides plenty of examples of pre-industrial civilizations collapsing because of an erosion of their resources.

Several applications of this method of analysis (land–time budget) of the metabolic pattern of rural communities have been presented elsewhere (Giampietro and Pastore 1999; Pastore *et al.* 1999; Grünbühel and Schandl 2005; Arizpe-Ramos *et al.* 2011; Scheidel *et al.* 2013; Serrano-Tovar and Giampietro 2014).

4.5.2 The metabolic pattern of rural societies practising HEIA

The metabolic pattern of rural systems practising HEIA is completely different and is represented in Figure 4.4. Note that input of human activity in the HEIA system is minimal (Giampietro 2004, 2008). Indeed, at present, 50 per cent of the world population is urban, and in post-industrial societies less than 3 per cent of the work force is engaged with agriculture.

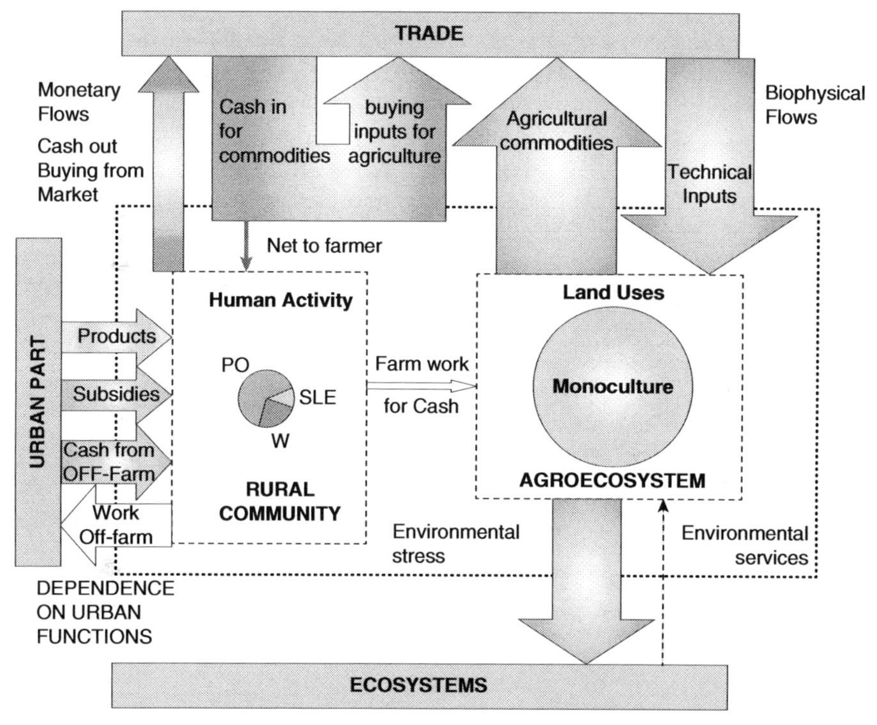

Figure 4.4 Template representing the metabolic pattern of rural communities practising high-external-input agriculture

Source: Adapted from Serrano-Tovar and Giampietro (2014).

Note: PO = physiological overhead; SLE = social, leisure and education; W = work.

As illustrated in Figure 4.4, the metabolic pattern of rural systems practising HEIA is unsustainable by definition for the following reasons:

1 It is *infeasible* in biophysical terms given the constraints at the local scale. The linearization of nutrient flows practised in HEIA, rather than respecting the natural cycles, overcomes the slow natural reproduction process of ecological funds, thus boosting the productivity of the biophysical production factors labour and land (Giampietro 1997a, 1997b). With many of the natural ecosystem services substituted by technical inputs, this choice results in a major stress on the ecological funds (biodiversity, soil, water funds), as well as pollution and emissions. Add to this that modern agricultural production is totally dependent on fossil energy (Giampietro 2002), a stock-flow input.

2 HEIA exists only by the grace of external inputs, the purchase of which is financed by selling the produced flows on the market. Therefore HEIA entirely depends on the market to stabilize its flows.
3 More in general, the processes taking place in the rural system are not functionally self-sufficient. HEIA depends on input flows generated elsewhere and produces flows consumed elsewhere. Therefore its sustainability depends on demand and policies (subsidies, price policies, regulations) decided 'elsewhere'. This makes HEIA rural systems vulnerable. It follows that it is essential that the representation of the metabolic pattern of rural societies practising HEIA includes the symbiotic relation with its urban counterpart and the international market or the relevant encompassing higher level of organization (e.g. the Common Agricultural Policy in the EU).

4.6 Conclusions

In this chapter we illustrated the use of Georgescu-Roegen's flow-fund model to implement the concept of societal metabolism and to assess the sustainability of socio-ecological systems. The use of the concepts flows, funds and stocks provides a flexible means to analyse the metabolic systems over multiple organizational scales. We further saw how the Odums' concept of ecosystem metabolism can be used to construct ecosystem impact indicators. In line with the general MuSIASEM philosophy we proposed an impact indicator based on a flow/fund ratio, the negentropic cost of standing biomass.

MuSIASEM can thus be used to establish a bridge between relevant characteristics of the metabolic pattern of societal systems and the metabolic pattern of ecosystems. The metabolism of the rural part of society can be conveniently singled out to highlight natural resource use by focusing on the fund element land use. The description of land systems, as a subcategory of socio-ecological systems, is further detailed in Chapter 5.

5 Land systems

Multi-scale dynamics of human and environmental systems

Richard J. Aspinall

Summary

This chapter describes the nature and functioning of land systems in the context of a multi-scale representation and analysis of coupled human–environment systems. This description is linked to resource accounting and the operation of the multi-scale integrated assessment procedure through a variety of mechanisms. Issues considered include: land as a coupled human and environment system; land cover and land use; land functions and ecosystem services (which include water, food and energy); and scale.

5.1 Introduction

Land is a fund element in the MuSIASEM approach to resource accounting. As a fund, land reflects not only the solid surface of the earth, including fresh water (Global Land Project 2005), but also land uses and land systems, which are the interactions of human activity and environmental resources. This chapter introduces the nature and functioning of land systems in the context of a multi-scale representation of land as a coupled human–environment system. Coupled human–environment systems are also termed socio-ecological systems, and the two names are considered equivalent here, both referring to the systemic coupling of human-controlled socio-economic processes to ecosystem-controlled biophysical processes (see also Chapter 4) and the importance of societal institutions, actors and actions in this coupling. The chapter describes several ways in which land and land systems link to resource accounting and to the operation of the multi-scale integrated assessment. Linkage is through representations of land as:

1. a geographical area, defined by the boundary of the study area of interest;
2. a production factor (in the Ricardian sense of land, labour and capital) that identifies a set of resources and their uses;
3. a set of geographically distributed human and environmental funds, qualities and processes; and
4. a geographical, place-based framework for an indexing system, based on location, that references human and environmental funds, qualities and processes (as in 3); the geographical representation using this indexing is formalized

within GIS (Chapter 10), but representations as sets of 'vectors' and 'arrays' of human and environmental conditions and qualities are also possible, and are used extensively, in MuSIASEM.

The second and third of these representations have evolved and expanded over time, and now there is wide recognition of natural capital as the fund that yields a flow of ecosystem goods and services (Daily 1997). In MuSIASEM, the role and importance of natural capital is incorporated though land systems and land use.

Understanding and use of land and land systems in each of these representations face a number of issues. These include:

1. the nature of land as a coupled human–environment system;
2. relationships between land cover and land use;
3. a wider suite of issues associated with the multiple uses and functions of land and land systems, increasingly presented and discussed as ecosystem goods and services (which include water, food and energy); and
4. the many and various definitions of scale (spatial, temporal, organizational, functional and local–regional–global multi-scales) as they relate to land, not least from the perspectives of different disciplines involved in multi-, inter- and trans-disciplinary studies of land, land systems and socio-ecological systems more generally.

This suite of representations is directly relevant to definitions and use of 'land' as a fund element in the MuSIASEM resource accounting framework presented in this book. Each of the representations is discussed in this chapter.

5.2 Land systems

5.2.1 Land systems: coupled human–environment systems

Land systems can be represented and understood as coupled human–environment (socio-ecological) systems (Global Land Project 2005; Foresight Land Use Futures Project 2010). A whole-systems approach to land represents not only the structures and processes that link human and environment sub-systems, but also the driving factors of land system change (Lambin *et al.* 2001), themselves a suite of social and biophysical processes that operate at multiple scales in space and time. Such a whole-systems approach thus necessarily embeds the different spatial, temporal and organizational scales of environment (Levin 1992; Chave and Levin 2003) and human (Gibson *et al.* 2000) system processes.

The environment sub-system includes the biophysical earth system, with climatic, biological, biogeochemical, hydrological and other sub-systems. In studies of land systems and land system change, environment systems have generally been linked to the human sub-system through analysis of land cover. The human sub-system includes economic, institutional, demographic, technological and political factors, and studies have been linked to the environment sub-system through land use. Both land cover and land use contribute to the ecosystem goods and services derived from land systems. The interaction of land use and land cover is recognized and investigated in research by international programmes such as Land Use and Cover Change (LUCC) (Lambin and Geist 2006), NASA Land-Cover/Land-Use Change (LCLUC) (Gutman *et al.* 2004) and the Global Land Project (2005), and in the elements of recent interdisciplinary research that has defined land systems and land change science, including observation and monitoring, impacts, and modelling (Aspinall 2006; B.L. Turner *et al.* 2007).

Processes in the environment sub-system are largely driven by biodiversity, energy and material flows, while processes in the human sub-system are driven by flows of finance, ideas, innovation, technology and human activity, implemented and executed by decisions. Land, as a coupled human–environment system, thus reflects fully both human and environment sub-systems, and their interaction. A systems model of land emphasizes these systems-level interactions, not only of factors that affect land, but also of the different activities and processes that have an impact on food, water and energy, as well as other goods and services provided. Although ecosystem goods and services are typically defined as the benefits society receives from environmental systems (Millennium Ecosystem Assessment 2005), and may also be considered the productive output of natural capital (Daily and Matson 2008), it is clear that the many ecosystem goods and services produced from land are not solely the product of environment systems; active land management and other human activities are central to delivery of ecosystem services (Global Land Project 2005). In the context of resource accounting for sustainability assessment, it is necessary to emphasize that continued societal access to ecosystem goods and services, such as food and water, is based on the persistence and resilience of land systems as functioning autopoietic systems encompassing stocks and funds of natural capital. Long-term sustainability of goods and services that arise from land systems is, therefore, not solely a property of land system functions based on biophysical system performance linked to biodiversity (Millennium Ecosystem Assessment 2005; UK National Ecosystem Assessment 2011), but also fully reliant on a hypercycle which maintains land as a fund element, the hypercycle in most land systems being dominated by the human sub-system (see Chapters 2 and 3 for more information on autopoietic systems and hypercycles, and Chapter 4 for examples of high- and low-external-input agricultural land systems).

Land systems also vary at local, national, regional and global scales, not only through the role and geographical differences of system elements (environment, labour, capital, knowledge, etc.), but also in contextual and substantive differences in the structural bases for land use (e.g. land tenure, regulatory, legislative and policy frameworks, etc.). Understanding these qualities of land systems is important for effective use of MuSIASEM, and further emphasizes why MuSIASEM should be used within participatory approaches that bring local and cultural knowledge to the analysis of resource accounts (Raquez and Lambin 2006).

5.2.2 Land cover, land use and land evaluation

5.2.2.1 Land cover

Land cover represents the biophysical characteristics of a unit of the physical land surface. Land cover types include habitat types and other classifications (Vogelmann *et al.* 2001; Aspinall 2002). The sources of data, and their scales, used for mapping land cover, are an important determinant of the nature of the classification that can be achieved, as well as its accuracy (Anderson *et al.* 1976). In this instance, scale refers to: 1) geographic scale of the representation; 2) the ability to resolve the land covers in the taxonomic classification defining the land cover types; and 3) the minimum geographic sizes of mappable units that it is possible to resolve from the source data. Satellite imagery is frequently used as a source for land cover mapping.

5.2.2.2 Land use

Land use represents the social and economic functions and purposes of land. With this definition, it can be seen that land use cannot be mapped directly using remote sensing, but, rather, has to be collected using field-based methods of social and economic survey and mapping. Land use is distinct from land cover, although land cover data, which are considerably easier to collect than land use data because of the utility of satellite imagery, are frequently used as a surrogate for land use. Strictly this is appropriate only for certain very general typologies of land use, such as agriculture versus forestry versus urban land uses, for which the differences between categories of land use are also associated with resolvable differences in land cover. Given that, in practice, there is widespread use of land cover data as a source of land use data, it is important to be aware of the limitations of any land cover or land use dataset being used as an input to MuSIASEM.

5.2.2.3 Land evaluation

Land cover and land use, although used and useful in MuSIASEM, are not sufficient as a complete description of the nature of land, and more holistic land evaluations can also be useful for MuSIASEM. Given the definition of land systems as coupled human–environment systems, the full range of environment and human sub-system characteristics have relevance for describing and understanding land systems and their use. For example, soils and geological parent material, topography, climate, and a variety of biological factors together influence land uses such as growth of different crops. Land capability and land suitability assessments are two forms of land evaluation that interpret the flexibility and capacity of land for different uses based on an ensemble suite of relevant environmental, social and technological factors (Klingebiel and Montgomery 1961; Bibby and Mackney 1969; FAO 2007). Land evaluation assesses the suitability of land for specific different crops or other land uses using expert opinion or a number of other analytical methods. Land capability assessments evaluate the capacity of land for a variety of related uses, for example different types of agriculture (Bibby *et al.* 1982; I. Brown *et al.* 2008, 2011) or forestry (Bibby *et al.* 1988). There are numerous examples of land capability and suitability assessments of land for different uses, and there are well-developed methodologies for land evaluation (FAO 2007; Costantini 2009).

These types of multi-dimensional assessments and evaluations of land, and its potential, are of great value in MuSIASEM, particularly in relation to use of MuSIASEM in simulation mode, where one or more potential alternative land uses are being assessed as part of the analysis. GIS-based land suitability assessment can be used to identify the location and extent of existing and alternative land uses in order to change the pattern of land uses in a study region, the GIS providing data on land mixes and areas for use in calculation of land as a fund for input to the MuSIASEM accounting data in multi-level tables (see Chapters 10 and 12).

5.3 Land systems and ecosystem goods and services

Land systems are used to provide a wide range of goods and services that support human well-being and society (Global Land Project 2005; Millennium Ecosystem Assessment 2005; Daily and Matson 2008; Carpenter *et al.* 2009). The Millennium Ecosystem Assessment (MEA) has popularized a categorization of these ecosystem goods and services into four main types: supporting, regulating, provisioning, and cultural services; other classifications are closely aligned to this typology, including the Common International Classification of Ecosystem Services (EEA 2010), which also explicitly recognizes abiotic services. These different types of services are not alternatives; multiple services can be, and are, delivered from a single block of land or land system. This is related to, but not the same as, multiple land uses. Both single and multiple land uses can produce multiple ecosystem goods and services. Additionally, it is important to emphasize that ecosystem goods and services obtained from land systems are not produced solely by the biophysical (environment) sub-systems, especially biodiversity; human sub-systems, and particularly land management activities, contribute to recovery and delivery of ecosystem goods and services (Global Land Project 2005; Carpenter *et al.* 2009).

The recovery of ecosystem services through land management also has economic, social and environmental costs. These are important, not only because energy, labour (human activity), money and other resources are expended on land management to recover goods and services, but also because investment in natural capital is necessary to ensure sustainability of goods and services. Recognition and treatment of land as a fund, rather than stock (see Chapter 4), and the need for appropriate land management to ensure the sustainability and resilience of the land fund, especially when considered as natural capital, are central to the perspective on sustainability presented in this book. This view is also compatible with a focus on delivery of multiple ecosystem services, and is essential for effective sustainability assessments. Thus, the MuSIASEM approach currently focuses primarily on food, water and energy, with certain environmental impacts also considered (for example greenhouse gas emissions – see Chapter 4). Other goods and services could be added within the MuSIASEM resource accounting framework.

5.4 Land systems: scale and multi-scale issues

The concept of scale refers to the spatial, temporal, thematic, quantitative, analytical or other organizing dimensions, including extent and resolution, of variables or models used to measure and study any phenomenon (Gibson *et al.* 2000). Thus, scale provides a framework that defines not only the geometric, thematic and information contents of a dataset, but also behavioural properties and limits of the dataset, which together circumscribe the use and utility of the data. This section addresses the dimensions for four main categories of scale relevant to MuSIASEM: spatial, temporal, organizational and functional. The section also describes the multi-scale, frequently hierarchical, nature of land across the different types of scale. This is particularly important, since MuSIASEM, as a multi-scale approach for resource accounting, encapsulates different elements of each of the types of scale, and their multi-scale interactions and dynamics. The effectiveness of land as an informative fund element in MuSIASEM is possible, in part, because of the ways in which land and land systems articulate to the different dimensions of scale.

5.4.1 Spatial

Spatial, or geographic, scale refers to the representation of geographic phenomena, for example on a map. The two most common ways to represent spatial scale are: 1) using map scale, the representative fraction which relates map distances to 'real-world' distances; and 2) using a conceptual terminology that embodies a hierarchical scaling, such as local–regional–national.

Spatial scale is most commonly encountered in relation to land systems in geographical representations of biophysical and socio-economic data. Biophysical data include representations of soils, land cover types, weather and climate, topography, geology, hydrology, vegetation, and so on. Socio-economic data include survey and census data, with associated spatial units, administrative regions, and maps of infrastructure, such as locations of power stations, electricity transmission lines, dams, roads, and so on. GIS can be used to present these data for use in MuSIASEM. Summary statistics of the number, length and area of these different environment and human system data for relevant regions may also be used in MuSIASEM.

With increasing use of GIS, the concept of map scale (representative fraction) has become less explicit, although it is still relevant in analysis, not only for representation of information within GIS and printed formats, but also because many of the source datasets used within GIS have an explicit scale at which the data were collected, represented and digitized. The appropriate heuristics and caveats, as well as considerations of error propagation (Burrough and McDonnell 1998), apply to uses of these data in GIS, even with the apparently limitless zooming in and out that GIS allows. A practical heuristic is that, nominally, map-sourced data should be used with other data only within a +/– 2.5 times range of source scales (thus a 1:100,000 scale source dataset can be used with other data within the range 1:40,000–1:250,000). Land, and other, data collected with GPS and entered into GIS provide a further challenge for traditional map-related concepts of scale, although the more general definition of scale given at the head of this section (5.4) applies to GPS data as much as to any other data. Indeed, GPS refers only to the locational accuracy of the data, not to the accuracy and relevance of measurements of any other variables made at GPS-fixed locations.

5.4.2 Temporal

Temporal scale refers to the time period over which data are represented or measured or over which a model applies (Gibson *et al.* 2000). The temporal scale refers, in part, therefore, to the measurement support for a dataset. This has two main elements: 1) the date or range of dates over which the source data were collected; and 2) the duration period for which those data are relevant. For many datasets with a short duration of relevance, because of change in the property being measured, the date at which the source data are collected provides a valuable practical indicator of the relevance of that dataset to analysis with MuSIASEM. This is particularly important for land use and land cover data, which can change rapidly and should be collected or available from dates compatible with the analysis being carried out with MuSIASEM.

Temporal scale also refers to the time period over which a model is applied and to the time period of interest for analysis of a phenomenon. In land systems, temporal scale is central to measurement, representation and understanding of change and dynamics. Land system dynamics, and especially land use and land cover change, are typically studied with a temporal scale of years and decades (Aspinall 2004), although land systems, land use and land cover all exhibit changes and dynamics over a wide range of temporal scales (Lambin and Geist 2006). For example, agricultural areas exhibit changes and dynamics that are associated with land and other management activities with seasonal cycles and that manage changes within a calendar year, as well as responding to longer-term trends and signals from markets, policy, regulation, legislation, and climate changes (Lambin *et al.* 2001). Additionally, land systems, land use and land cover themselves each can exhibit different dynamics over time within a single location. Thus, an agricultural land system (e.g. mixed farming) at a location can remain the same type of land system for decades, although land use (e.g. crops versus livestock production) may change on yearly time scales, while land cover (e.g. bare ground, cereals, legumes or fodder crop) changes seasonally, especially in places with multiple crops per year (e.g. Punjab – Chapter 13). Technology may also change within the land system over time: a mixed farming system today is very different to a mixed farming system of a century ago! Spatial scale and the scale of the taxonomic categorization of land systems, land uses and land covers are also relevant in these examples.

5.4.3 Organizational

Organizational scale most often refers to a hierarchical level at which different organizations or other taxonomies operate. In the context of organizational scale, these hierarchical levels represent a conceptual scale that is often based on functional or geographic relationships.

Hierarchies can be either exclusive or nested, nested hierarchies being either inclusive or constitutive (Gibson *et al.* 2000). In an exclusive (non-nested) hierarchy, groups of objects or processes that are ranked as lower in a hierarchy are neither contained in, nor subdivisions of groups that are ranked as higher in the system. In nested, inclusive hierarchies, phenomena are grouped into levels such that phenomena grouped together at any one level are contained in the category used to describe higher levels, although there is no particular organization at each level. In constitutive hierarchies, groups of objects or processes at one level are combined into new units at another 'higher' level, and so on at higher levels. In a constitutive hierarchy, each level has characteristic functions and emergent properties. The hierarchical organization of government and governance within a nation is often an example of a constitutive hierarchy, as are metabolic systems, for example, with cells, organs and organisms as the different levels.

Certain taxonomies of land systems provide examples of inclusive hierarchies. For example, individual farms may be classified into groups defining specific types of farm, and these may then be geographically organized into a nested series of agricultural regions. Agricultural statistics are frequently organized with this type of hierarchical aggregation. For land systems, and for agricultural land systems in particular, the distinction between an inclusive hierarchy and a constitutive hierarchy may become blurred, largely because aggregation based on administrative and/or geographic regions produces a constitutive hierarchy. This hierarchical aggregation of agricultural data into geographic regions, with characteristics of constitutive hierarchies, is then associated with constitutive hierarchies of institutional structures and policy making that mirrors the geographic differences between regions and their imputed and perceived functional and emergent properties. Policy-making and institutional processes that operate in the human sub-system of land systems then link to the individual farms and farmers through the constitutive hierarchy of institutions. This is important, not because of the taxonomy of organization scale, but because it illustrates the multi-scale nature of land systems as coupled human–environment systems (see section 5.5).

5.4.4 Functional

Within each of the human and environment sub-systems of land systems there may be characteristic functional scales, or ranges of scales, at which specific processes apply and operate. These functional scales may have characteristic extents, in both spatial (distance or length, area) and temporal (duration as second, hour, season, year, decade, etc.) scales. In relation to spatial scales of land systems, government regulation, legislation and policy typically are developed for application at national scales; hydrological processes operate at hillslope and catchment scales; and agricultural land management is applied at field and farm scales. Similarly, although most processes operate continuously through time, there are often temporal scales, measured as duration, over which processes are most clearly manifest. For example, land management is concerned with short to medium time scales, while policy related to food and farming refers to longer time scales (e.g. CAP and CAP Reform in Europe).

5.5 Land systems: multi-scale systems and MuSIASEM

Land systems operate – irreducibly – at multiple scales at the same time, and they do this for each of the dimensions of scaling described. In land systems, human and environmental processes operate across spatial, temporal and organizational scales. These scalar (cross-scale) dynamics are fundamental to understanding land systems and land system change (Geist and Lambin 2004; B.L. Turner *et al.* 2007). Importantly for resource accounting and this book, this property of land systems means that they display characteristics of constitutive hierarchies associated with complex adaptive systems (see Chapters 2 and 4). Specifically, land systems show the importance of 'local–regional/national–global' sequences and relationships in their multi-scale dynamics.

Further, if we consider scale as a continuously varying function with four different dimensions, as described in section 5.4, we recognize that the different sub-types of scale neither exist nor operate independently of one another, and that there are characteristic associations between scale types which are consistently apparent. These characteristic associations include repeatably revealed correlation between spatial and temporal scales of processes and forms in biophysical systems and anthropogenic disturbance processes (Walker and Walker 1991), and the logic of hierarchical multi-scale sequences of micro–meso–macro (Doing 1997) and local–regional/national–global (Easterling and Apps 2005).

The interrelations of scaling dimensions mean that, for practical operational purposes of study and analysis, we can unite the scale dimensions for analysis of land systems. The multi-scale nature and cross-scale dynamics of land systems are treated as jointly and collectively represented by a hierarchical scaling which describes a 'local–regional/national–global' sequence (approximately equivalent to micro–meso–macro scales; see Chapter 3). This organizes and unifies management of scale in relation to land systems, serving as a shorthand for the spatial, temporal, organizational and thematic dimensions of land system variability and measurement, as well as encapsulating functional links between human and environment system processes that produce scalar dynamics.

The same sequence of 'local–regional/national–global' hierarchical multi-scaling is implemented in MuSIASEM. MuSIASEM explicitly presents interconnections between land, population, economy, food, water and energy simultaneously at multiple scales, reporting and analysing the multi-scale use of land systems to society, treating land as a fund element. In both land systems and MuSIASEM, therefore, the hierarchical levels 'local–regional/national–global' are used to refer to a series of inclusive, constitutive, spatial/geographic scales.

Despite this shared and unified scaling terminology for land systems and MuSIASEM, it is important to remain aware of differences between the dimensions of scale, and the underlying individual scale types and their properties. As Chapter 3 makes clear, the pre-analytical step of MuSIASEM requires the choice of a given level of analysis, and makes it possible to monitor the characteristics (at the micro and meso scales) and the relative size (at the macro scale) of land as a fund element making up one functional compartment determining the dimension of flows across different levels of analysis. Note that, in using this sequence, we reaffirm the principles that relate to scale which were expanded in Chapter 3:

1 Each of the levels operates at its own scale and must be observed and described at that scale.
2 Use of multiple levels requires the simultaneous use of non-equivalent descriptive domains.
3 Assumptions of linear relations between inputs and outputs cannot be made.

Similarly, as described in Chapter 4, time scales are of considerable importance in resource accounting and MuSIASEM. The definition of land as a fund element requires that the identity of land has to remain the same over the time scale of the analysis. MuSIASEM operates using one year as the basic temporal scale, a duration that accommodates annual cycles of land use and land management activity related to food production, hydrological cycles and energy usage.

Part II

The toolkit

6 Accounting for human activity and socio-economic characteristics

Zora Kovacic and Jesus Ramos-Martin

Summary

This chapter shows how human activity and socio-economic characteristics can be integrated in the MuSIASEM accounting to assess the feasibility and viability of a given socio-ecological system. It presents a comprehensive grammar for human activity to represent and quantify the allocation of this fund element within human societies and couples it with the most widely used variables in economics, the gross domestic product, a measure of production, and its components, such as gross value added, a measure of production of individual economic sectors, and import–export values, a measure of the openness of the economic system. In MuSIASEM, monetary flows are output flows resulting from the combination of funds (labour, land, power capacity) and input flows (energy, water and other natural resources). The inclusion of this variable in the biophysical accounting scheme of MuSIASEM is essential to establish a link with other accounting methods.

6.1 Introduction

Society can be studied from both the social science point of view and a more technical point of view looking at the biophysical processes associated with its reproduction. In the former case, the analysis focuses on *social* characteristics by looking at the social values and perceptions that shape the concept of desirability of the development path, while, in the latter, *societal* features are examined by studying how the hierarchical organization of the various components of society results in the expression of an integrated set of functions. The consideration of demographic and economic variables, relevant in both these complementing views, helps in integrating the two approaches. For example, living standards can be seen as an interface between social and cultural values on the one hand, and as constraints emerging from demographic factors (e.g. life expectancy, dependency ratio, infant mortality) and economic factors (e.g. monetary income) on the other hand.

Demographic characteristics are key to the identity of a society. For this reason, the fund element human activity lies at the core of the analytical framework of MuSIASEM. In section 6.2, we show this representation of society as a hierarchical organization of human activity closely linked to the definition of the set of socio-economic compartments of society. Following, in section 6.3, we present a comprehensive accounting system (a grammar or accounting scheme) for human activity that explains how to quantify the profile of allocation of human activity in accord with the other MuSIASEM grammars. In section 6.4 we look at the possible use of economic variables to characterize the pattern of societal metabolism in terms of monetary flows (gross domestic product, value added, imports and exports). As noted earlier, monetary flows provide a key piece of information to link the reading of biophysical flows, described in the next chapters, to economic analysis. In particular, monetary flows are of great interest for complementing biophysical analysis related to international trade (imports and exports) of biophysical flows.

6.2 Human activity as the focal fund element of society

We saw in Chapter 3 that human society is a metabolic system, that is, a complex self-organizing system reproducing itself. Then, if we adopt a representation of human society on the basis of the flow-fund model (Chapter 4), it logically follows that the most important fund element for society is human activity: this is what has to be reproduced to keep the society alive. We thus use human activity, closely associated with population, as the external referent defining the identity of our fund element; this makes it possible to define, across levels, the size and structure of the whole socio-economic system and its lower-level compartments. In the framework of MuSIASEM, human activity is categorized according to the *functions* it expresses in the reproduction of society, for example paid work in agriculture or leisure in the household. To quantify the pattern of human activities associated with the expression of these different functions we describe society as a hierarchical structure of functional compartments, whose size is also assessed in terms of human activity (hours per year). When integrating the pattern of human activity over different compartments with the metabolic rate of these compartments (the flow-fund ratio) we can define the metabolic pattern of the various flows. In this way, it becomes possible to study the feasibility of the metabolic pattern (compatibility with external constraints), its viability (compatibility with constraints determined by the internal organization of society) and its desirability (compatibility with the expectations and normative values keeping together the social fabric).

A metabolic system expresses an emergent property: the generation of a complex and integrated set of functions that stabilizes the metabolic pattern required for its reproduction. No individual human being alone can express that property. Hence, in contrast to societal aggregates, where the whole is defined as the sum of the characteristics of individual human beings, MuSIASEM describes how emergent properties of the system are generated from the interactions of lower-level functional components observable only at the local scale (the concept of exosomatic metabolism proposed by Lotka and discussed in Chapter 3). To this purpose, we express flow rates in the different compartments and on the different scales *per hour of human activity and not per capita* (Giampietro *et al.* 2012). The size of a society, in relation to this fund, can be conveniently assessed by the total human activity (THA) available to the population. The fund human activity, in terms of allocation of human time, also lends itself extremely well to structuring the analysis through the quantification of the size of the functional compartments of society. For example, in accordance with the economic view, we can divide the society into two large compartments: the paid work sector (PW), which consists of the working time of the economically active population, and the household sector (HH), which includes the activity of the dependent population and that of the employed population when not working. Note that in this way the time of individual human beings who are employed is allocated to more than one compartment (to both the household and the paid work compartments). Both the paid work and household sectors can be further subdivided into lower-level compartments (e.g. urban household versus rural household). Again, the identity given to these compartments is defined by the specific functions they express in the reproduction of society, while their size is measured by the allocated human time in hours. In general, allocation of human activity (the dynamic budget of human time) to the different compartments is obtained by multiplying the number of workers in a sector by their specific work load (expressed in hours per year).

Mapping human activity to the various functional compartments of society, we find that the population age structure is an important factor in defining the relative size of the paid work and household sectors. For example, China's population presently has a large proportion of adults and hence exhibits a low dependency ratio and a large proportion of human activity in the paid work sector. Italy, on the other hand, with its ageing population (a large proportion of retired people in the population) is an example of a country with a high dependency ratio, meaning a lower relative size for its paid work sector. To make things more difficult, the population age structure tends to change in time, which is a potential source of internal instability in the medium to long term. For instance, the large proportion of adults in China, now a major plus for the economy, will eventually become a liability when they retire. In fact, a massive ageing of the population will result in:

1. a shortage of the labour supply, demanding larger investments of technological capital and energy carriers to boost labour productivity;
2. a demand for a larger proportion of the available work force in the service sector to provide assistance to the growing number of elderly;
3. the generation of immigration pumps (to cover low-paid jobs). Indeed, shortage of work supply in an economy implies that lower-paid jobs tend to remain uncovered, attracting foreign workers. Immigration pumps, while being short-term solutions to labour force scarcity, may represent medium-term challenges for resource use, as they also imply a higher overhead (i.e. the direct consumption of the dependent population and the relative services) to the whole society if the dependent population also increases. This is the case for the USA, where economic growth is largely driven by a rising population, which in turn increases the overall overhead of the country, translated into an ever increasing need for natural resources.

The dependency ratio is an important variable reflecting both demographic and economic characteristics. It is defined as the ratio of the population not of working age to the population of working age (15 to 64 years old). In MuSIASEM we use the ratio between the number of hours allocated to the household sector and those allocated to the paid work sector to address the implications of the demographic characteristics of a given society. This ratio tends to increase with the level of development of a society (meaning a lower fraction of working population has to support the non-working population). In fact, development is associated with higher life expectancy, lower child mortality and higher enrolment in education (UNDP 2013). The more developed the society, the smaller the fraction of human activity invested in PW.

The characteristics of the fund human activity and their evolution in time are key to the assessment of the feasibility and viability of the metabolic pattern. The method of accounting for working hours in MuSIASEM is also suitable for studying the complex effects of population growth in future scenarios. Population growth affects not only population size (a quantitative characteristic) but also the demographic structure and dependency ratio (qualitative characteristics). Depending on the dynamics of births, deaths and migration, a similar increase in population size (and THA) may have widely different effects on the dependency ratio in society. For example, in the short term, immigration decreases the dependency ratio (immigrants are mainly adults). However, in the medium term, it increases birth rates and reduces mortality rates, leading to an increase of the dependency ratio (Giampietro *et al.* 2012).

6.3 Human activity accounting

We describe here the accounting for human activity over the various functional compartments in society, as applied in the case studies presented in Chapters 12, 13 and 14 and as illustrated in Figure 2.1.

The overall population size determines the THA available to society and is defined at level n as follows:

$$\text{THA} = \text{population size} \times 8{,}760 \text{ hours/year}$$

As described before, the THA is then split between the two compartments defined at level ($n-1$): the PW and HH sectors. The human activity allocated to the PW sector is then further divided over two lower-level compartments, both defined at level ($n-2$): the production sector (PS), including the primary and secondary production sectors, which express transformation activities, and the service and government sector (SG), comprising transaction activities. The PS is further subdivided into two compartments, both defined at level ($n-3$): the building and manufacturing (BM) and the primary flows (PF) sectors. The latter sector, producing food and exosomatic energy carriers and corresponding to the primary sector in economics, can be still further divided into the agriculture and fishing (AG) and energy and mining (EM) sectors, both defined at level ($n-4$).

It is absolutely essential in the accounting system of MuSIASEM that the size, defined in hours of HA per year, of any one given compartment equals the sum of the sizes of its immediate lower-level compartments that compose it (observing a closure constraint). For example:

$$THA\ [\text{level}\ n] = HA_{HH} + HA_{PW}\ [\text{level}\ n-1]$$

$$HA_{PW}\ [\text{level}\ n-1] = HA_{PS} + HA_{SG}\ [\text{level}\ n-2]$$

The definition of functional compartments employed in MuSIASEM is similar to the one used in economics, which distinguishes between the primary (equivalent to AG and EM), secondary (equivalent to BM) and tertiary (equivalent to SG) sectors. The MuSIASEM representation emphasizes the biophysical reading of the economic process across the hierarchical scales of analysis, thus facilitating the identification of internal constraints imposed by the societal organization. For instance, even though the agricultural and the energy and mining sectors in most developed countries do not contribute much to the gross domestic product (GDP), their combined contribution accounting for no more than a small percentage of the total, their functions (providing food and energy carriers) are of uttermost importance and cannot be substituted by any other human activity. We do have the option to import food and energy, thus relying on the AG and EM sectors of other societies, but we cannot do without them!

The definition of functional compartments adopted in the MuSIASEM grammar is flexible and can be adapted (by aggregation or further subdivision) depending on the focus of the case study. This is illustrated by our three case studies (Chapters 12, 13 and 14), in which we opted for different definitions of the compartments at the lower levels. For instance, in the case study of South Africa we focused on alternative energy sources and singled out the EM sector by simply dividing the PW sector into EM and the remaining sectors in paid work (labelled as PW*). In the case of Mauritius, we examined the openness of the system and added the 'export sector' by refining the subdivision (at level $n-2$) of the paid work compartment. Similarly, a focus on the agricultural sector may require a further subdivision (at level $n-5$) of the agricultural sector by crop type, where in other studies we may want to single out other economic compartments, such as the tourism or financial sector within the service and government sector.

The human activity for each economic sector i is calculated as follows:

$$HA_i = (\text{employed people}) \times (\text{hours of work per week}) \times (\text{work weeks per year})$$

In order to estimate the number of work weeks per year, national holidays, sick leave and part-time workers have to be taken into account. The average hours of work per week range from 35 to 48 hours depending on the country and the activity analysed (ILO 2007). In our case studies, data have been taken from national statistics, but data availability may vary from country to country. For example, in the case of Punjab, no sub-national data are available on hours of work per week for the various sectors, so that figures published by the ILO for India were used as an approximation. South African statistics, on the other hand, provide human activity figures in hours per week for each economic sector and already include part-time workers. Rearrangement of categories used in national statistics may be necessary to fit the definition of functional compartments used in MuSIASEM. An example

Table 6.1 Correspondence between categories of human activities and functional compartments in MuSIASEM and economic sectors in the national statistics for Mauritius

MuSIASEM	*National statistics*
AG	Agriculture, forestry and fishing; sugarcane; tea; other primary sector
EM	Mining and quarrying; electricity, gas and water
BM	Manufacturing; sugar; food; textiles; other manufacturing; construction
SG	Wholesale, retail trade, repair of vehicles; hotels and restaurants; financial intermediation; real estate; public administration, defence; education; health and social work; transport, storage and communications; other services

Source: Ministry of Finance and Economic Development of the Republic of Mauritius (2012c).

is given in Table 6.1. Problems may arise when national statistics present data at a much aggregated level. For example, employment in utilities is reported as one single category, comprising both water handling and electricity and gas distribution. In this case, we have assigned the relative human activity to the EM compartment in our representation, resulting in an overestimation of its size.

Finally, human activity in the HH sector is calculated by difference as follows:

$$HA_{HH} = THA - HA_{PW}$$

At times, we may want to single out the tourism sector, as in our case study of Mauritius (Chapter 12), to study its impact on the local economy and on environmental resource consumption. In this case, tourists may be considered as an addition to the dissipative sector of the local population, so that the total human activity consists of local activity and the 'resident equivalent' of tourist numbers. Georgescu-Roegen (1971) called this category a 'process-fund': something that is not the main fund giving identity to the system, but that in any case has to be reproduced to guarantee the stability of the actual metabolic pattern. In fact, tourists are required for the proper operation of the economy of Mauritius because they add to the consumption of food, water, energy and so on, and to the generation of GDP by increasing the tourism sector. They increase the societal overhead (the dissipative part) that needs to be sustained. To account for tourists in the total human activity we calculate the 'resident equivalent' human activity from the number of tourists and the length of their stay as follows:

$$THA = HA_{PW} + HA_{HH} + HA_{tourists}$$

where $HA_{tourists}$ = no. of tourists × length of stay (days) × 24 hours/365 days

Data on the number of tourists and length of stay may be obtained from the Ministry of Tourism of the country analysed. Data are generally published annually. An example of the quantification of relevant demographic variables is given in Figure 6.1 for the case study of Mauritius.

Population structure

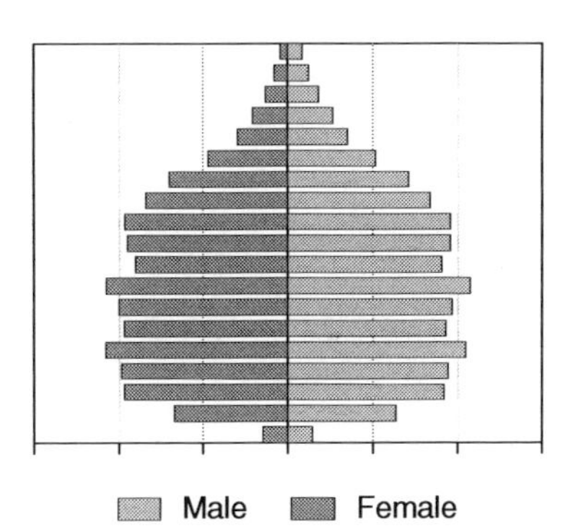

Demographic variables

Total population	12.8 million
Labour force	6 million
Employed population	5.6 million
Unemployment	7%
Dependency ratio	57%
Tourists (resident equivalent)	630,000
Urban population	42%
Rural population	58%

Figure 6.1 Overview of relevant demographic variables for MuSIASEM of the Mauritius case study

Data sources: Ministry of Finance and Economic Development of the Republic of Mauritius (2010, 2012c, 2012d, 2012e).

Having completed the accounting for human activity over the various functional compartments we obtain a first characterization of the society under study. The profile of allocation will show which sectors absorb the larger shares of human activity, and this alone will tell something about the level of development of the economy. Indeed, in the more developed societies a large proportion of human activity is generally allocated to the SG and BM sectors, while the AG and EM receive only a minor share. In addition, a large proportion of THA in the HH and SG sectors is indicative of a diversified economy. Giampietro *et al.* (2012) showed that SG and BM accounted for almost 8.5 per cent of human activity in Germany in 2005, of which 5.6 per cent was in SG, and only 0.2 per cent in AG, and that 91.2 per cent of THA was in HH. A larger societal overhead generally allows the reproduction and expansion of institutions and activities in the SG sector and more time for leisure and education, thus enhancing the adaptability of the system.

6.4 Accounting for economic variables

Monetary flows are accounted for as one type of flows associated with the economic process. Monetary flows are essential, as they affect both the desirability of a given metabolic pattern (a high GDP tends to translate into desirable material living standards) and its economic viability (the production of a monetary surplus makes it possible to import resources from abroad, thus reducing the internal pressure on domestic funds, e.g. labour, and flows, e.g. water). The main difference between monetary and biophysical flows is that monetary flows do not provide information about the feasibility or the biophysical viability of the system. In fact, the generation of monetary flows is more closely related to the characteristics of institutions regulating the economic activities, which do not necessarily reflect biophysical processes. For example, property rights make it possible to obtain income from a piece of land through agricultural production (a biophysical process) but also through a rent on its value (a financial operation) (Kapp 2011). Especially in post-industrial societies, the monetary flows generated by financial activities are becoming more important. For instance, according to OECD National Accounts (OECD 2013), in 2010 the combined share of GDP for the euro area (17 countries) of the AG sector (1.5 per cent), industry (16.7 per cent) and construction (5.3 per cent) – the monetary value associated with biophysical processes – was smaller than the share of GDP of the financial sector (26.3 per cent).

As regards the categories of accounting, at level *n*, the MuSIASEM representation refers to GDP as the flow produced by society over the period of the representation (e.g. measured in US dollars for a given year). At lower levels – the meso and local levels – gross value added (GVA) is adopted as a measure of the monetary flows produced by the compartments of human activity. GDP can be calculated following different approaches, such as the production approach:

$$\text{GDP} = \text{GVA} + \text{Taxes}$$

The sum of GVA of all the economic sectors considered is not equal to GDP at level *n*, because taxes are not taken into account in the MuSIASEM representation. An exception is presented by the case of Punjab (see Chapter 13), where:

$$\text{GDSP} = \text{GVA} - \text{FISIM (financial intermediation services indirectly measured)}$$

The gross domestic state product (GDSP) is calculated after deducting financial intermediation services that presumably are accounted for at the national level. In relation to data sources, GVA is available from national statistics and has to be organized according to the categories of human activity defined in the grammar. Incompatibilities between the two accounting systems may arise depending on the level of aggregation used in national statistics. We have already mentioned the case of the utilities sector in which ‘electricity, gas and water supply’ is reported as a single sector that does not map on to the definition of EM. In case of necessity, this problem can be solved by breaking down the aggregated data that are incompatible with the MuSIASEM categories, although this may involve having to look for additional sources or using ‘guesstimates’. Finally, published statistics often present inconsistencies, owing to rounding, to changes in accounting procedures from year to year or to the use of multiple sources of data, such as different ministries.

Other monetary flows considered are those associated with foreign trade. Exports can be seen as monetary flows generated elsewhere that enter the economy in exchange for goods and services produced at home. Imports imply a surplus of value added that needs to be generated in order to acquire goods and services that are not produced domestically. An assessment of imports and exports is needed to characterize the level of openness of the system, information that is essential to study the stability of the metabolic pattern in biophysical terms. In fact, the trade balance gives an indication of how monetary flows contribute to the feasibility, viability and desirability of the biophysical economy. A negative trade balance suggests that domestic metabolism is sustained by importing primary flows from abroad and requires the domestic economy to increase transfers and capital outflows or issue an equivalent amount of debt in order to sustain the biophysical economic process. When considering imports and exports we refer to the alternative expenditure approach for the calculation of GDP:

$$GDP = C + G + I + (X - M)$$

where C stands for private consumption expenditure, G is government expenditure, I represents investment, and the trade balance is given by exports (X) less imports (M). In the standard calculation of the GDP, the quantification obtained with the expenditure approach is equivalent to that obtained with the production approach, so that the final value of GDP does not change with the system of accounting. Therefore, exports and imports are already accounted for in the estimation of GVA. As a consequence, the sum of monetary flows of the different compartments at level $n - 2$ (SG, export sector, BM, AG and EM) does not add up to the GDP because the different monetary flows used in the representation would result in double accounting of exports.

Remittances are another example of how economic surplus generated abroad may help sustain the domestic metabolism. In this case, the surplus from abroad is transferred to the domestic economy in order to support domestic consumption and support, or make up for, the public welfare system in the form of support for non-working family members, forgone income from children enrolled in school, and so on. A representation of all monetary flows considered is given in Figure 6.2.

In the grammar of monetary flows, the paid work sector can be seen as the hypercycle, as it is responsible for the generation of value added and surplus, with which access to resources is gained. The household sector, on the other hand, can be seen as the dissipative part of the system responsible for final consumption and including all those activities involved in the reproduction of the fund human activity, such as sleep, personal care, education, childcare and care of the elderly. Living standards of society are positively correlated with the size of the household sector (measured in hours of human activity) for three reasons: 1) a longer life expectancy increases the dependency ratio (ageing of the population); 2) wealthy countries with abundant technological capital (power capacity) exhibit a reduced work load for the working population (e.g. less than 1,800 hours per year); and 3) wealthy countries have a high level of education, which delays entrance into the paid work sector.

The profile of contribution of the economic sectors to the total GVA provides an indication of the economic development of the society under study. For example, economic growth goes hand in hand with an increasing share of the economic

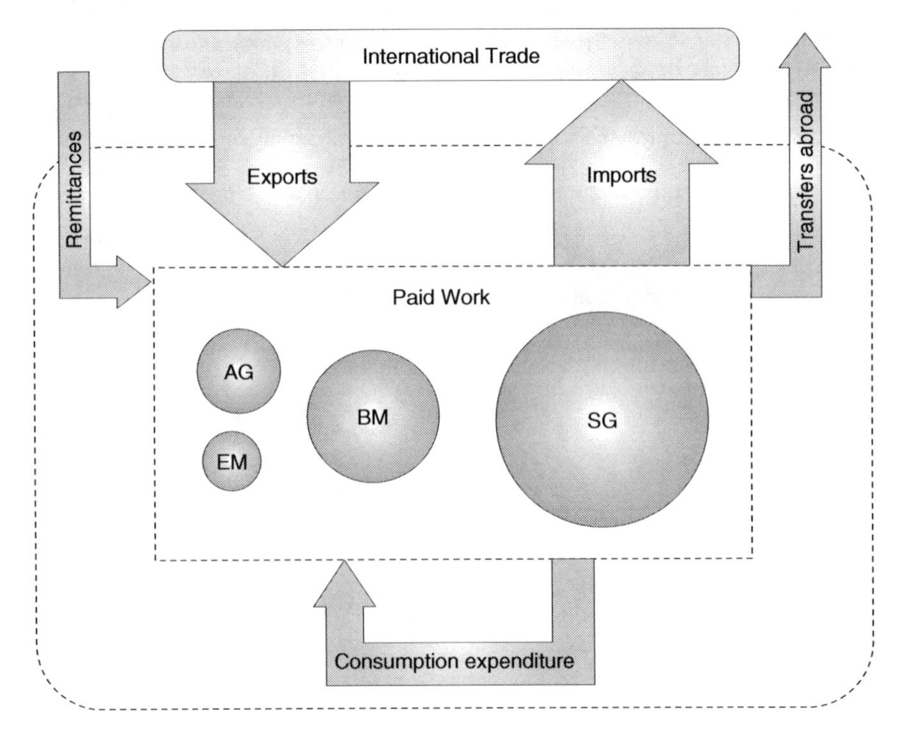

Figure 6.2 Conceptual example of a grammar of monetary flows

Note: The relative sizes of the discs reflect the relative share of GDP of the economic sectors considered.

activity carried out in the SG sector and a decreasing contribution of the AG sector. However, the notion of relative size of societal compartments in economic terms does not necessarily coincide with that in biophysical terms. For example, even though the AG sector in high-income countries tends to account for a very small share of GVA (less than 3 per cent), the share of managed land used (more than 90 per cent) as well as water consumed (often around 70 per cent) in agriculture can be large. For this reason, an integration of quantitative assessments based on an economic narrative and monetary variables with those based on a biophysical narrative and biophysical variables results in a richer representation of both the characteristics and the performance of a given socio-economic system, by providing information on the environmental impact and resource use of different economic activities.

Finally, the definition of monetary flows for compartments defined within MuSIASEM can be used to derive intensive variables (flow/fund ratios) similar to the ones used in biophysical accounting. For example, for activities taking place within the paid work sector we can define the economic labour productivity (ELP_i), calculated as the value added generated per hour of human activity in each economic compartment:

$$ELP_i = GVA_i/HA_i$$

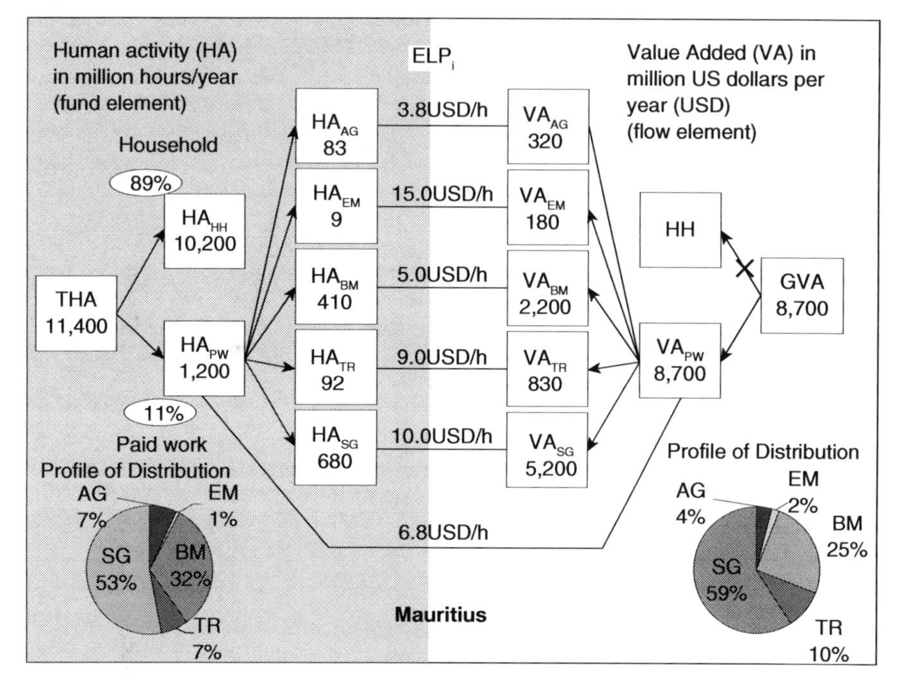

Figure 6.3 Assessment of economic labour productivity (ELP) of the different economic compartments of the Mauritius islands

Data sources: Ministry of Finance and Economic Development of the Republic of Mauritius (2012c, 2012e, 2012f).

This qualitative factor allows the comparison of the economic performance of different economic sectors or different subsectors independently of their relative size. This assessment is based on the same rationale of coupling of dendrograms (illustrated in Figure 2.2 for the assessment of energetic metabolic ratios) and is illustrated in Figure 6.3.

As illustrated in the example of the Mauritius islands (Figure 6.3), different economic sectors exhibit different values of ELP_i. The profile of ELP_i is useful to characterize the level of economic development. In high-income countries the AG sector has a much lower ELP than the other sectors of the economy. In the same way, in post-industrialized countries, the ELP of the financial sector is much higher than the ELP of the BM sector. Gradients in ELP (which are reflected in the relative wages paid in these sectors) help explain why with economic growth job seekers tend to move from the AG sector to the BM and then to the SG sector. This continuous internal shift across sectors may result in a shortage of labour in the AG sector in the long run and prime immigration pumps, bringing foreign workers from poorer countries.

6.5 Conclusion

Socio-economic variables are directly related to the profile of distribution of human activity over the various functions required for expressing a given societal metabolism. The characteristics of the population are reflected by demographics (age structure and dependency ratio), which in turn affects the split of human activity between PW and final consumption, that is, the ratio HA_{HH}/HA_{PW}.

Social characteristics can be used as a first assessment of the desirability of the system. In a first approximation we can say that the larger the fraction of human activity in SG and HH the better (Giampietro *et al.* 2012). However, for specific cases and for a more accurate assessment a thorough analysis based on participatory evaluations should be carried out with the involvement of local actors to individuate an integrated set of indicators reflecting local perceptions of desirable attributes.

Economic variables can be integrated in the representation of the metabolic pattern given by MuSIASEM as a means to compare and contrast economic valuation against the biophysical characterization of the system. In this way, we can link economic variables to the analysis of energy, water, food flows and land use patterns, as illustrated by Table 12.7.

This integration of quantitative information referring to an economic narrative and to a biophysical narrative implies facing a few challenges when searching for data and dealing with data from official statistics. Often the categories used by statistical offices have to be adapted to match the MuSIASEM categories. Depending on the chosen grammar, one has to handle inconsistencies between MuSIASEM and GDP accounting; for example, accounting for foreign trade while using GVA figures results in double accounting of imports and exports. That is, the monetary flows created for the MuSIASEM representation (referring to the local and the meso scale) do not necessarily add up to GDP (referring to the large scale – level n), but rather they should be used as an indication of how biophysical and monetary variables relate to each other at the level of economic processes or economic sectors (level $n-i$). Last but not least, there is the problem of missing data, especially at lower levels of analysis. This problem was very relevant for this exercise of applications of MuSIASEM to case studies using secondary data. Clearly, in a real application the possibility of directly collecting the required primary data in the field will dramatically improve the quality of data used.

7 Food grammar

Juan José Cadillo-Benalcazar, Mario Giampietro, Tarik Serrano-Tovar and Sandra G.F. Bukkens

Summary

This chapter presents a grammar for the integrated accounting of food energy flows across the various compartments of society defined at different scales. The internal view on food metabolism focuses on food consumption and flows of nutrient carriers; the external view focuses on food production and flows of agricultural commodities. The food grammar bridges the internal and external views and takes into account the complications introduced by the internal autocatalytic loop of food (consumption of food for production of food). The application of the food grammar to a specific case is illustrated with data from the Mauritius case study.

7.1 Introduction

In this chapter we discuss the difficulties encountered in the accounting for food flows for the complex system of human society, difficulties that are inherent in the hierarchical organization of the system, the coexistence of distinct scales and dimensions of analysis, and the legitimate distinct views (internal versus external) on the system. Taking into account these pitfalls and accommodating a link to the other elements of the nexus (exosomatic energy, water and monetary flows), we propose here a comprehensive accounting for food flows, the so-called food grammar. This grammar, like the other grammars proposed in this book, consists of a conceptualization of food flows and is based on the flow-fund model, discussed in Chapter 4, and the basic hierarchical structure of society proposed in Figure 2.1, and encompasses both the external and internal views on the food system. The external view focuses on the supply side (the production of food), while the internal view focuses on the end uses (consumption of food). As we will see in this chapter, both are essential to studying the metabolic pattern of society.

7.2 Terminology

The study of the food system encompasses various scientific disciplines, including ecology, agronomy, economy and nutrition, each with its own specific narrative, conventions and jargon. To avoid possible confusion, we provide here a series of definitions of categories of accounting used in our grammar (the 'MuSIASEM semantics') and their relation to commonly used terms and statistics. It is essential to comprehend the often subtle difference in the meaning of the terms used in order to understand the underlying rationale of the proposed trans-disciplinary food grammar:

- *Food energy* is the chemical energy contained in a food item, commodity or supply. It is directly related to the food macro-nutrient composition (protein, fat, carbohydrates and alcohol). We report food energy content either as a single number (a quantitative assessment in J) or as a vector of these macro-nutrients (an array of quantitative assessments in J). The latter notation conveys information on the qualitative aspects of the food in question (the mix of macro-nutrients in the diet).
- *Endosomatic energy* is synonymous with food energy. This term is used to highlight the role of food in the societal metabolism, by emphasizing that food energy is destined for metabolization *within* (endo) the human body, as opposed to exosomatic energy (such as petrol), which is metabolized *outside* (exo) the human body (see section 3.4.2 in Chapter 3).
- *Food (energy) requirement* is a normative concept that we define as the food needed by a population or a segment of the population in order to safeguard its nutritional and health status. It depends on the population age and gender structure and physical activity patterns. It is comparable to such concepts as the recommended daily allowance (RDA) or dietary reference intake (DRI) in the fields of public health and nutrition.
- *Food intake or dietary intake* refers to the amount of food actually consumed (ingested) in the diet. National statistics on actual food intake are rarely available. However, small-scale studies (household surveys, food diaries), providing some rough indications at the local level, can be found in the scientific literature. For this reason, the food intake is approximated by the final consumption (see below).
- *The net food supply or final domestic consumption at the household level* is defined as the food *available* to the population for consumption that disappears at the level of the household. This quantity refers to the *end use* of the food flow and is equal to the food intake plus the losses incurred and waste produced at the household level. Even though food losses and food waste within the household are not actually consumed, they still imply the use of resources in their production, and hence it is essential to include them in the accounting for food flows (see also FAO 2013b). Statistics on the net food supply are available from the FAO Food Balance Sheets (FAO 2013a). Final consumption is used as a proxy of food intake.
- *The gross food consumption at the level of society* is defined as all the food consumed in society (in the sense of disappearance) for the endosomatic metabolism. This quantity includes: 1) final domestic consumption; 2) food used in the operation of the food system itself (animal feed, seeds, and eggs for broiler); and 3) losses and waste in processing, distribution and storage. Food that is exported is not included in the analysis of the metabolic pattern, as it fulfils an economic function, not a biophysical requirement of the

endosomatic metabolism. The production factors used in agriculture (quantities of land, labour, power capacity) for producing food exports are not available for the production of the domestic supply. The gross consumption at the level of society can be estimated from the statistics in the FAO Food Balance Sheets (FAO 2013a) by summing the quantities of food belonging to the three categories listed above: final consumption, internal investment in the autocatalytic loop of food used to produce food, and losses.

- *The gross food supply to society* (which should match the consumption) is the total food supply entering the domestic food supply chain. It can be calculated from the statistics published in the FAO Food Balance Sheets (FAO 2013a) by summing the following categories: local production, imports, change of stocks and subtracting exports.

7.3 The internal versus the external view

In Table 12.7 we illustrate the internal and external view on the food system for the Republic of Mauritius using aggregate food flows. The upper block (first six rows) of this table represents the internal view on the system; the household compartment defined at level $n-1$ (HH) and five paid work compartments defined at level $n-2$ (within PW): PW*, AG, EM, export PW* and export AG. It tells us the amount of production factors (either flow or fund elements) consumed by the various functional compartments within society. The first column refers to the consumption of food energy. The row in the middle represents the total size of flow and fund elements of the society as a whole. The lower two rows represent the external view. They tell us how the flows are supplied. Some caution is due in the handling of these data.

When focusing on the data referring to food energy, our definition of the household sector is based on human activity and includes the time of the economically inactive *as well as the non-working time of the economically active population.* For this reason, *all* final consumption of food energy is assigned to the household sector. We assume that no final food consumption takes place during paid work hours, and therefore food consumption (including waste and losses) in restaurants and other away-from-home outlets (e.g. canteens) is assigned to the household sector. In fact the end use of the household sector and the food flows in the endosomatic metabolism is the reproduction of human activity (people).

A second observation concerns the food system's internal food consumption. A certain share of the gross food consumption is accounted for by the food system itself to guarantee its functioning. Indeed, the agricultural sector consumes a part of the gross food supply in the form of seeds and eggs, as well as feed crops (e.g. corn) used in animal production (Table 12.7). Therefore, there is an internal loop of food products used to make food products within the food metabolic pattern (see Figure 11.2). The proportion of the gross supply that ends up in this internal loop can be significant because of the so-called double conversion involved in animal products. For instance, in 2009 in the USA the net supply of grains (direct consumption at the household level) was 33MT or about 110 kg per capita per year, whereas the gross supply of grain was ten times larger, that is, 333MT or almost 1,100 kg of grain per capita (FAO 2013a). The difference between the direct consumption at the household level and the gross domestic supply of grain from the agricultural sector is 'eaten' by the huge internal loop of the US food system!

Additional food 'consumption' also takes place in the secondary production sectors, for example losses in processing in the food industry (included in building and manufacturing) and in distribution (included in service and government), as illustrated in Table 12.7. These concern the so-called post-harvest losses. Furthermore, in most societies a share of the food produced is exported abroad for economic reasons (to make value added) or political reasons (e.g. foreign aid). Hence, export 'consumes' a fraction of the production factors used in the agricultural sector. However, note that in Table 12.7 no food consumption is associated with export. Indeed, the production of sugarcane, the principal export commodity of the agricultural sector of Mauritius, does not form part of the *endosomatic* metabolic pattern of Mauritius. Within the integrated analysis of the metabolic pattern the production of sugarcane is included in a special category of accounting – agricultural exports – and not in the food system (the exported sugar is not eaten by the people of the Mauritius islands). Exports in agriculture concern economic activities that require production factors (land, labour, water, energy) in the agricultural sector and provide a source of economic revenues. Thus, in the integrated analysis of the metabolic pattern, export of agricultural commodities implies a reduction in the potential for domestic food supply (by reducing the availability of production factors) on the one hand but an inflow of added value on the other hand.

By summing over the different categories of food consumption (the functional societal compartments), we can assess the aggregate flow of food consumption (internal view) that has to be matched by the gross food supply (external view). Note that in the analysis of the metabolic pattern we inevitably face a bifurcation in the meaning of the 'quantities' assessed in the grammar. In the observing of existing metabolic patterns (using MuSIASEM in diagnostic mode), the observed flows are the result of a dynamic equilibrium; a given food consumption generally implies that the food supply matches the food requirement. However, in scenario analysis (using MuSIASEM in simulation mode) the characteristics of the end use (referring to the internal view) define 'required' quantities that are not necessarily matched by the supply side (external view). In this latter case, we are dealing with an unviable scenario.

The external view on the food metabolic pattern (the bottom two rows in Table 12.7) focuses on the supply side. Indeed, the flows of food consumed by the whole of society (summed over the functional compartments) must be made available in one way or another through the interaction of society with its context, be it through the exploitation of land systems (Chapter 5) using natural resources within the system's borders (domestic supply) or by importing food from abroad (using monetary resources or benefiting from donations).

Combining the internal view (to describe how the available food is consumed) and the external view (to describe how the food is made available) in the representation, we can – in principle – generate an integrated analysis of the sustainability of the food metabolic pattern. This characterization is essential in order to identify those factors determining the establishment of a dynamic equilibrium between the requirement for and the supply of food flows. However, the simultaneous handling of quantitative information related to the internal and the external view on food metabolism introduces a series of systemic complications in the relative accounting for food flows. These complications are well known in the field of hierarchy theory and are detailed in the next section in relation to the food grammar.

7.4 Epistemological complications

7.4.1 Contextualizing aggregate flows

Aggregate assessments of food flows, as shown in Table 12.7, expressed using individual numbers, do not carry sufficient information to assess whether the nutritional requirements of the population are met (on the consumption side) nor whether this food consumption pattern is sustainable in time (on the production side). If we want to give meaning to these assessments we must contextualize them in relation to both the internal and the external view: Are the nutritional requirements of the population met? Is there an equitable distribution of the net food supply over all segments of the population? What factors constrain the food supply? Do shortages of natural resources limit the domestic food production? Are imports too expensive to guarantee an adequate supply of food to the population?

Addressing all these questions requires different types of data; to check whether dietary requirements are met (internal view) we must measure food flows in terms of 'nutrient carriers' (macro- and micro-nutrients), while a check on the sustainability of domestic food production (external view) requires us to measure food flows in terms of output of tons of commodities (e.g. tons of cereals, vegetables, animal products). Tons of commodities can be further described in biophysical terms (looking at agronomic characteristics) and in economic terms (looking at prices and costs of production). Indeed, according to the flow-fund model, the identity of the food flow is specific for the identity of the compartment (fund) consuming or producing it. Therefore, the need to distinguish and at the same time reconcile the internal view (flows of nutrient carriers) and external view (flows of food commodities) is one of the epistemological challenges we face in the food grammar.

In the bottom table of Figure 7.1 we illustrate how to link the accounting for the food flow in terms of nutrient carriers with that for flows of agricultural commodities (breaking down the flows of nutrient carriers over a set of food commodities). First of all, this complexification of the assessment requires replacing a single quantitative assessment (5.9PJ of food energy) with a vector disaggregating this number into quantities of energy referring to different types of macro-nutrients (the vector [3.6, 0.7, 1.6] PJ/year of carbohydrate, protein

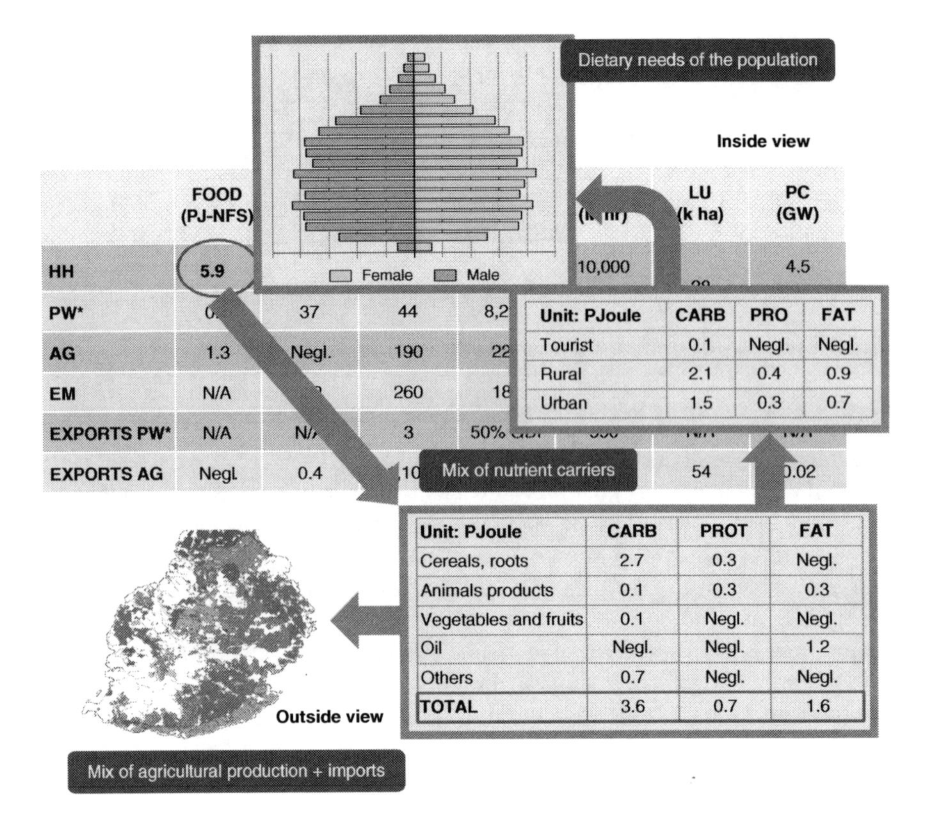

Figure 7.1 The set of complex relations between quantitative assessments expressed in the form of individual numbers, vectors and multi-level tables

Source: Data from the case study presented in Chapter 12.

and fat, respectively). The specific columns and rows in this table reflect the pre-analytical choice of, respectively, a set of relevant nutrient carriers (to interface this information with dietary requirements) and a set of relevant food commodities (to describe the food supply). The choice of how to disaggregate the assessment of food energy flows will vary from case to case. For illustrative purposes, we have kept the selection of nutrients and food commodities in our example to a minimum (e.g. alcohol has been included in carbohydrates, and pulses have been included in grains).

Note that the 'net food supply'/'final domestic consumption' refers to the hierarchical level of the household sector ($n-1$). If we want to assess whether this net food supply meets the food requirement, it is often useful to disaggregate this sector and look at lower-level characteristics further down the hierarchy (level $n-2$ and below). This is illustrated in the upper table of Figure 7.1, where we have disaggregated the vector characterizing the flow of food energy for the household sector

([3.6, 0.7, 1.6] PJ/year) into three vectors characterizing the flow of food energy going into the subsectors: urban residents, rural residents and tourists. At this level, we can check against the proper external referent (an observable metabolic element associated with the expected flow), determining whether or not the supplied flow is congruent with the expected flow. This procedure of moving across levels or scales is always possible in MuSIASEM, provided closure is observed (see Chapters 2 and 6). The value at any given hierarchical level (e.g. the household compartment at level $n-1$) is always a weighted average of the characteristics of lower-level compartments (rural and urban residents and tourists, defined at level $n-2$). Of course, other criteria of disaggregation or further disaggregation of the fund element human activity can be applied (e.g. by age and/or gender), depending on the focus of the analysis.

The assessment of the gross food supply (aggregate value at the societal level) is of limited use in the outside view. What we need here is to capture and refine the interface of society with its context, in particular the interferences with the ecosystem metabolism. Two interrelated pieces of information are particularly important here: the degree of openness of the food system (what share of the gross food supply is imported) and the local biophysical limits to domestic production (the actual local environmental impact). This information is defined on different hierarchical levels ($n+i$) and across non-equivalent descriptive domains (local, meso, large), and therefore requires complementary spatial analyses (and preferably the use of GIS).

As illustrated in Figure 7.1 (bottom left), an analysis of the feasibility of the metabolic pattern in relation to the food supply (outside view) requires us first to locate the food production in space and time. Different crops require different types of soil, climate, slope, water supply and labour input. Hence, only after having characterized the production pattern at the local scale can we study the existence of biophysical limits, the impact on local ecosystems, and the requirement of production factors (input of labour, machinery, fertilizers, pesticides, etc.). As discussed in Chapters 4 and 5, when analysing the interface between the metabolic patterns of society and ecosystems it is essential to be able to scale up and down the quantitative analysis according to our interests and needs (e.g. analysing damage to ecological funds, such as soil at the local scale or watersheds at the meso scale, or the relation to the labour market). At last, to get the big picture – placing the socio-ecological system within the larger (political) context – we must be able to effectively integrate all the various pieces of information gathered at the different scales and from the different points of view (see, for example, the Punjab case study, Chapter 13).

7.4.2 The internal loop of food products for food products and lack of linear relation

Confronting the gross supply and final domestic consumption for different countries, we discover that, no matter how we measure these flows (in terms either of nutrient carriers or of food commodities), they are not linearly related (Table 7.1).

Table 7.1 Yearly per capita gross and net grain consumption for the USA and China

Country	*Gross supply*	*Net supply*	*Ratio gross/net*
USA	1,100	110	10
PR China	300	150	2

Source: FAO (2013a).

Note: Data refer to 2009 and are expressed in kg per capita per year.

For example, the per capita gross grain consumption (gross grain supply/population) of the USA is three times that of China, but this relation is no longer found when considering the final domestic consumption (per capita net grain consumption is higher in China than in the USA). This phenomenon is explained by the marked difference in the societal metabolic pattern of food between the two countries. In the USA, the larger share of the gross grain supply does not flow into the household sector for direct consumption, but flows within the agricultural sector for the production of animal products and into the processing industries for alcoholic beverages, while in China the bulk of the gross grain supply made available at the level of society ends up directly in final consumption in the household sector.

Hence a first explanation for the non-linearity in the relation between the gross food supply and the final domestic consumption is the existence of an internal loop of food consumption to generate the desired food mix at the household level. The US food system has a strong internal loop that transforms raw grains into animal products and that, in this process, consumes a large share of the gross food supply (in the form of corn for animal feed). Therefore, our grammar makes a distinction between food that is consumed in the food system because of the internal loop and food that is consumed by the households. The rationale for implementing this distinction is the following: when a certain quantity of food that has been produced using production factors (a food product) is used to generate a different food product that is consumed in the diet and when this implies a large loss of that flow, then we can say that the flow is consumed in the internal loop of the food production.

A second explanation for the lack of a linear relation between gross supply and final domestic consumption lies in the food losses incurred in the food system (post-harvest losses). In relation to this assessment it is impossible to apply a flat rate of losses for the metabolic flow of food, as food losses vary greatly depending on the commodity and the relative importance of processing, packaging, distribution and storage in the food system (e.g. losses of fresh vegetables may reach up to 40–50 per cent depending on the distribution system). This is especially true when quantitative assessments are based on food energy rather than mass. So this assessment can be obtained either as a top-down assessment – when statistics about both the gross supply and the final domestic consumption are available – or as a bottom-up assessment (e.g. when dealing with scenarios) by characterizing the gross supply (starting from known technical coefficients and the mix of products) and by applying estimates of losses in relation to the set of operations taking place in the food system.

7.4.3 So how do we approach the accounting for food flows?

The pitfalls discussed above emphasize the need for a coherent protocol of accounting for the metabolic pattern of food in modern societies. In particular, a food grammar is needed to organize effectively the various pieces of information into a general conceptualization of an expected set of relations among quantities determined by the metabolic characteristics of modern societies. In this way, we obtain a representation based on semantic categories including a set of primary resources (the production actors required), a set of food commodities in production (the supply in the external view), a set of nutrient carriers within the metabolic pattern (the flows of food in the internal view), and characteristics of the internal autocatalytic loop and losses (introducing non-linearity between the gross supply and final domestic consumption), and final domestic consumption (the requirement to be matched). This semantic framing of the quantitative analysis can then be translated into a formal quantitative representation (accounting system) by tailoring the template of the accounting procedure (the grammar) on to the specific characteristics of an observed instance of the class (a specific country expressing a metabolic pattern). The food grammar and the translation into a specific accounting system are illustrated in the following sections.

7.5 A protocol of accounting for food metabolism

7.5.1 A grammar for characterizing the metabolic pattern of food in semantic terms

The metabolic pattern of food of a modern society refers to the expected modalities of its endosomatic metabolism. An effective representation of this metabolic pattern in terms of semantic categories must take into account the two complementing views outlined in section 7.3. A food grammar generating this dual representation, based on categories of accounting relevant for both the external view (left side) and the internal view (right side), is given in Figure 7.2.

In relation to the outside view we need information on:

- The gross supply of food products to society.
- The relative contribution of domestic agriculture (biophysical processes) and imports (economic and biophysical processes) to the gross food supply of society. This gives us an idea of the openness of the food system and, therefore, of the degree of food self-sufficiency of society. The characteristics of the domestic production of food commodities are essential to analyse the actual stress on local ecosystems and the biophysical constraints to changes in or expansion of the existing metabolic pattern.

In relation to the internal view we need another three pieces of information:

- The final household consumption. This is the flow that sustains the dissipative part of the endosomatic metabolic pattern.

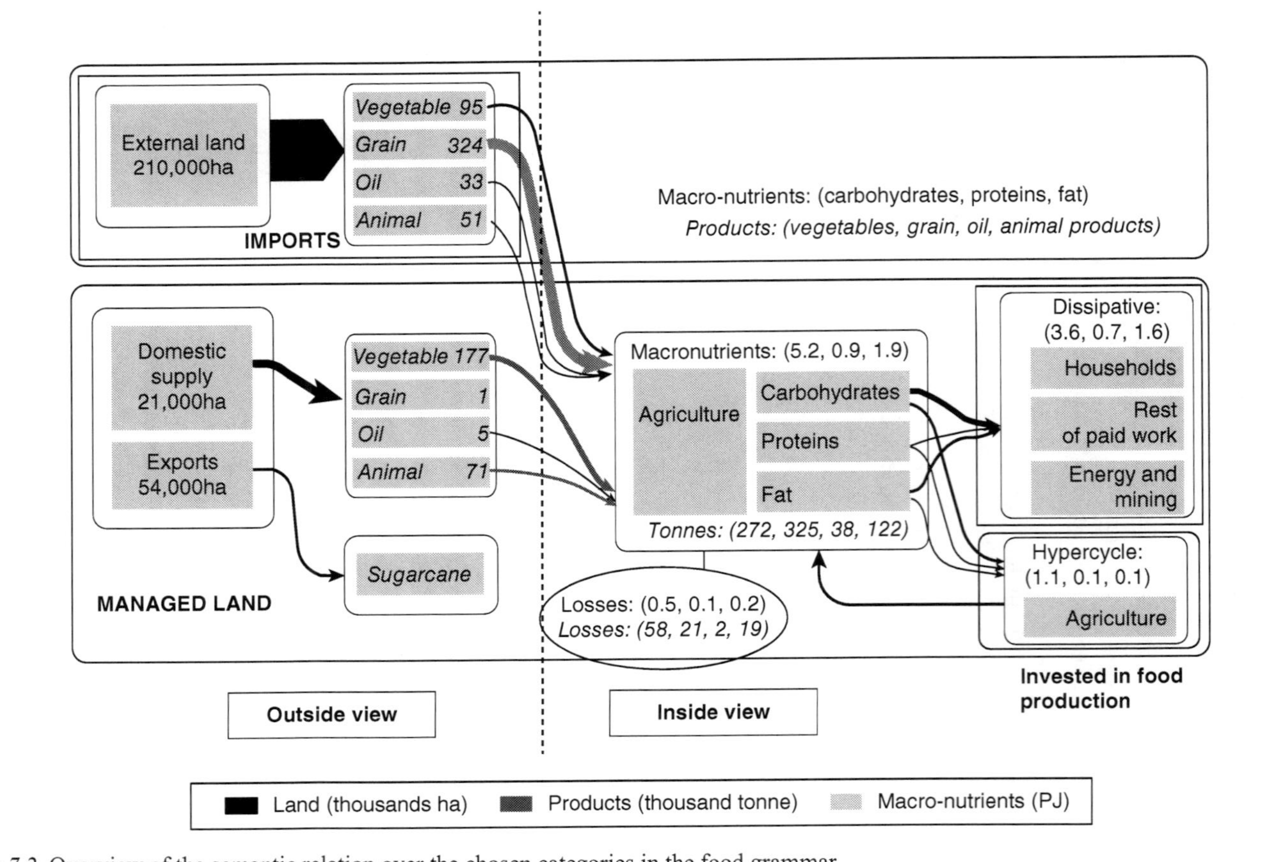

Figure 7.2 Overview of the semantic relation over the chosen categories in the food grammar

- The share of the gross food supply that is invested in local food production in the agricultural sector (AG), such as seeds, eggs and feed crops. This flow represents the 'overhead' consumed by the hypercyclic part of the endosomatic metabolism (the internal loop of food consumed to produce food). In most modern societies, the endosomatic hypercycle is reinforced by food imports (feeds for animal production tend to be imported in many developed countries).
- The post-harvest losses, that is, the share of the gross food supply lost in the food system during processing and distribution (including transportation and storage). These losses take place across the various components of the food system, but do not include the household losses, the latter being included in the final food consumption at the household level.

In order to translate this semantic framing of the endosomatic metabolic pattern (the grammar) into a formal accounting system we must also define the set of categories used to represent the flow of food commodities (production side/outside view) and that to represent the flow of nutrient carriers (consumption side/internal view). For instance, in the case study of Mauritius we selected four categories for the accounting for food commodities ('cereals' [grains and pulses], vegetables, oils and animal products) and three for the accounting for nutrient carriers (proteins, carbohydrates and fats). The pre-analytical choice of closure of the accounting space must be made with the specific characteristics of the case study in mind and should allow the analyst to single out relevant aspects of the system and to establish the desired relations between the outside and the inside view. This process will inevitably introduce a certain arbitrariness and approximation in the analysis and leave some aspects out of focus. For this reason, all pre-analytical choices should be declared and motivated so as to generate a transparent analysis.

7.5.2 The internal loop: a slippery interface between the inside and the outside view

The existence of the internal autocatalytic loop of food energy flows represents a major complication for the accounting for food flows, especially when trying to establish a bridge between the external view (production) and the internal view (consumption). We show here how to approach this problem for the double conversion involved in animal products. In our simplified example we consider a food system in which only the following two conversions take place:

- *Conversion of grain into beef:* We assume that the production of 1 kg of beef meat (6,300 kJ of food energy) requires an input of 7 kg of grains (105,000 kJ of energy) (L.R. Brown 2006). Hence, in terms of energy we have that 1J of beef requires an input of 17J of grains.
- *Conversion of grain into chicken:* We assume that the production of 1 kg of chicken meat (5,000 kJ of food energy) requires an input of 2 kg of grains (29,000 kJ of energy) (L.R. Brown 2006). Hence, in terms of energy we have that 1J of chicken meat requires an input of 6J of grains.

Even in this simple example, with only two types of animal products (beef and chicken), one type of feed (grains) and two corresponding conversion efficiencies (17/1 and 6/1, respectively), we cannot define an expected *flat conversion efficiency* for a generic category 'meat' (grain energy consumption per unit of gross energy supply of meat) without knowing the relative contribution of chicken and beef to the overall meat production. If meat production in the food system consists of 50 per cent chicken and 50 per cent beef, then the conversion efficiency of grain energy into meat energy at the level of society will be 11/1. But, if it consists of 80 per cent chicken and only 20 per cent beef, then the conversion efficiency becomes 8/1. Thus, the overall conversion efficiency of grain energy into meat energy reflects characteristics defined on two different scales of analysis: the technical coefficients of production defined at the local scale and the relative contribution of meat types in the production and consumption in the food system of society at the meso scale.

This example illustrates that it is tricky to perform calculations in generic terms of 'food energy'. Depending on the question, a given flow has to be quantified in different ways. For example, 1J of meat has to be assessed at 1J of chemical energy contained when accounted for as dietary intake (input for the human body in the internal view), but, as discussed above, at several joules of embodied energy of grains when accounting for the biophysical cost of its production in the external view. In fact, when considering the external view, the 'energetic value' of 1J of meat is no longer the same as that of 1J of grain. We encounter the same problem if we do the quantitative analysis in terms of nutrient carriers (rather than food commodities): in the external view the 'energetic value' of 1J of animal protein is not the same as that of 1J of vegetable protein. Hence we must be extremely cautious in the quantitative analysis of the metabolic pattern of modern societies in order to properly define and handle the different semantic categories used for the accounting. As will be shown also in the energy grammar, not all joules are the same!

Thus, in order to generate useful quantitative assessments we should always describe the flows of both food commodities and nutrient carriers through the food system, using the whole set of semantic categories defined by the grammar, and keep in mind how the pattern of production affects the pattern of consumption and vice versa. But even if we use a grammar (Figure 7.2), describing a set of expected features of the metabolic pattern of food in modern society (a typology), any metabolic pattern expressed by a given society will be special (a special instance of that typology). For this reason the general semantic representation (conceptualization) provided by the grammar must be formalized to tailor the system of accounting to the specific case under study. This involves the following pre-analytical choices:

- Definition of the set of categories used to describe the flows in relation to both the internal and external view. These categories must reflect the nature of the flows in relation to the characteristics of the fund elements consuming the flows (human beings) and producing the flows (physiological and agronomic characteristics of the plant and animal species used in production, technical characteristics of the industrial processes involved) at the local scale.

- Specification of the expected relations among the different flows, including the effect of internal autocatalytic loops and losses.
- Data sources used to assign numerical values to the chosen categories. In this regard, a multi-scale analysis provides a major advantage, as it combines and confronts different data sources (bottom-up and top-down information).

7.6 Formalization of the food grammar

In this section we illustrate the formalization of the food grammar drawing on the data of our case study of Mauritius and following the semantic conceptualization illustrated in the text. The quantitative information presented in Figures 7.3 and 7.4 shows two possible formalizations to quantify the various flows of the metabolic pattern of food in the Mauritius islands across different scales and compartments in relation to both the internal and the external view. Note that the formalization of the grammar presented in these two figures is part of the diagnostic step (description of the actual situation), which is a prerequisite for subsequent scenario analysis. The application of the grammar to scenario analysis is described in Chapter 12.

In the formalization shown in Figure 7.3, the accounting for the food flows made available or consumed by the various functional compartments is based on joules of nutrient carriers, disaggregated into carbohydrates, proteins and fats. In the formalization shown in Figure 7.4 the accounting is based on tons of food commodities, disaggregated into cereals, vegetables, oils and animal products. The bridge from one mode of accounting to the other can be established by applying food composition values (the value of nutrient content per kg of food product) to the various flows of food products (FAO 2001). However, some caution is due in the use of food composition data. The food composition of a given product (e.g. chicken meat) can vary considerably depending on the breed or variety, the conditions of production (e.g. feed used), and the fraction of the product considered (e.g. entire chicken versus chicken breast). Caution and some expertise are needed when handling the statistical data. For instance, the assessment of 1 kg of a given animal product (e.g. pork meat) can refer either to the edible part or the live weight; 1 kg of paddy is different from 1 kg of rice; and so on. For this reason, the quantification of flows of food products in terms of energy and nutrients has to be based as much as possible on local data covering the specific characteristics of the food system under study.

In this respect, *imported* food flows pose a particular challenge. In fact, a modern food system is extremely complex, and a detailed tracking of all food flows may not always be possible. For example, how do we account for the exportation of food products (meat) for which the raw materials (livestock feed) were imported (e.g. a common case in Belgium and the Netherlands)? Even though it is impossible to provide the 'right' answer to all these questions, in general it is better to generate an approximate representation of relevant flows based on a set

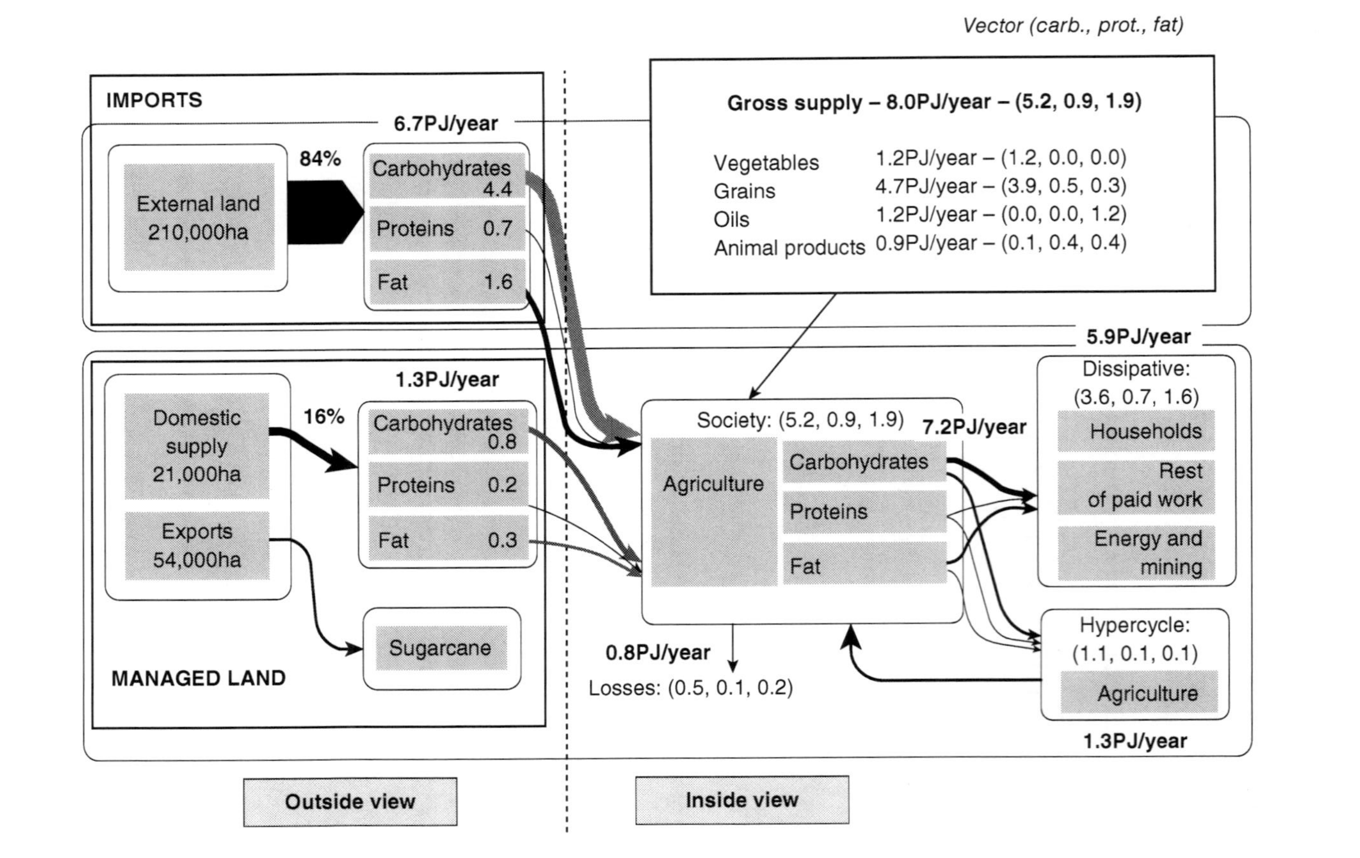

Figure 7.3 Formalization of the food grammar for Mauritius based on an accounting for joules of nutrient carriers

Source: Data from the case study presented in Chapter 12.

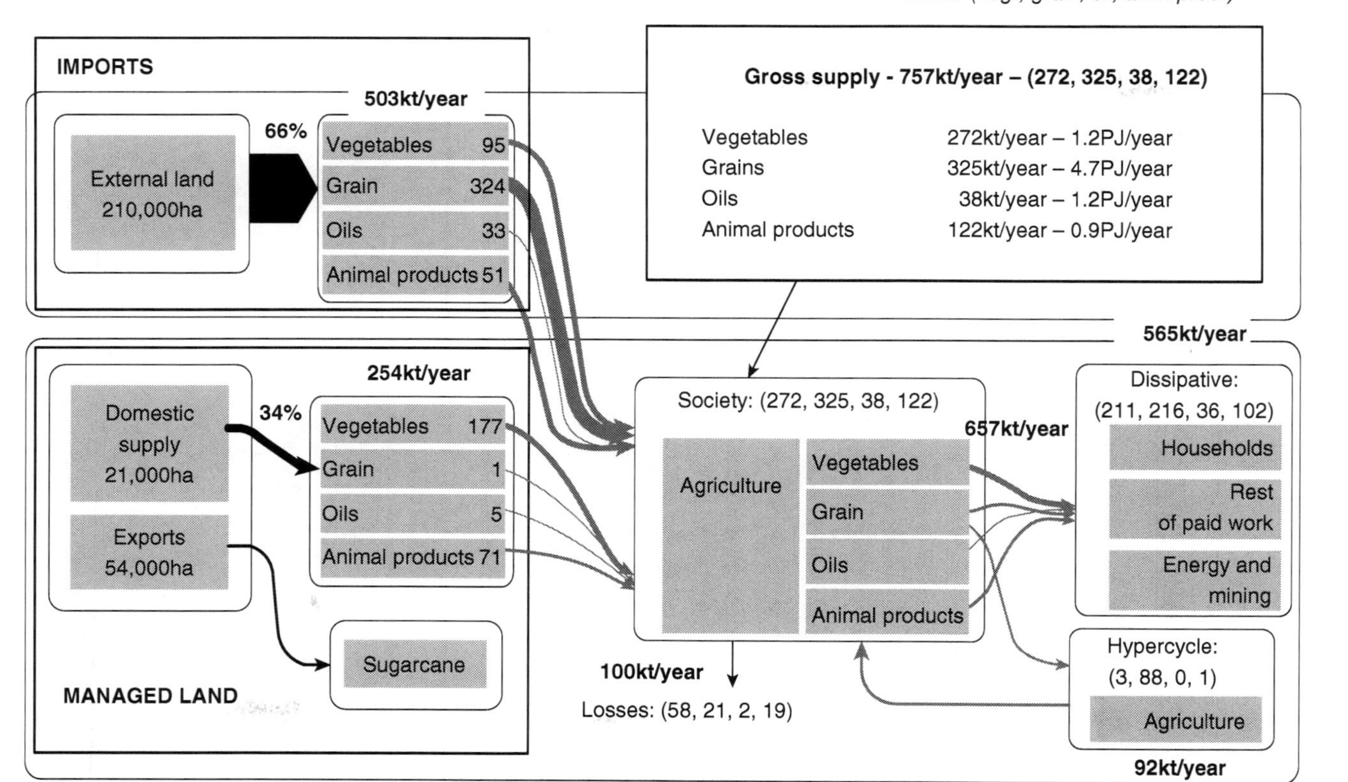

Figure 7.4 Formalization of the food grammar for Mauritius based on an accounting for tons of food commodities

Source: Data from the case study presented in Chapter 12.

of expected relations over semantic categories (the grammar proposed here) than to try to mingle an enormous amount of data referring to different accounting categories without establishing first a clear distinction among them. In the absence of location-specific data, the Food Balance Sheets of the FAO (2013a) are the best option for this task, since they are organized using the same logic of accounting as our grammar (when adopting the top-down view).

The use of two distinct formalizations for the same set of semantic relations allows us to store a lot of relevant information on the present food metabolic pattern of Mauritius. In particular, a detailed analysis of the flows of nutrient carriers from the internal perspective allows us to address issues of food security and health (nutrition), for instance by looking at heterogeneities in the pattern of consumption among segments of the population (e.g. urban versus rural) at the local scale. On the other hand, an accounting based on food commodities (e.g. animal products) allows us to focus on the use of natural resources and technical inputs in production and to study bottlenecks in the pattern of production. This feature is extremely important when characterizing and assessing scenarios (discussed in Chapter 12).

Clearly, the most important feature of the grammar is that it is designed for use with similarly organized data on exosomatic energy (Chapter 8), water (Chapter 9), and socio-economic variables (Chapter 6). This common logical structure makes it possible to arrive at a comprehensive representation of the societal metabolic pattern. Moreover, the organization of information across scales can be effectively used in spatial analysis (Chapter 10). Combining the characteristics of the food flows (Figures 7.3 and 7.4) with those of the other flows and fund elements (see Table 12.7) we obtain a representation of the *actual* metabolic pattern in terms of a set of flow/fund ratios (diagnostic step), in which different flows share the same endowment of fund elements. These characteristics can then be compared to expected values associated with a typology of metabolic patterns.

Subsequent scenario analysis for the food system is based on the use of these observed values for the metabolic characteristics of known typologies of metabolic pattern. For instance, at the local scale we have for each land use a series of observed or typical flow/fund ratios, such as the crop yield per hectare, evapotranspiration per hectare, labour and fertilizer input per hectare, and labour productivity. Note that metabolic characteristics of newly introduced crops in the area are necessarily based on reference (typical) values observed in similar systems. Based on these metabolic characteristics at the local scale we can analyse the effects of proposed changes in land use (e.g. cropping pattern) by working our way up in the hierarchy (scaling up) and assessing the aggregate effect that these changes imply on the flows (e.g. gross and net food supply) and funds at a larger scale. In a similar way, one can study the effects of changes in population growth, immigration, the tourist industry or food preferences both on the required food supply and on the availability of fund elements to be used as production factors. Thus, while the diagnostic step involves mostly a top-down approach – starting out from national and sub-national statistics to describe the breakdown of flows and fund elements across compartments – scenario analysis is typically based on a bottom-up approach.

7.7 Conclusion

In conclusion, the food grammar allows us to study the biophysical limits to the existing local food supply (diagnosis of the compatibility of the local pattern of food production with the metabolic pattern of the exploited ecosystems) or check the feasibility, viability and desirability of future scenarios (simulations). Examples of these applications are given in the Mauritius case study (Chapter 12). Analysis of the food metabolic pattern is also a powerful tool to link local-scale information (e.g. characteristics of rural households, water and soil conditions) with large-scale processes, such as (inter)national policies related to food imports and exports or agricultural subsidies. The latter application requires us to interface biophysical analysis with a complementing analysis of economic processes (see Chapter 6), which is illustrated in the Punjab case study (Chapter 13).

8 Energy grammar

Mario Giampietro and François Diaz-Maurin

Summary

This chapter illustrates the integrated accounting for exosomatic energy flows across different scales of analysis bridging the internal and the external view on the societal energy metabolism. The energy grammar deals with: 1) the presence of an internal autocatalytic loop of energy carriers; 2) the coexistence of two distinct energy forms, mechanical and thermal energy, whose quantities cannot be summed; 3) the requirement of biophysical production factors, including exosomatic energy, power capacity, human activity and managed land, for the conversion of exosomatic energy flows into applied power (end uses); and 4) the impossibility of calculating a simple output/input ratio (energy return on investment) to assess the quality of energy sources.

8.1 Introduction

In spite of the fact that *all* assessments of energy can be expressed in joules – the official SI unit of energy – not all joules of energy are of equal quality. In short, not all joules are the same! For example, depending on the goal of the analysis, we can link a given number of joules of electricity to non-equivalent rationales of accounting. Depending on *how* the electricity is produced, 1J of electricity will (coal-fired plant) or will not (hydroelectric plant) result in CO_2 emissions; depending on *where* it is produced (distance between production and consumption of electricity) there may or may not be significant losses of energy involved; and depending on the required end use (different voltages) different types of technology will be needed. Indeed, the meaning and the usefulness of any one quantitative assessment of 'energy' depend on the pertinence of the semantic category used for the accounting in relation to the goal of the assessment. As explained by Maddox (1978, p. 136), "there is no unambiguous energy measure that allows one energy form to be compared to another. Energy cannot be treated as a single entity, because its various forms possess irreconcilable qualitative distinctions."

Are we looking for an assessment to understand how the energy input is used (internal point of view) or for an assessment to understand the required conditions for stabilizing the supply of energy inputs (external point of view)? A sound energy analyst must always ask her/himself: 'Joules of what?', 'Why do we want to know this quantity?' and 'What is the most appropriate categorization for this type of information?'

In this chapter we provide an energy grammar to help the energy analyst and other practitioners make the appropriate choices so as to achieve a useful and coherent energy accounting system.

8.2 The exosomatic energy grammar at a glance

The basic structure of the exosomatic energy grammar is similar to that of the food (endosomatic energy) grammar – not surprisingly so, given the existence of a common set of expected characteristics of energy transformations in the metabolic pattern of a complex self-organizing system.

Thus, the *internal view* of the exosomatic energy grammar focuses on the conversions of different types of exosomatic energy carriers (fuels, heat and electricity) into end uses taking place within society. These energy conversions reflect the specific characteristics of exosomatic devices (the various forms of power capacity such as bulldozers, refrigerators and cars) performing specific tasks (such as moving material, cooling food and transporting passengers) at the local level.

The *external view*, on the other hand, focuses on the locally available primary energy sources plus imports that are required to guarantee the supply of energy carriers to society. Primary energy sources consist both of stocks of biophysical energy resources, such as fossil energy and uranium ores, and of fund-flow renewable energy resources, such as solar, hydro, wind and biomass. Imports may refer either to primary energy sources, such as coal and crude oil, or to energy carriers, such as electricity or petrol.

The template of the energy grammar is shown in Figure 8.1. It provides three pieces of information: 1) the three basic semantic categories (primary energy sources, energy carriers, and end uses) needed for the analysis of exosomatic energy flows; 2) the set of functional compartments within society (e.g. the energy and mining sector, the household sector, etc.); and 3) a semantic description of the complex relations across these flows and compartments in relation to both the internal viewpoint (right side of the grammar) and the external viewpoint (left side of the grammar). As we will show in this chapter and in the case studies (Chapters 12–14), this grammar allows us to create a coherent dataset that describes the expected relations over 'quantities of energy' using different semantic accounting categories referring to different hierarchical levels and scales and reflecting the adoption of different views on the system.

8.2.1 Relevant semantic concepts for the external view

- *The gross energy throughput of society:* This concept is defined as the throughput of 'energy' taken from outside the society that is dissipated within. Depending on the goal of the analysis, the gross energy throughput of society can be perceived (and referred to) as the *gross supply* or the *gross requirement* of exosomatic energy. The former perception is typically adopted to

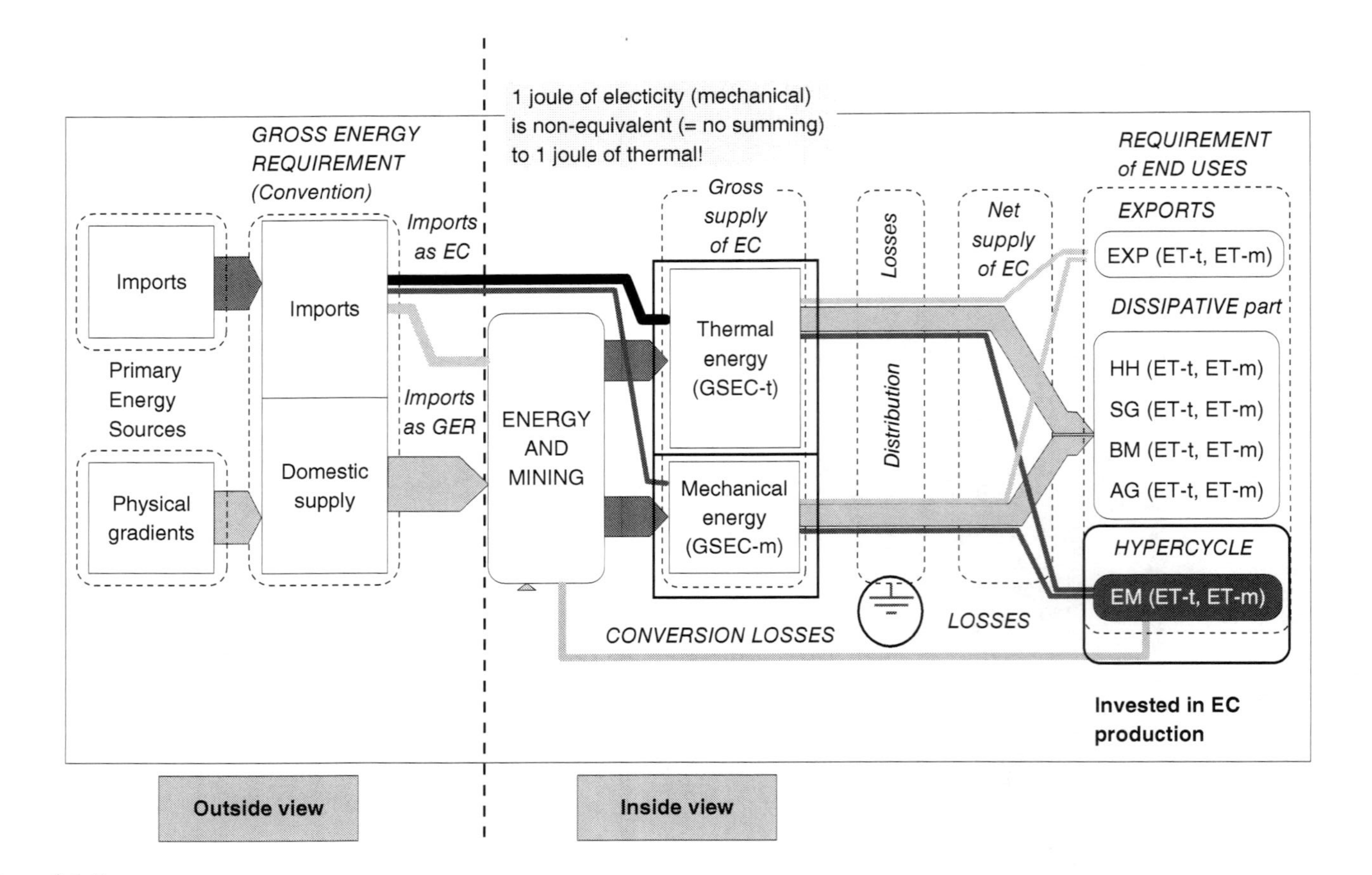

Figure 8.1 Energy grammar

study the characteristics of an established metabolic pattern from the supply side (diagnostic mode), while the latter is typically used to check the feasibility and viability of a projected metabolic pattern (scenario analysis). In an established metabolic pattern the gross supply and the gross requirement of exosomatic energy must match.

- In the external and internal view we adopt distinct narratives about what should be observed as an instance of 'energy flow' and, as a result, we also adopt distinct accounting protocols. We saw in the food grammar (Chapter 7) that food energy can be measured in joules of macro-nutrients (internal view) or joules of food commodity (external view) and that these two accounting methods may result in distinct quantitative assessments. In the energy grammar we have a similar bifurcation in the accounting between energy carriers (internal view) and primary energy sources (external view). Being on the interface between the external and the internal view the quantification of the energy throughput of society is by far the most problematic aspect of energy accounting (see section 8.3).
- *The openness of the energy sector or degree of energy self-sufficiency of society:* This semantic concept is defined as the proportion of the gross supply of energy carriers obtained from the exploitation of domestic primary energy sources as opposed to imports. Note that imports enter into the energy metabolism in the form of primary energy sources (notably crude oil, gas and coal) and/or energy carriers (such as fuel and electricity).
- *Characteristics of the domestic supply of primary energy sources:* This information concerns the interaction of society with the ecosystems contained within its boundaries (e.g. national borders) with regard to the exploitation of primary energy sources. It is essential to assess the sustainability or *feasibility of the metabolic pattern* by analysing the current degree of stress on the exploited ecosystems (diagnostic analysis), as well as the existence of biophysical constraints to further expansion of or changes in the metabolic pattern (scenario analysis).

8.2.2 Relevant semantic concepts for the internal view

- *The gross supply of energy carriers (GSEC):* This concept is defined as the supply of the various forms of energy carriers actually made available to society (electricity, fuels, heat) by the energy and mining sector and by direct imports of energy. It is best represented by a vector/matrix notation (as illustrated in Figure 8.3).
- *The net supply of energy carriers (NSEC):* This concept refers to the flows of the different forms of energy carriers (electricity, fuels, heat) that are consumed in end uses by the various functional compartments of society. It is best represented by a matrix, as shown in Figure 8.3. NSEC may also be referred to as the net consumption (diagnostic analysis) or net requirement (scenario analysis) of energy carriers. The final consumption of energy carriers – the end use of the net supply – is observable only at the local scale,

where we can thus assess the performance of the various functional compartments of society in terms of the efficiency of the energy conversion and the productivity of the production factors involved. As shown in the exosomatic energy grammar (Figure 8.1), the net supply of energy carriers is divided into two flows: one to sustain the hypercyclic compartment (energy and mining sector) and one to sustain the dissipative compartments of society (those functional compartments that are net consumers of energy carriers, such as building and manufacturing, households, agriculture, and government and service).

- *The strength of the exosomatic hypercycle (SEH):* This concept concerns the share of the NSEC that must be invested by society in the domestic energy and mining sector (EM or simply 'energy sector'), or *hypercycle*, for the production of energy carriers from primary energy sources. The smaller the investment of energy carriers needed for a given supply of energy carriers, the stronger the hypercycle. The exosomatic hypercycle is also referred to as the autocatalytic loop of energy carriers for energy carriers.

  The compulsory investment in the hypercyclic compartment is needed for: 1) the domestic production of energy carriers (electricity, fuels and heat) from domestic primary energy sources; 2) the domestic production of energy carriers from imported primary energy sources; and 3) the handling and distribution of imported energy carriers. That is, the energy and mining sector itself must consume energy carriers for these operations. This is illustrated in Figure 8.1, at the right, by the final consumption of the hypercycle (EM), which is feeding back to the production of energy carriers. The openness of modern economies allows society to reinforce the strength of its exosomatic hypercycle (defined as the total GSEC divided by the flows of energy carriers feeding into EM) by importing energy in the form of primary energy sources and/or directly in the form of energy carriers. Note that imported energy carriers must be paid for in economic terms (by taking advantage of favourable terms of trade or international aid, or by issuing debt), but do not require a direct investment of energy carriers for their production. Therefore, in the case of favourable terms of trade the imports of energy carriers may require much less biophysical resources than the domestic production of energy carriers from domestic or imported primary energy sources.
- *Energy losses (of energy carriers):* Losses are defined as the proportion of energy carriers made available to society (GSEC) that is not consumed in end uses but lost within the metabolic pattern because of energy transformations (processing losses) and because of transportation, storage and distribution of energy carriers (distribution losses). Therefore, the conversion of primary energy sources into energy carriers (e.g. coal used to generate electricity) should not be included in this category, but in the category of energy going into the hypercycle. Losses are specific for each form of energy carrier and are best represented by a matrix of proportional loss coefficients, as illustrated in Figure 8.3.

8.2.3 Formalization of the grammar

In order to operationalize (and quantify) this general framing of the exosomatic metabolic pattern we must define first of all the specific sets of formal categories used to represent: 1) the size of relevant societal compartments; 2) the primary energy sources supplied or required on the production side (outside view); and 3) the flow of energy carriers consumed or required on the consumption side (inside view). Useful categories of societal compartments must include as a minimum the energy and mining sector (hypercycle) and the dissipative compartment (the rest of the economy plus final consumption). Clearly, the latter can be further disaggregated according to the aim of the study. Formal categories of primary energy sources may include: coal, oil, natural gas, nuclear, wind, concentrated solar power, biofuels and biomass residues for electricity generation. Formal categories for the accounting of energy carriers can be defined according to two distinct criteria. Considering the nature of the energy forms, we can use the classic distinction between thermal energy (fuels and process heat) and mechanical energy (electricity). However, energy carriers may also be categorized according to the typology of energy converters linked to the end uses (consumption-side view), such as fuels for transportation, high-temperature heat processes, low-temperature heat processes, high-voltage electricity and low-voltage electricity. Both logics for defining categories of accounting are valid provided they observe closure; that is, the quantities of energy accounted for in the various categories at one level (high-temperature and low-temperature process heat) must be equal to the quantity of energy accounted for in the higher-level category (process heat).

Depending on the socio-economic system under study, not all possible categories of accounting are relevant or needed. As this pre-analytical choice is necessarily arbitrary, the selection of the formal categories used for the accounting should be transparent and discussed carefully in relation to its relevance to the research question (singling out specific compartments and/or flows) and its pertinence to data handling (concordance with the classifications used in available energy statistics). The pre-analytical step of choosing categories capable of closing the accounting space is essential to tailor the quantitative representation to the specific characteristics of the society in question and to the specific objectives of the study.

8.3 Energy accounting from the external point of view

8.3.1 Primary energy sources

From the external point of view, the assessment of 'how much energy' is used by society is done in terms of supply by assessing the primary energy sources (PES). This form of accounting is important for studying the compatibility of the societal metabolic pattern with its context and hence for studying the *feasibility* of societal energy use in relation to the stability of boundary conditions (existence of external constraints).

Unfortunately 'primary energy source' is an elusive concept and very tricky to handle for quantification. In fact, a primary energy source represents an interface between the external and the internal view. We talk of a primary energy source when there is an energy system (requiring the investment of production factors) that can exploit 'physical gradients' (not measured in energy terms in the external view) to generate a given quantity of energy used by humans (measured in energy terms in the internal view). Looking at the characteristics of the physical gradients described in the outside view, primary energy sources are of three types: 1) quantities of materials that can be associated to quantities of thermal energy because of either their potential chemical energy (coal, gas, biomass) or their fission energy (uranium); 2) physical processes associated with kinetic energy (falling water, blowing wind, waves, tides) or solar radiation associated with quantities of mechanical energy; and 3) physical processes such as concentrated solar power or geothermal phenomena that can be associated to quantities of thermal energy. In relation to quantities of 'energy' observed in the internal view (the produced energy carriers), these three types of PES produce either joules of mechanical energy (e.g. kinetic energy and electricity) or joules of thermal energy (e.g. fuels and process heat).

Owing to this heterogeneity, primary energy sources per se cannot be quantified in a single accounting category of energy in relation to either the external or the internal view. Moreover, the relation between a given quantity of material (e.g. coal, oil or uranium) or a given physical process providing mechanical energy (falling water, waves) and the resulting quantity of energy usable by humans depends on the capacity to take advantage of the chemical potential or kinetic energy of a given resource or natural process. For example, a hydroelectric plant (the energy system capable of taking advantage of the physical gradient) transforms the kinetic energy of falling water (natural process) into electricity (J of energy carrier) with a given efficiency. Similarly, a coal-fired power plant (the energy system) can use the chemical energy (potential energy) contained in coal (natural resource) to generate thermal energy (J of energy carrier). It is the combination of an exploitable physical resource and a process of exploitation under human control that defines a primary energy source. A good understanding of this notion is crucial for a sound use of energy statistics for the analysis of the metabolic pattern of energy of societies.

Given the heterogeneity of the possible natural resources and processes on which the various energy systems feed we have to be careful when establishing an interface between the external view (the resources used) and the internal view (the energy carriers produced in the exploitation). An example of this interface is illustrated in Figure 8.2 (which will be described in detail below). Indeed, the physical characteristics of natural resources and processes used as primary energy sources are independent from the identity of the energy system making use of them. Therefore they can be measured in biophysical units other than joules. For example, we can have tons of coal, uranium or biomass, cubic metres of gas, and km/h of wind. We use this assessment as a 'proxy' for primary energy sources in the analysis of the supply side (external view). Biophysical quantities other than

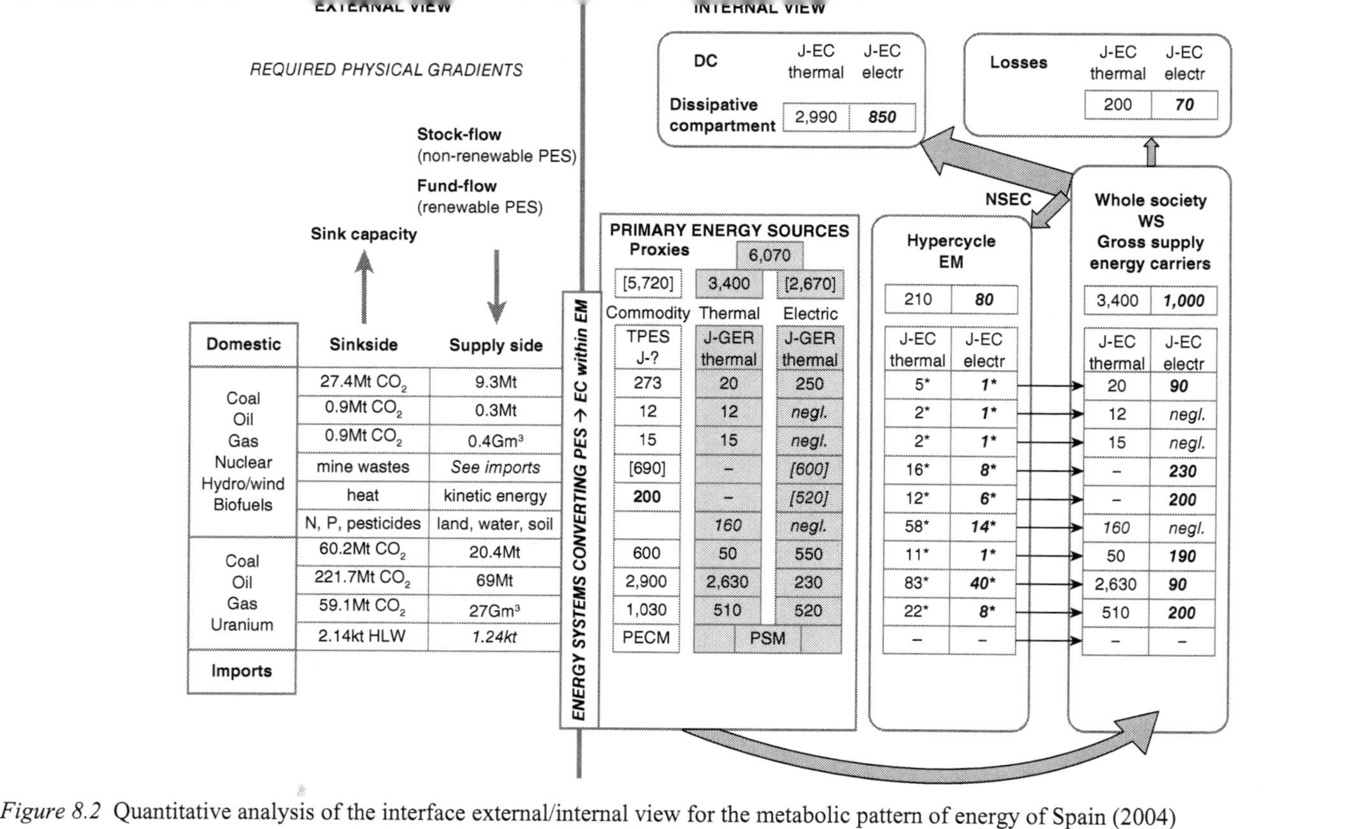

Figure 8.2 Quantitative analysis of the interface external/internal view for the metabolic pattern of energy of Spain (2004)

Source: Elaboration from Eurostat Fact Sheet, http://ec.europa.eu/energy/energy_policy/doc/factsheets/mix/mix_es_en.pdf.

Notes:

Energy data in PJ.

Numbers in square brackets represent virtual flows (thermal equivalent); numbers in bold represent mechanical (electricity) flows.

Abbreviations used: PES = primary energy source; EC = energy carrier; TPES = total primary energy supply; GER = gross energy requirement; GSEC = gross supply of energy carriers; PECM = physical energy content method; PSM = partial substitution method; negl. = negligible.

* These data are approximated and have the sole purpose of illustrating the approach.

energy are included in the external view of our energy grammar (see the left side of Figures 8.1 and 8.2). In this way we can also easily verify the existence of external constraints by confronting the requirement of these resources and processes with their availability. As a result, primary energy resources assessed in this way cannot be summed (we cannot add tons of coal to km/h of wind).

If we want to express primary energy sources also in terms of energy we must link the available or required natural resources and processes (external view) to the corresponding energy carriers produced or required by society (internal view) by analysing the interface. Expressing the supply of primary energy sources in terms of a corresponding amount of 'energy' getting into society is a conundrum haunting statisticians. Thus far two categories of accounting have been developed for this task: the 'total primary energy supply' (TPES) and 'gross energy requirement' (GER). The accounting problems with these categories will be discussed in subsection 8.3.2.

In the external view of our energy grammar, we distinguish between two different forms of exploitation of primary energy sources (see the left side of Figure 8.2):

- *stock-flows*, in which the energy carriers are obtained from the depletion of non-renewable resources (transformation of the potential chemical energy of coal, oil and gas reserves and the potential nuclear fission energy of uranium and thorium);
- *fund-flows*, in which the energy carriers are obtained from the exploitation of natural processes that can be considered stable in time (renewable resources), such as falling water, waves, tides, blowing wind, solar radiation and biomass production.

Stock-flow exploitation is by definition unsustainable in the long term since the size of the stock is reduced by the flow. In order for fund-flow exploitation to be sustainable, the flows of energy carriers produced must be compatible with the characteristics of the fund elements (water bodies, land, soil) generating or sustaining the exploited primary energy sources.

Note that besides useful energy (end use) the concept of energy metabolism implies another output of energy transformations, that is, the flows of wastes released into the context, such as CO_2 from coal and high-level waste (HLW) for nuclear power (see the left side of Figure 8.2). Hence a check on the feasibility of the metabolic pattern must also consider the compatibility between the flows of waste produced and the sink capacity of the embedding ecosystems. Thus, the *feasibility* of the metabolic pattern of exosomatic energy is determined by the *external constraints* (processes beyond human control) to the availability of renewable and non-renewable primary energy sources and to the sink capacity of society's context.

As we will see in detail in section 8.4, the exploitation of primary energy sources is also subject to *internal constraints*. These constraints are related to the demand for limited production factors (e.g. human labour, technological capital, land, energy carriers) that have to be allocated to the energy and mining sector for the exploitation of primary energy sources. Production factors invested in producing energy carriers are not available for investment in other societal compartments. Hence, these internal constraints determine the *viability* of the metabolic pattern of exosomatic energy. Indeed, if the exploitation of a primary energy source calls for a huge investment of production factors, it will result in being impracticable.

External and internal constraints to the exploitation of primary energy resources can be overcome by importing primary energy sources or energy carriers, provided of course that these imports are economically feasible. Thus, the openness of the metabolic pattern adds another dimension (economic and political) to the analysis of its feasibility and viability. That is, if the gross supply of energy carriers of a socio-economic system is secured predominantly through imports, it is necessary to check the economic viability of this solution.

8.3.2 Navigating through the energy statistics

Having explored the various concepts involved in an effective accounting of the metabolic pattern of exosomatic energy of modern society we can understand the 'mission impossible' of statistical offices. Energy statistics generally provide a single category of accounting to assess the size of the 'energy throughput' of society for comparative purposes. However, as we have seen in the external view, it is impossible to sum the mix of primary energy sources used in terms of biophysical quantities. The alternative is to express the primary energy sources in terms of an energy equivalent, so as to establish a link with the internal view on the energy metabolism. However, this operation is extremely treacherous, as it must necessarily blur the distinction between the internal and the external view – and their corresponding logic of accounting – and between mechanical (electricity) and thermal energy.

Indeed, there is no agreement, not even among the major statistical offices, on how to measure the total energy throughput of a society (Giampietro and Sorman 2012). Two distinct accounting methods presently coexist, the partial substitution method (PSM) and the physical energy content method (PECM). The former is in use by the US Energy Information Administration (EIA) and British Petroleum (BP) Energy Statistics, the latter by Eurostat and the International Energy Agency (IEA). Both accounting methods are based on the application of a set of flat conversion factors to condense the raw datasets about energy flows into a single number. Both methods acknowledge the need for making a distinction between 'primary energy' (external view) and 'secondary energy' (internal view). But this is where the similarities between the two end. The differences of the two accounting systems are explained below using the data shown in Figure 8.2.

The *partial substitution method* (PSM) provides the thermal energy equivalent (in joules) of the gross energy *requirement* of society as a proxy of the demand for primary energy sources. In this protocol, in use by BP and EIA, the assessment of the gross energy *requirement* of society is based on the characteristics of the mix of energy carriers (electricity and thermal) actually consumed (or required) within society. This hybrid approach is thus rooted in the internal view and establishes a link between the internal and external view by translating the information about the gross requirement of energy carriers (secondary energy flows referring to the internal view) into an equivalent amount of *thermal energy* that must be supplied by primary energy sources (referring to the external view). Given this logic, this protocol does not use any information about the actual mix of primary energy sources supplied to and used by society. In this protocol, 1J of electricity is considered equivalent to a flat 2.6J of thermal energy independently of how and where this electricity is produced (2.6/1 is the average conversion factor observed in fossil-fueled power plants in OECD countries nowadays). This conversion factor assumes that all electricity is produced using only one single primary energy source of reference, that is, fossil energy.

This protocol was developed at the time the supply of fossil energy was abundant, which may explain the adoption of fossil energy as the reference to calculate the thermal equivalent of mechanical energy. Thus, the protocol maps a given quantity of thermal energy on to a given type of primary energy source used as standard. In the past it used to be 1 tonne of coal equivalent (tce), equivalent to 29.4GJ of thermal energy; later on it became 1 tonne of oil equivalent (toe), equivalent to 42GJ of thermal energy. This implies that the expression 'tonne of oil equivalent' refers to a quantity of thermal energy accounted for in the category of primary energy and not to the mass (an actual tonne) of oil. In Figure 8.2 the accounting of joules of gross energy requirement referring to electricity production is indicated in the grey columns labelled J-GER thermal (expressed in PJ). This quantity is divided into a column of actual quantities of thermal energy delivered in the form of energy carriers (left), and in quantities of energy equivalents (right, indicated by values in square brackets) for the supply of electricity provided by nuclear power (230PJ of electricity in GSEC [in bold] = 600PJ of thermal equivalent of GER [in square brackets]) and by hydroelectric and wind power (200PJ of electricity in GSEC [in bold] = 520PJ of thermal equivalent of GER [in square brackets]). For the electricity produced with fossil energy, the method simply refers to actual physical conversions (1J of electricity in GSEC [in bold] = 2.61J of thermal equivalent of GER).

The *physical energy content method* (PECM) provides the gross energy *supply* in joules of 'primary energy commodities', a generic semantic category proposed by OECD/IEA/EUROSTAT (2004, pp. 17–18) as the proxy of primary energy sources. This protocol, in use by Eurostat and IEA, bases the accounting on the characteristics of the mix of primary energy sources (e.g. fossil energy, nuclear and alternative sources) actually supplied to and used by society. Starting from this mix the protocol calculates the TPES to society. This hybrid approach is rooted in the external view, as it is based on information about the mix of primary energy sources used by society (primary energy supply) to generate energy carriers. Given this choice, this protocol does not provide reliable information on the actual mix of energy carriers used in society. This limits the usefulness of such assessment. Given the way it is calculated, the total primary energy supply does not provide useful information for the accounting for energy flows in the internal view nor about the required primary energy sources.

In this protocol, 1J of electricity (mechanical energy; an energy carrier or secondary energy) is accounted for in different ways, depending on the primary energy source used to produce electricity:

- 1J of electricity is accounted for as 2.6J of primary energy supply for fossil energy sources (note this is the same conversion factor as the one used in the partial substitution method);
- 1J of electricity is accounted for as 3J of primary energy supply for nuclear energy sources (the accounting of the 'primary energy supplied' by the plant refers to the heat dissipated in the nuclear reactor);
- 1J of electricity produced by wind or falling water (hydroelectric) is accounted for as 1J of primary energy supply. Indeed, when dealing with non-thermal alternative energies such as wind or hydroelectric power, the accounting of the 'primary energy supplied' refers to the kinetic energy converted into electricity without heat losses.

The physical energy content method is illustrated in Figure 8.2 in the column labelled 'TPES J-?'. The question mark refers to the fact that we cannot and should not sum the numbers in this column (some values refer to J of thermal energy, others to J of mechanical energy). It is evident that this approach has two serious problems:

1 The overall assessment of TPES is obtained by summing joules of thermal energy (from fossil and nuclear sources) and joules of mechanical energy (from water and wind sources). This sum is not admissible according to the laws of thermodynamics. This may explain why quantities of TPES are expressed under the bizarre label 'joules of energy commodities'. The equivalence class to which this category refers is unclear. In fact the category energy commodities comprises both primary and secondary energy and, at the same time, thermal and mechanical energy.
2 The total primary energy supply (outside view) does not map on to the gross supply of energy carriers (inside view). For example, in Sweden in 2005, renewable sources (mainly hydro) provided 25.5 per cent and nuclear sources 25.3 per cent of the electric supply (actual supply of electric power to the grid, an energy form that can be measured). However, according to the TPES assessment (obtained with the physical energy content method), nuclear power was claimed to supply 30.4 per cent of the electricity, whereas renewable sources (mainly hydro) were claimed to supply a mere 10.4 per cent (Giampietro and Sorman 2012). This mismatch can also be seen in Figure 8.2 for Spain. Looking at the domestic supply, we have that 230PJ-EC of electricity in GSEC was generated from nuclear sources whereas 200PJ-EC of electricity in GSEC was generated from wind and hydro (the ratio between these two values of electricity supplied to the grid is 1.15/1). However, if we look at the TPES the corresponding ratio between the two is 3.4/1!

In conclusion, neither of the two methods is satisfactory. The partial substitution method estimates a total requirement of thermal energy (GER-thermal) – to be supplied by primary energy sources – on the basis of information that considers only the internal view. Therefore it does not provide any information on the quantity and quality of primary energy sources actually used or required. The physical energy content method, on the other hand, estimates a TPES of joules of 'energy commodities' to assess the contribution provided by primary energy sources. This protocol does take into account the mix of primary energy sources but does not provide a useful interface between the external and internal view because of: 1) the choice to aggregate the contribution of different primary energy sources by summing joules of mechanical and thermal energy; and 2) the lack of any useful information about the supply of the various energy carriers used in society (internal view).

Whatever the chosen method of accounting is, it is important to realize that the assessment of the aggregate throughput of energy at the level of society (GER-thermal or TPES) no longer refers to measurable flows of energy carriers. Flows of energy carriers can be measured only at the local scale (e.g. we can directly measure the joules of electricity consumed by a refrigerator, but not the embodied energy in that electricity). Thus, both the gross energy requirement (in J of thermal energy) and the total primary energy supply (in J of energy commodities) are *virtual* quantities of energy obtained by using conversion factors and defining ad hoc categories of accounting reflecting a given convention (perception) over energy flows. They are not measurable physical quantities in the external ('real') world.

This discussion over the two approaches used by statistical offices and their shortcomings clearly shows that quantitative information referring to different perceptions (internal view versus external view logic of accounting) and different definitions of equivalence class (thermal versus mechanical energy) cannot be compressed into a single number. The metabolic pattern of energy of modern society is extremely complex and cannot be represented with the traditional linear approach to energy flows based on analytical tools developed within the paradigm of reductionism. As shown in Figure 8.2, statistical offices have established a shaky 'interface' between the internal and external views and across distinct energy forms.

To avoid these pitfalls our energy grammar seeks to maintain information relevant to both the external and internal views:

- When dealing with primary energy sources (external view) we adopt measures based on non-energy physical quantities. This information is used to generate an interfacing table in which energy equivalences are mapped on to non-energy quantities (as done also in the food grammar presented in Chapter 7) referring to the required natural resources and processes. In this way, we can also define an environmental impact matrix to check the severity of external constraints on the metabolic pattern.
- When dealing with energy carriers (internal view) we use measures referring to their specific category of accounting (either thermal or mechanical) and maintain this distinction across different compartments.

These two quantitative representations can be effectively integrated with MuSIASEM, thus establishing a bridge between quantitative assessments across different levels and scales.

8.4 Energy accounting from the internal point of view

The internal point of view focuses on the representation of the flows of *energy carriers* so as to study the complex dynamics between requirement and supply of exosomatic energy *within* society. The flows and concepts relevant for the internal view have been defined earlier, in subsection 8.2.2. Here we concentrate on the complex relation among flows of energy carriers and on establishing a link with the external view. The factors determining the *viability* of the metabolic pattern (internal constraints) will be discussed in sections 8.5 and 8.6.

Energy carriers are consumed in society either in the energy and mining sector (the hypercyclic compartment), which by definition is the sole sector exploiting primary energy sources, or in the dissipative compartment, comprising all other functional sectors of society (see right-hand side of Figures 8.1 and 8.2). Energy carriers can also be exported, but in this case they should not be included in the exosomatic metabolism of society, but accounted for as products or services exported for economic reasons. In the internal view, we observe and represent *actual* flows of energy carriers at the local scale and, depending on their characteristics, we measure them in joules of distinct qualities, either electricity, process heat or fuel. Energy carriers belonging to different categories cannot be summed and, as we prefer to avoid the use of flat conversion factors, we consider them separately throughout the accounting. The easiest way to do so is by using vector and matrix representations.

Our approach to characterizing energy flows from the internal point of view is illustrated in Figure 8.3, using the data for Spain for 2004. We want to flag to the reader that the data in the figure are approximated and have the sole purpose of illustrating the approach. The representation given in this figure is divided into two parts; the upper part provides information that is relevant from the internal viewpoint, while the lower part provides information that is useful to establish a link with the external viewpoint.

The vector-based representation illustrated in Figure 8.3 makes it possible to analyse the use (or requirement) of energy carriers within society. In each matrix, the columns represent the categories of accounting for energy carriers, while the rows represent the metabolic flow of energy through functional compartments of society (generating closure across levels). In this way, each horizontal vector is composed of three elements, referring to quantities of electricity (x_{i1}), process heat (x_{i2}) and fuel (x_{i3}), where i refers to the selected compartment of society. Each vertical vector describes the consumption pattern of a given type of energy carrier (j) in society: $[x_{1j}, x_{2j}, x_{3j}, x_{4j}, x_{5j}]$, where the sum of the flows accounted for at each lower-level compartment (rows 2 to 5) must equal the total for the whole system given in the first row (WS). In this example, society is divided into the household sector (HH), the service and government sector (SG), the

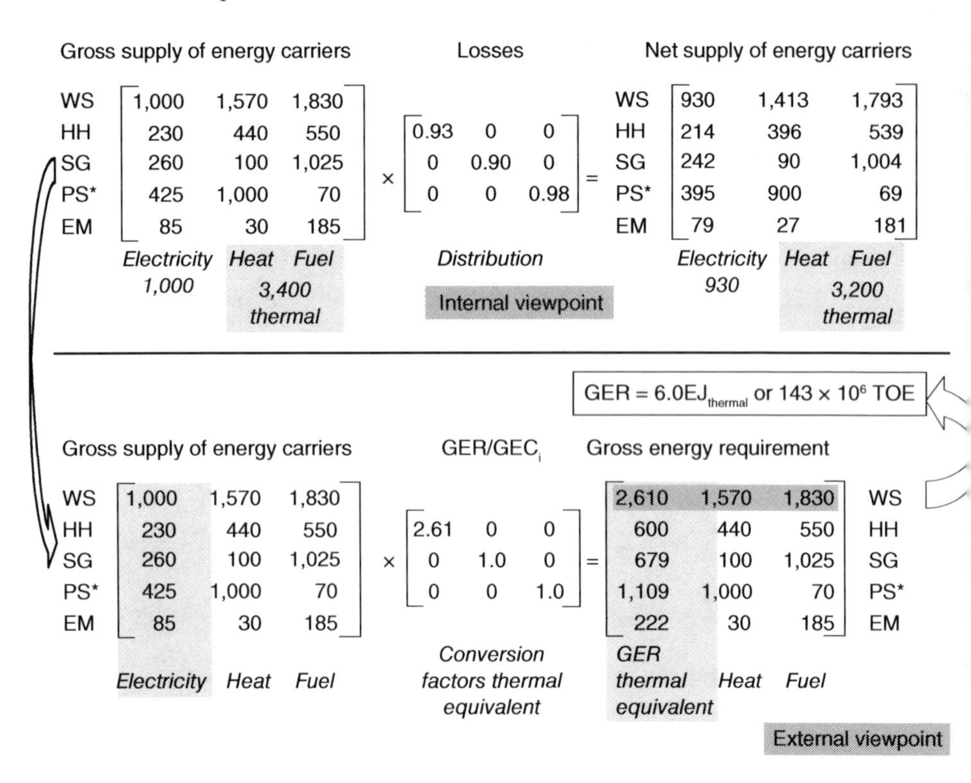

Figure 8.3 Relation among the gross supply of energy carriers (GSEC), net supply of energy carriers (NSEC) and gross energy requirement (GER) using a vector-based representation of the metabolic pattern

Source: Adapted from Giampietro *et al.* (2013) and Eurostat, Spain – Energy mix fact sheet (http://ec.europa.eu/energy/energy_policy/doc/factsheets/mix/mix_es_en.pdf).

Notes:
All data are expressed in PJ/year, unless stated otherwise.
Societal compartments are abbreviated as follows: WS = whole society; HH = household sector; SG = service and government sector; PS = primary and secondary production sectors except for energy and mining; EM = energy and mining sector.

primary and secondary production sectors except for energy and mining (PS*), and the energy and mining sector (EM). The latter sector has been singled out because it is of special interest. The energy and mining sector is the sole sector responsible for the exploitation of primary energy sources. Therefore, a thorough study of this sector is key to understanding the complex interface between the internal and external views.

- *The internal view point:* The matrix in the upper left part of Figure 8.3 refers to the gross supply of energy carriers available for final use. The GSEC to society as a whole is represented in the first row (WS [1,000, 1,570, 1,830]

PJ-EC/year). This representation is based on two categories of thermal energy carriers (together 3,400PJ-GER), including process heat (1,570PJ-EC thermal) and fuel (1,830PJ-EC thermal), and one category of electric energy carriers (1,000PJ-EC electric). Note that these values correspond to those reported in the box 'Whole society' in Figure 8.2, with the difference that here we further disaggregate the generic accounting category 'thermal energy' into the categories 'heat' and 'fuel' (see Figure 8.3). In this way we can better characterize the typology of energy carriers in relation to the tasks performed: fuels are mainly used in transportation, whereas process heat is typically used in industrial processes. Note that the gross supply of energy carriers in Figure 8.3 does not include the joules of gross energy requirement used within power plants to generate electricity. Also, as indicated in Figure 8.2, the gross energy requirement to make electricity within the energy and mining sector (2,670PJ-GER thermal) remains in this sector and is considered only in relation to the internal operation of this sector.

As shown in the upper part of Figure 8.3, multiplying the GSEC matrix by a vector representing an estimate of the loss coefficients for each category of energy carrier, we obtain the matrix of the net supply/consumption of energy carriers (NSEC). The latter matrix describes the net supply/consumption of the various energy carriers in end uses at the local scale for the whole society and its lower-level compartments.

- *Link to the external viewpoint:* The same matrix representing the GSEC is also shown in the lower left part of Figure 8.3 to illustrate how we can generate a large-scale assessment of the energy requirement of society relevant for the external view. As we started out from the internal view, the logical choice is to use the partial substitution method. Thus, we convert the assessment of electricity reported (in joules of mechanical energy) in the first column of the GSEC matrix into its thermal equivalent by multiplying with the flat conversion factor 2.61 (see subsection 8.3.2). The result is the matrix of gross energy requirement, shown in the lower right part of Figure 8.3, in which all values are expressed in joules of thermal energy. This matrix represents how much 'thermal energy equivalent' would be required to sustain the metabolic pattern of society (row 1) and its lower-level compartments (rows 2–5) if electricity was produced only from fossil energy. As all elements of the GER matrix belong to the same category of accounting (thermal) and are expressed in the same unit (joules of thermal energy), they can be summed across the rows *and* the columns. Doing so, we obtain the overall gross energy requirement of Spain, 6.0EJ-thermal or 143Mtoe. As discussed in subsection 8.3.2, this assessment is of limited relevance for the external view (to study the feasibility of the metabolic pattern), but is useful in comparing the energy throughput of countries – both in absolute terms and in per capita terms – using a defendable set of assumptions and reference standards. One important feature of the MuSIASEM accounting system is that it establishes a bridge between distinct types of quantitative assessments of energy, referring simultaneously to the local and large scales and to the internal and external views. Indeed, combining the information provided in Figures 8.2 and 8.3, we can identify the corresponding gross and net actual supply/consumption of energy carriers for the whole society (WS) and for each of the lower-level compartments by keeping the distinction between thermal (fuels and process heat) and mechanical (kinetic energy and electricity) energy.

8.5 Accounting production factors to characterize end uses

Within the exosomatic metabolic pattern, different types of energy carriers (electricity, fuels, heat) are converted outside the human body by exosomatic devices (technology) capable of carrying out defined tasks through flows of applied power (useful energy). Examples of exosomatic devices include tractors, aeroplanes, and electronic devices capable of processing information. Exosomatic energy conversions have the goal of amplifying the output of useful work per unit of human activity. Indeed, the biophysical productivity of one hour of human labour can easily be amplified thousands of times when combined with the use of fossil energy and technology. For example, a farmer with an endosomatic (muscle) power capacity of 0.1hp driving a tractor with an exosomatic power capacity of 300hp controls a power level that is 3,000 times his/her own. Therefore, in a society that heavily relies on exosomatic power the amount of useful work performed is no longer proportional to the hours of human labour invested in a given task, but depends mainly on the level of power capacity (the characteristics of the exosomatic devices) and the flow of energy input (the energy carriers consumed by the exosomatic devices) used to carry out that task. For this reason, an effective characterization of the exosomatic metabolic pattern has to focus on the combined use of all three biophysical production factors:

1 *Power capacity:* the fund element representing exosomatic devices operating in the functional compartments of society. It is defined as the ability to convert a flow of energy carrier input into a flow of applied power at the local scale in order to perform a defined task (function). Power capacity is measured in watt (kW) or horsepower (hp). We prefer the SI unit – watt (kW) – because it is compatible with our assessments of energy flows in joules. Note that, in this approach, power capacity refers to the ability of devices to consume (dissipate) energy carriers – power capacity (PC), measured in kW-REU (REU = requirement of end use). This should not be confused with the ability of converters (e.g. power plants) to generate energy carriers within the EM sector – power capacity hypercyclic (PCH), measured in kW-GSEC.
2 *Human activity:* the fund element that controls the generation and effective delivery of the applied power generated by exosomatic devices. Human activity (a proxy of the presence of humans in the functional compartment) is measured in hours and, when accounted for within the paid work compartments, is also referred to as human labour.
3 *Input of energy carriers:* any flow element that represents an input for local conversions into applied power.

Clearly, other production factors (e.g. land, water) are also needed to stabilize the metabolic pattern. They are not considered here, as we focus on the metabolic pattern of exosomatic energy flows.

Considering power capacity and human activity in addition to exosomatic energy flows complements our picture of the metabolic pattern of exosomatic energy. It also allows us to establish a bridge with socio-economic variables and to scale up the analysis across hierarchical levels. To achieve this result, we combine the information shown in Figure 8.3 with: 1) the number of hours of human activity that must be coupled to the various flows of energy carriers in order to control the flows; and 2) the amount of power capacity that must be coupled to the flows of energy carriers to enable their conversion into useful energy. An example of this approach, referring to the same dataset used in Figures 8.2 and 8.3, is illustrated in Table 8.1.

The assessments of the fund elements' power capacity for the various flows of energy carriers consumed in the various compartments are obtained starting from the assessments of the flow of energy carriers. This can be done using the following relation (Giampietro *et al.* 2013):

$$PC_{maximum} = ET_{year} \times \eta \times 1/OL \times 1/CL$$

where:

$PC_{maximum}$ is the maximum level of power that can be generated by the exosomatic device converting the input of energy carriers into a flow of applied power, measured in kW (per year);

ET_{year} is the flow of energy input feeding the power capacity, measured in J-EC per year;

η is the thermodynamic efficiency, the ratio 'applied power'/'energy input';

OL is the operation load, the hours of operation per year of the converter divided by 8,760 (hours in a year);

CL is the capacity load, the fraction of the maximum power capacity used (averaged over the year) during the operation.

Therefore, by defining these factors it is possible to assess the size of the fund power capacity (PC) for different types of energy carrier conversions (electricity, heat and fuel) and different compartments, as illustrated in Table 8.2. A detailed example of the application of this method is available in Diaz-Maurin (2013, chap. 3).

Looking at the differences in the values taken by these factors in Table 8.2 one can realize the importance of analysing the characteristics of the metabolic pattern at the local scale. In fact, only at this scale does it become possible to use bottom-up information about a specific data array describing the end uses of a given compartment: how power capacity is used, for how long and at which power level, depending on the type of energy carrier, the required input of labour and the task

Table 8.1 Characterization of end uses of production factors across functional compartments of society

	Production factors (flow and fund elements expressed per capita per year)							*Metabolic characteristics (flow/fund – average in year)*	
	HA (h)	*Electricity*		*Heat*		*Fuel*		*EMR (MJ-GER/h)*	*IPC (GJ-GER/kW)*
		End use (GJ-EC)	*PC (kW)*	*End use (GJ-EC)*	*PC (kW)*	*End use (GJ-EC)*	*PC (kW)*		
Whole society	8,760	23	6.5	30	4	50	10.5	16	6.7
Household sector	7,825	5	5	10	3	13	6	5	2.6
Service and government	598	6	0.9	0	0	27	4	70	8.6
Building and manufacturing	280	9	0.5	19	0.8	0	0	159	33
Agriculture	48	0.5	0.04	1	0.1	2	0.2	90	14
Energy and mining	8	2	0.1	0	0	7	0.3	1,537	31

Source: Elaboration of data from Figure 8.3 and from Giampietro *et al.* (2013).

Note: Data refer to Spain, 2004.

Table 8.2 Factors for calculating the fund element power capacity (PC) for different types of energy carriers in different societal compartments

	Conversions of EC electricity				*Conversions of EC heat*				*Conversion of EC fuels*			
	η (%)	*OL (%)*	*CL (%)*	*UF (%)*	*η (%)*	*OL (%)*	*CL (%)*	*UF (%)*	*η (%)*	*OL (%)*	*CL (%)*	*UF (%)*
HH	80	5	50	3	80	10	80	8	25	8	20	2
SG	80	40	50	20	80	20	80	16	25	20	30	6
BM	80	75	80	60	80	75	80	60	–	–	–	–
AG	80	40	80	32	80	40	80	32	25	20	40	8
EM	80	75	80	60	80	75	80	60	25	50	40	20

to be performed. In this way, when making scenarios, we can use previous knowledge of metabolic patterns to check whether the combination of values in a given data array is compatible with the expression of the expected function. This quality control (the horizontal check in the Sudoku effect) is described in Chapter 11.

Returning to the multi-scale analysis, Table 8.1 provides information on the required combination of production factors for the expression of expected functions at the level of the whole society and at the levels of the individual lower-level compartments. The production factors (on the left side of the table) include: 1) human activity (HA), expressed in hours per capita per year; 2) the net supply/consumption of electricity (end $use_{electricity}$), expressed in GJ-EC electric per capita per year; 3) the power capacity used to dissipate this electricity, expressed in kW per capita per year; 4) the net supply/consumption of process heat energy carriers (end use_{heat}), expressed in GJ-EC thermal per capita per year; 5) the power capacity used to convert heat into applied power (useful work), expressed in kW per capita per year; 6) the net supply/consumption of fuels (end use_{fuel}), expressed in GJ-EC thermal per capita per year; and 7) the power capacity used to convert fuels and heat into applied power, expressed in kW per capita per year.

The integrated characterization across hierarchical levels of analysis shown in Table 8.1 is important for two reasons. First, at the local scale, we can use the information listed in the rows to study the specific characteristics of a given compartment in relation to its expected functions. This feature is extremely useful in scenario analysis, in which we need to know the expected endowment of production factors used by the various compartments to be able to express their typical functions. Second, at the large scale, we can use all the information provided by the entire table to check the congruence of the profile of allocation of fund and flow elements over the columns, making use of the closure of the accounting system. For instance, in a post-industrial economy, less than 1,000h/year of human activity per capita are available to the whole paid work sector, making up all the economic sectors (see Chapter 6). At the same time, the service and government sector and the primary and secondary production sectors (minus energy and mining) require together almost 900h/year per capita of human labour. In this situation, it is obvious that the energy and mining sector must exploit a set of primary energy sources that demands only a very small investment of labour among the production factors. Therefore, we may also expect that in this type of metabolic pattern the energy and mining sector must be characterized by a large input of power capacity to compensate for the reduced amount of labour hours. This type of forced relations is discussed in Chapter 11 under the header 'Sudoku effect'.

The closure of the accounting system used in Table 8.1 also makes it possible to define a series of metabolic characteristics (flow/fund ratios) for the whole system and its components, such as the exosomatic metabolic rate and the intensity of the power capacity (see the right side of Table 8.1). Again, these characteristics are essential to assess the viability of the exosomatic metabolic pattern of energy. In fact, cross-sectional and longitudinal studies have shown that the metabolic characteristics of societal compartments (in terms of flow/fund or fund/fund ratios) of similar socio-economic systems tend to converge to defined benchmark values (Giampietro *et al.* 2012, 2013). Hence, we can construct 'viability domains' for the metabolic characteristics for different types of socio-economic systems, which can then be used in diagnostic and scenario analysis.

Thus, the data describing the end uses for the various societal compartments (left side of Table 8.1) can be used to highlight important quantitative and qualitative characteristics (right side of Table 8.1). In fact, at this level of disaggregation, Table 8.1 clearly shows that the functional compartments of society do not simply 'consume a certain amount of energy'. When they are perceived and represented at the local scale, we can see that functional compartments require *an expected mix of energy carriers, in the right quantities*, which must be converted *at a given power level*, using *a defined mix of exosomatic devices* (guaranteeing the required power capacity) using *a given amount of human labour*, capable of providing *the required quality of control* (adequate skill) for the operation of these exosomatic devices. When perceived at the large scale, the various data arrays describing the local characteristics of the end uses of the various compartments must result in being compatible with the total size of the fund and flow elements assessed at the level of the whole society. At the same time, the metabolic characteristics of the various functional compartments must stay within the viability domain defined for the type of socio-economic system under study.

8.6 The energy return on investment (EROI) within the energy grammar

The concept of the energy return on investment (EROI) (at times also referred to as the energy return on energy invested, EROEI) has been put forward in the field of energy analysis as an indicator of the 'quality' of energy sources (Hall *et al.* 1986). This indicator has rapidly gained popularity in the field of energy analysis (see Hall *et al.* 2009; Hansen and Hall 2011). The rationale of EROI is based on the concept of optimal foraging strategy developed in ecology (i.e. for an animal the best food is the one providing the maximum energy with the minimum effort – see

Pyke 1984 for an overview of the concept) and that of net energy return developed in energetics (Cottrell 1955), applying the same idea to the assessment of energy sources. Indeed the rationale of the energy return on investment seems to be a good starting point to assess the performance of energy systems exploiting physical gradients. According to this rationale, a 'good' primary energy source should return much more 'energy' than that invested in its exploitation. However, in spite of the simple logic when the concept is stated in semantic terms, the implementation of the EROI in quantitative terms has proven to be quite problematic (Giampietro *et al.* 2013).

We can use the overview provided in Figure 8.2 to explain why. The use of a simple ratio referring to a given 'quantity of energy' produced (output) and a 'quantity of energy' invested (input) clashes with the epistemological impasses discussed earlier (the mission impossible faced by the statistical offices!). A single number cannot handle all the information needed to describe the differences in quality of primary energy sources. The first problem is that a simple ratio (e.g. 10:1) does not carry any information about the size of the flows involved; it can refer to the relation between the two quantities 100,000,000 and 10,000,000 as well as to the relation between 1 and 0.1. That is, such a ratio lacks an external referent. The information about the actual sizes of the flows is essential in assessing the requirement of physical gradients (feasibility in relation to external constraints) and the requirement of production factors (e.g. labour, power capacity required for handling the internal loop of energy for energy) and hence the viability of the dynamic equilibrium between the hypercycle and the dissipative compartment (internal constraint). So the assessment of the flows has to be related to an assessment of the fund elements processing them. The second problem is that energy flows considered in the assessment of the output and the input often belong to different semantic categories of accounting; for example, different primary energy sources use different physical gradients as input, such as mechanical energy from wind and hydro and chemical potential energy from fossil, and they generate energy carriers as output of a different nature such as electricity or fuels.

The adoption of the MuSIASEM approach makes it possible to generate an alternative characterization based on a set of factors determining the EROI. An example of this alternative accounting, based on four distinct output/input ratios, is provided in Figure 8.4:

1 The first two 'output/input ratios' (labelled 'environmental impact' in Figure 8.4) reflect the characteristics of the energy systems exploiting the PES, and refer to the interface internal view/external view. The inputs are represented by physical gradients not measurable in energy terms, and the outputs are represented by the amount of energy that the exploitation makes available for the generation of energy carriers. This quantity can be in the form of either mechanical energy (e.g. wind, hydro) or thermal energy (biomass, concentrated solar power). This amount of energy is used only by the EM sector (it is not used by the rest of the society), so it refers to an 'internal energy output' that is fully consumed as an 'internal energy input' by default.

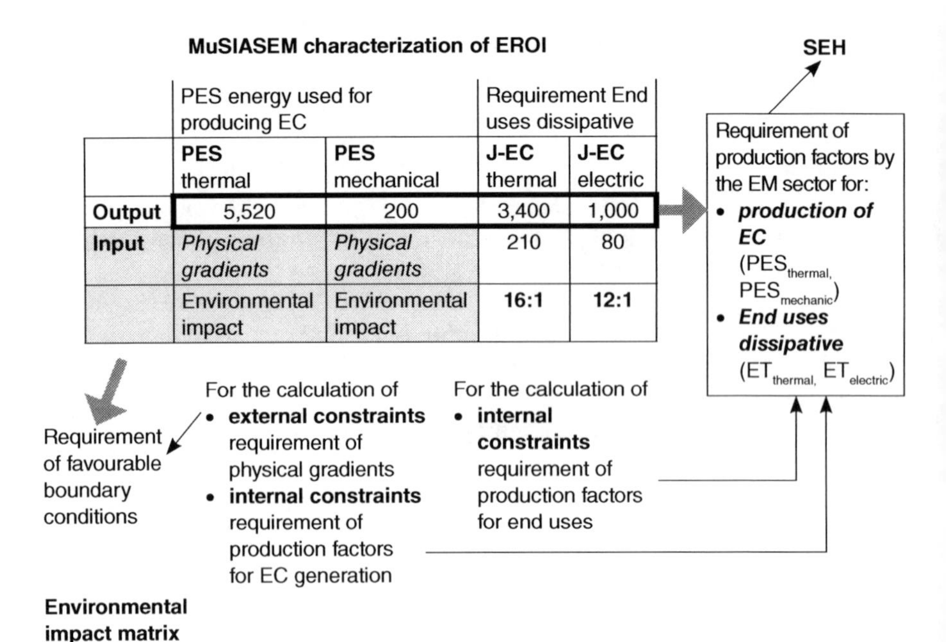

Figure 8.4 Implementation of the EROI rationale using the MuSIASEM accounting (Spain, 2004)

Source: Data from Figure 8.2.

However, this internal flow of energy is essential in assessing the severity of external constraints. In fact, this flow depends on the quantity of physical gradients available on the supply side (natural resources) and on the sink side (capability of handling the environmental impact of wastes), an availability that is beyond human control.

2 The second two output/input ratios (16:1 and 12:1) represent the ratio of energy carrier flow generated and that consumed by the EM sector. Following the scheme given in Figure 8.2, the flows of energy carriers can be divided into two categories of accounting, GSEC thermal and GSEC electric, which together represent the total consumption of society and, therefore, the total output generated by the energy sector. In the same way, the consumption of energy carriers in the EM sector can be divided into J-EC thermal and J-EC electric, the sum of which represents the total input of energy carriers required for the operation of this sector. Thus, the assessment of these two output/input ratios is based on homologous categories of accounting.

The quantitative analysis of EROI given in Figure 8.4 provides all the information required to analyse the relevant characteristics of the EM sector in relation to the external (feasibility) and internal (viability) constraints:

- *In relation to external constraints:* The assessment of the size of physical gradients makes it possible to generate an environmental impact matrix to analyse the severity of external constraints.
- *In relation to internal constraints:* We can assess the total power capacity used in the EM sector from the information about the quantities of energy handled by this sector – 5,520PJ GER thermal used to produce electricity and 200PJ GER mechanical used to produce electricity, plus 210PJ EC thermal and 80PJ EC electric to run the other operations.

As is evident from the set of relations illustrated in Figure 8.2, given a gross supply of energy carriers the smaller the share of energy carriers consumed by the hypercyclic compartment (EM), the greater will be the surplus of net energy carriers available to the dissipative compartment of society. This relation between our characterization of EROI and strength of the exosomatic hypercycle (SEH) will be discussed in Chapter 11 and illustrated with a quantitative example in the case study of South Africa in Chapter 14. The possibility of establishing a link between the characteristics of the whole metabolic pattern of society and the factors determining the EROI confirms the validity of the EROI rationale as a quality criterion for the performance of energy systems. However, studying the EROI within the MuSIASEM accounting system is not about calculating a simple ratio over two numbers, but about characterizing the relation between four distinct types of outputs and inputs. When dealing with the assessment of PES the inputs are physical gradients *beyond human control*, whereas, when dealing with the assessment of EC flows, both inputs and outputs refer to energy carriers *already under human control*. This implies that the two ratios of output/input of energy carriers – 16:1 for EC thermal and 12:1 for EC electric – are meaningless if not integrated by the other information shown in Table 8.4.

Having made this distinction, it is also possible to better discuss the role of imports. In Figure 8.2 we divided the energy flows within the energy and mining sector into the domestic supply (upper rows) and imports (lower rows). Looking at the relation between the energy carriers consumed in the EM (joules of EC thermal and EC electric) and the energy carriers delivered to society (GSEC in joules of EC thermal and EC electric) we can appreciate the huge difference made by imports. Imported flows of energy carriers (e.g. petrol) require only production factors in their handling, whereas imported flows of primary energy sources (e.g. crude oil) also require production factors for their conversion into energy carriers (e.g. refineries and power plants). Note that the numbers describing the breakdown of the consumption of energy carriers within the energy and mining sector over different energy systems and in relation to imports and exports are based on 'guesstimates' and have the goal only of illustrating the approach. However, it is reasonable to assume that imports of energy avoid the investment of production factors for the search of new resources and for the exploitation process (e.g. oil drilling and refineries). Thus, when dealing with imported energy the bulk of the internal autocatalytic loop of energy carriers for energy carriers is avoided (externalized!).

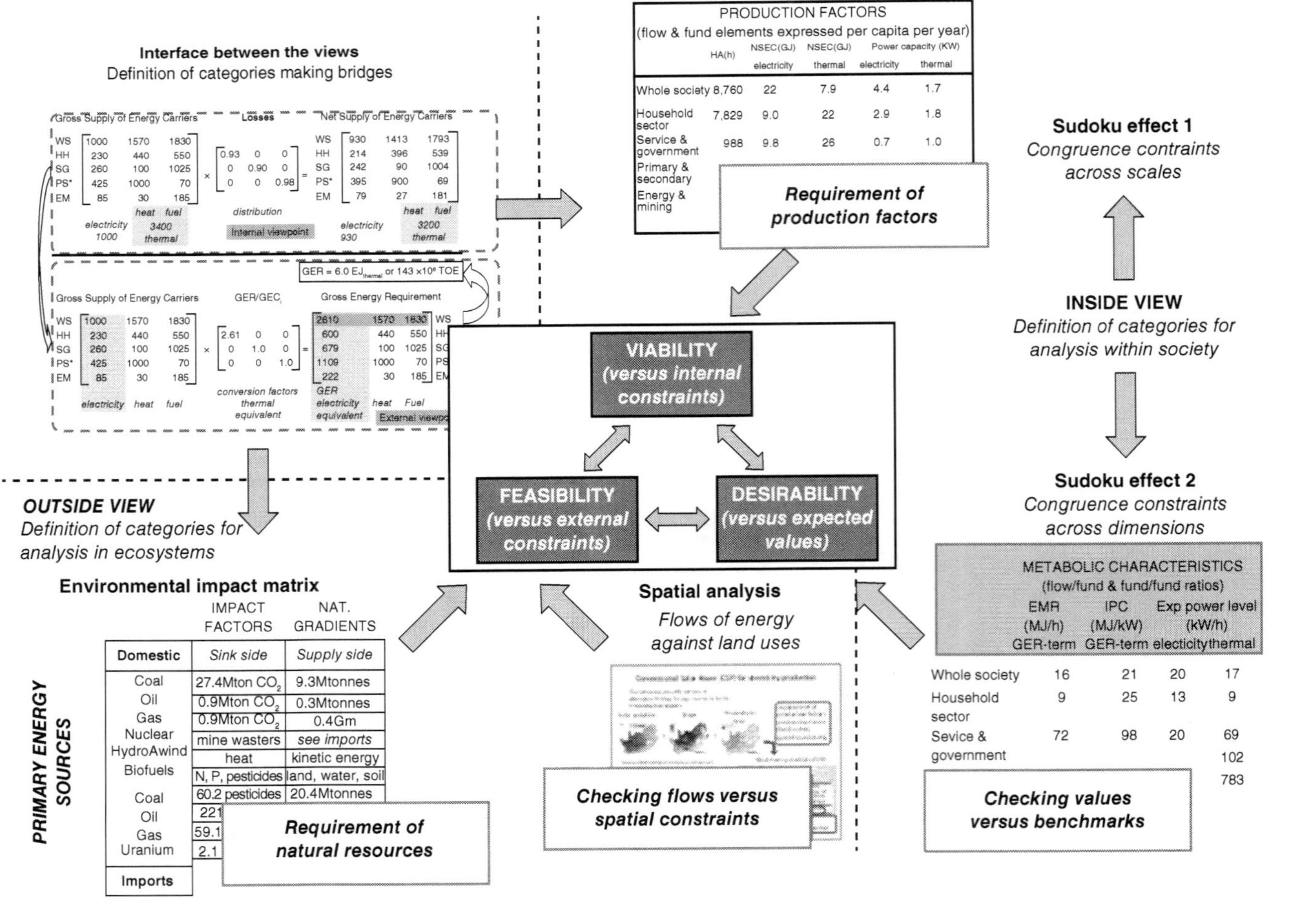

Figure 8.5 An overview of the toolkit developed within the MuSIASEM accounting system to check the feasibility, viability and desirability of the exosomatic energy metabolism

8.7 Conclusions

An overview of the application of the energy grammar to assess the feasibility, viability and desirability of the metabolic pattern of exosomatic energy is shown in Figure 8.5.

Four different pieces of information are needed to effectively characterize the total energy throughput of society and establish an interface between the internal and external views and across the local and large scales of assessment:

1 *The mix of primary energy sources used and their relative contribution:* This information is important because a great number of different processes (with different conversion efficiencies) are being used simultaneously to convert primary energy sources into energy carriers (e.g. electricity can be generated from coal, natural gas, oil, uranium, falling water, wind, waves or solar radiation). So, first, we have to define all the mix of primary energy sources used for producing the various energy carriers to be able to assess their resulting gross and net supply.
2 *The mix of energy carriers eventually consumed in end uses in society:* This information (referring to the internal view) is essential in order to establish a useful interface between the internal and external views. The quantity and mix of energy carriers required and consumed will eventually define the compatibility with external and internal constraints in relation to the chosen mix of primary energy sources.
3 *Distribution losses within the society:* Different flows of energy carriers imply different types and quantities of losses determined by the specific circumstances of the conversion processes, such as distance between places of production and consumption and temporal mismatches. This factor complicates the accounting. If a more efficient plant for generating electricity is placed further away, then larger distribution losses may offset a better performance. If a lot of electricity is produced when it is not needed or it is not produced when needed, its supply becomes less effective (e.g. wind power when deployed locally). We did not touch on technical aspects of this assessment, because this type of analysis cannot be carried out by applying a set of flat conversion rules to aggregate data, but has to be tailored to the specificity of the metabolic pattern under study.
4 *The importance of imports and exports:* The characterization of the energy throughput of society also has to consider the imports and exports of energy quantities, according to the chosen set of categories of accounting used in the grammar (i.e. primary energy sources, physical gradients, thermal and electric energy carriers, etc.).

Numerical applications of the energy grammar to case studies are provided in Chapters 12–14.

9 Water grammar

Cristina Madrid-Lopez and Mario Giampietro

Summary

The water grammar integrates the multiple societal and ecosystem dimensions of water metabolism into a coherent accounting method. It combines the distinct narratives for the analysis of ecosystem and societal metabolic pattern, including the different definitions of hierarchical levels of organization, functional compartments, and semantic accounting categories. Within the societal view, definitions are based on socio-economic criteria (water flows per hour of human activity and per hectare of land use), within the ecosystem view, on the role of water as a fund. We show how to check feasibility and viability of both water supply and water use. The grammar is implemented using practical examples.

9.1 The two non-equivalent narratives used in the water grammar

The metabolic patterns of water in societies and ecosystems are closely interwoven through biophysical and economic/societal processes. Connecting and combining them into a single quantitative representation has proven difficult, because this requires combining distinct scales of analysis and dimensions relevant for an integrated assessment (Madrid *et al.* 2013). Any given perception of water, such as production asset or rainfall, is tied to a specific disciplinary narrative used for its representation (specific scale, dimension of analysis, and set of causal relations – Giampietro *et al.* 2006). Therefore, any representation necessarily neglects other potentially useful perceptions focusing on other aspects of the metabolic pattern (e.g. sanitary aspects of drinking water, recreational aspects of a waterfall). The simultaneous existence and use of non-equivalent perceptions (and corresponding narratives) of different aspects of the metabolic pattern of water has resulted in a proliferation of analytical definitions of water that are mostly logically independent and incommensurable. For instance, water has been defined as a climatic phenomenon, a geological element, an ecosystem element, a human right, a production factor, a commodity, a chemical element and a public service, among others.

Hence, as is the case with the other nexus elements, what we need for a comprehensive accounting of water within MuSIASEM is a grammar that is able to accommodate and integrate the non-equivalent perceptions of water and the corresponding quantifications that are relevant for the specific goal of the analysis. The flow-fund model fulfils this need by providing a semantically open definition of fund and flow elements in which the description of the role of 'water' changes with the hierarchical level and scale of analysis. For example, lakes, rivers or aquifers represent structural ecosystem elements, thus ecological funds, whereas socio-economic water uses such as drinking, irrigation and cooling represent societal flows. This distinction allows us to define whether or not a quantity of water has been consumed in the metabolic pattern. The water flowing in a river represents the identity of this fund and it is not 'consumed' by the river, whereas water used by an industry has lost at least one of the attributes required by the local metabolic process and therefore it has been 'consumed' by the industry.

Thus, according to the MuSIASEM rationale, water can be represented as either a flow element or a fund element, depending on the hierarchical level and associated spatial-temporal scale used in the analysis. This will be reflected by the label given to the category used for its accounting: water belonging to an ecological fund, or water belonging to a societal flow. In the *internal view*, in terms of the processes taking place within society and defining what society does, water is perceived as a flow element (water use by humans), while, in the *external view*, in terms of large-scale ecological processes defining the identity of the ecosystem, water is perceived as a fund (processes beyond human control) (Madrid *et al.* 2013). In this section we explain how to operate simultaneously with these two different narratives about the role of water and how to handle the resulting dual role of water in the representation of the metabolic pattern of society and ecosystem.

9.1.1 Internal view: water as a flow in the societal metabolism

In the internal view the expected characteristics of water flows perceived at the local scale are determined by the characteristics of the societal funds using these flows. This follows the same logic used in the food and energy grammars. Depending on the particular use of water made by the structural fund elements (human activity, land use, power capacity) in the functional compartments of the socio-economic system, there is a set of specific attributes that a given quantity of water must possess for it to qualify as an input for the metabolic process. For example, a given quantity of water good for irrigation might not be suitable for drinking. A given fund element of society (e.g. human being, industrial plant or area of land) 'consumes' the resource water when a given quantity going through it loses at least one of the specific attributes required by the metabolic identity of that fund element. Thus, every time we identify a change of relevant attributes in a quantity of water due to the interaction with a fund element of society, we have a *flow* of water within the societal metabolism.

For example, a quantity of water held by a dam (attribute: great potential energy) is an input for a hydroelectric plant (fund: power capacity) and thus a flow in relation to this plant. Falling through the turbine, this volume of water loses much of its potential energy and with it the original usefulness for the plant. This same quantity of water can still be used as an input (flow) for irrigation of agricultural fields (fund land) or even a hydropower station downstream, yet not again for the same station at the same height. That is to say, after each use, the quantity of water under consideration loses its usefulness (the relevant attribute) for the task carried out by the specific fund using it. This explains why it is important in a water grammar to define a set of categories of 'water flows' (mapping on to water uses) and of 'ecological funds' (mapping on to the favourable boundary conditions guaranteeing the feasibility of these flows) and to keep track of these flows separately. Naturally, as the total amount of water is more or less constant on earth, a given mass of water that has lost its original attributes will during its course through the hydrological cycle regain these attributes and be capable of providing the same expected services again, but not during the time horizon of the analytical representation.

9.1.2 External view: water as a fund in the ecosystem metabolism

In the external view, volumes of water assume the role of fund element determining the ecosystem structure (e.g. lake, river). The classification of a given quantity of water as a fund within the metabolic pattern of ecosystems is rooted in the role that the given quantity of water plays in the stabilization of the ecosystem. Does this quantity of water form part of the ecosystem itself? When considered as a fund element, in the duration of the representation, the water body in question does not (and should not) lose any of the relevant attributes associated with the integrity of the specific type of ecosystem. When considering the interface of ecosystem and society, the quantitative aspect of this assessment is essential. In order to express their ecological and physical functions, water funds must have a critical volume of water that is needed all at once. A lake, for example, needs to have a determined water volume in order to provide the expected support for aquatic life. In the same way, a river must have a predictable water availability pattern to maintain the riparian ecosystem. The categories of accounting and scales to be used to describe the integrity of a lake or a river are entirely different from those describing water flows in society.

9.1.3 Linking the internal and external views

This distinction between societal flow elements and ecological fund elements is extremely useful in connecting the water use and environmental impact. Indeed, when describing water as an element that is required simultaneously by the metabolic pattern of societies and by the metabolic pattern of ecosystems, we provide an essential bridge between the internal and external views in the analysis of the nexus. This is shown in Figure 9.1.

Thus, the internal reading provides information on water-related societal processes and allows us to perform the *viability check* on the societal metabolism. As explained above, this typically focuses on water flows in relation to human

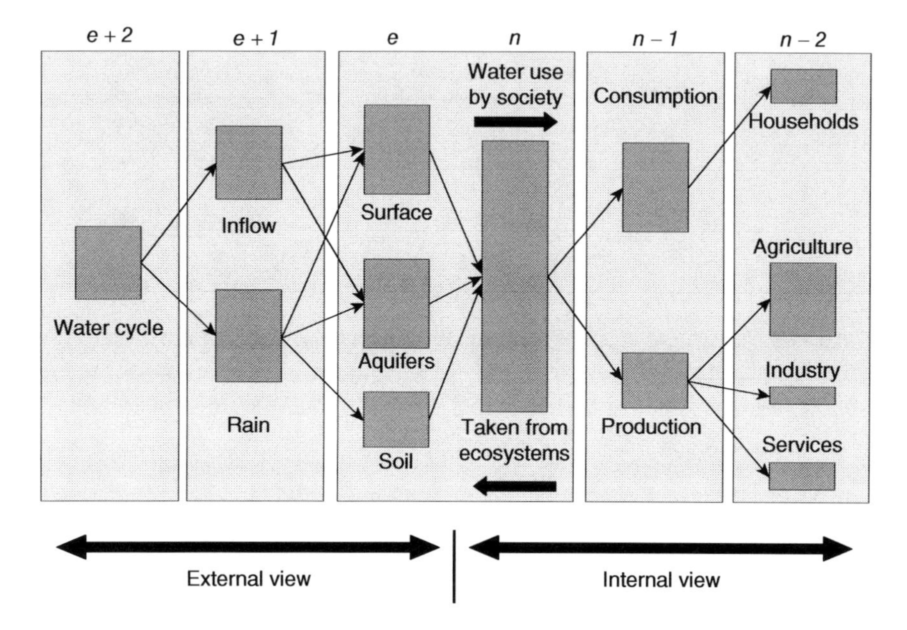

Figure 9.1 Overview of the metabolic pattern of water combining the hierarchical levels of organization of the societal metabolic pattern ($n/n-i$) and the ecosystem metabolic pattern ($e/e+1$)

Source: Adapted from Madrid *et al.* (2013).

activities (water use per hour) and land uses (water use per hectare) across different socio-economic compartments that are defined at lower levels of analysis ($n-1$, $n-2$, etc.). The external reading, on the other hand, allows us to individuate how much water can be appropriated by the metabolic pattern of a society as a whole without damaging ecosystem funds. This assessment of the *feasibility* of society's metabolic pattern must be carried out across different levels and scales (e, $e+1$, etc.). Because it considers the specific characteristics of geographical elements, the feasibility check involves the use of GIS techniques, as we explain in Chapter 10. The two different logics (narratives) used in our water grammar are illustrated in Figure 9.2.

Figure 9.2 refers to the application of MuSIASEM to the analysis of the rural metabolism of Punjab (see Chapter 13). As the focal level of our accounting system can be defined as a socio-ecological system (SES), both the ecological and the societal narratives of the metabolic pattern are relevant for the analysis. As discussed in Chapter 4, the concept of SES refers to the interface between two non-equivalent perceptions of the external world. As a consequence, the perception of the metabolic pattern of society and the perception of the metabolic pattern of ecosystem refer to two logically independent definitions of hierarchical levels associated with different scales. This becomes evident when comparing Figures 9.1 and 9.2. In Figure 9.1 the different levels of

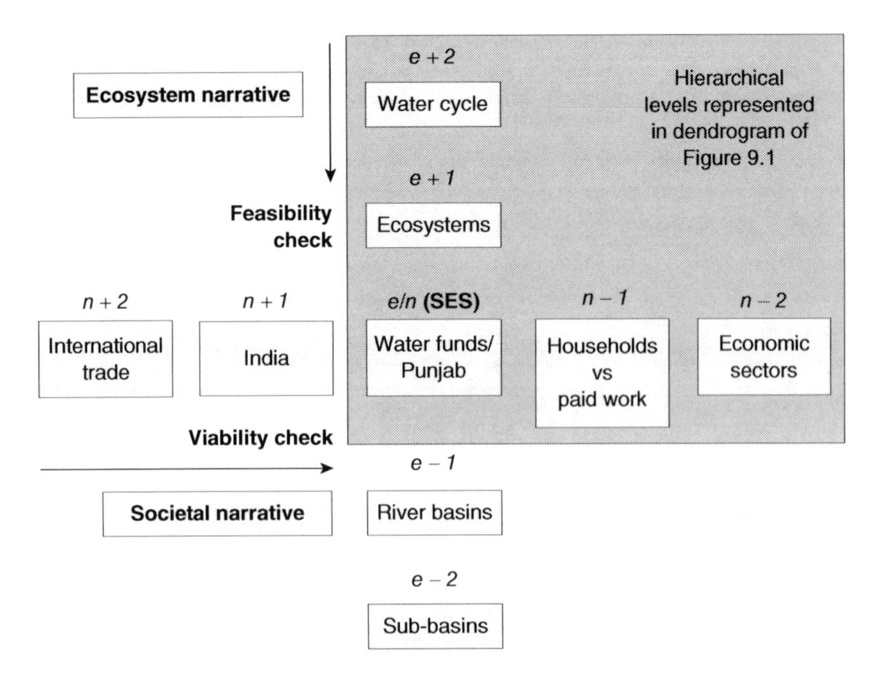

Figure 9.2 The two logically independent definitions of hierarchical levels of organization for the analysis of societal metabolism of water (horizontal, $n+i/n/n-i$) and ecosystem metabolism of water (vertical, $e+i/e/e-i$) for the Punjab case

analysis for the societal metabolism are represented horizontally: the hierarchical levels ($n/n-i$) of the 'inside view' on the right of Figure 9.1 correspond to the hierarchical levels on the right ($n/n-i$) of Figure 9.2. As regards the outside view, the hierarchical levels ($e/e+i$) on the left of the focal level in Figure 9.1 correspond to the levels represented vertically above the focal ecosystem level (e) in Figure 9.2. At these levels the quantification refers to: water funds (water bodies, such as rivers, aquifers or lakes); the ecosystem boundary conditions ($e+1$), including the processes recharging the water funds, such as rain or water inflows; and large-scale processes of the water cycle stabilizing the recharging of water funds, which are usually assumed to be stable in the wider context ($e+2$). Therefore, in the representation given in Figure 9.1 – representing the interface between the two metabolic patterns composing a socio-ecological system – we do not have information about socio-economic characteristics of processes taking place above the focal level (levels $n+i$) and the characteristics of ecological processes taking place below the focal level (levels $e-i$).

For this reason it is important carefully to tailor the choice of the focal level when implementing the grammar. For example, in the case studies of Mauritius and South Africa, the focal level matches the national level of the societal hierarchical structure, while in the Punjab case study (illustrated in Figure 9.2) the societal focal level coincides with an administrative unit at the sub-national level (a state of India). Given the different logic behind the definition of structural compartments for the societal and the ecosystem water metabolism, the extension of the societal level *n* rarely matches the extension of the ecosystem level *e*. The geographical extension of the focal level chosen for the analysis must follow the delimitation of one of them. This frequently results in mismatches between categories of water accounting (Moss and Newig 2010) and favours the proliferation of accounts that use the social logic to arrange water data, owing to the fact that the data requirement to assess the water metabolism is frequently arranged following a societal logic.

As mentioned earlier, the size of the lower-level societal compartments in MuSIASEM is defined by the size of societal fund elements, notably human activity (Chapter 6) and/or managed land (Chapter 4, section 4.5). Water flows in a given compartment of society are assessed as the product of: 1) intensive variables (flow/fund ratios) per hour of human activity (rate of water use) or per hectare of managed land (density of water use) of a given category of accounting; and 2) the size of the fund element belonging to that compartment (hours of labour in a given economic activity consuming water, hectares of crop cultivation evapotranspirating a known amount of water per year). Total compartmental water use is then obtained by scaling up the various flows of end uses by weighting the relative sizes of the funds. In this way, the total water throughput of a given compartment can always be represented and obtained in two different ways, based on either human activity or land use. The quantitative assessment in relation to land use is essential for the analysis of the feasibility of the metabolic pattern in relation to external constraints on both the supply side and the sink side.

In the societal narrative the focal level is determined by the boundary defining 'available land' (e.g. national borders at level *n* or administrative borders at level $n-i$). In the ecological narrative, the focal level is determined by the water funds included within it (e.g. a river). However, the delimitation of the focal level according to the ecological narrative seldom or never coincides with the administrative or functional boundaries used to define the categories of accounting of human activity, land use, or power capacity, the funds consuming flows of water in the socio-economic metabolism. The issue of how to handle this mismatch of categorizations within MuSIASEM has been addressed in theoretical terms by Serrano-Tovar and Giampietro (2014).

9.2 The semantics of the water grammar

Given the complexity of the water metabolic pattern outlined in section 9.1, the idea of developing a universal protocol (of the type 'one size fits all') for its quantification is unrealistic. In fact, as with the other elements of the nexus, the first step is about defining a set of useful *semantic categories* of accounting. Then, depending on the case under study, these categories have to be tailored to the specific situation and context. This two-layer system of categorization, associated with the very concept of a grammar, provides a solid foundation for comparability studies of water metabolic patterns and for linking water to the other elements of the nexus. The semantic categories for water used in MuSIASEM are shown in

Table 9.1 Semantic categories and water types used for the accounting of water in the three case studies

Role	*System definition*	*Semantic categories*	*Water types*	*Mauritius*	*Punjab*	*South Africa*
Fund	Water cycle *e+2*	Not applicable	–	–	–	–
	Ecosystem *e+1*	Ecosystem water recharge	Rain and other precipitation	X	X	
			External inflow		X	
	Water funds Focal level *e*	Societal appropriation of water	Surface water	X		X
			Ground water	X	X	
			Soil water	X	X	
			Qualitative loss		X	
			Virtual imported water	X	X	
Flow	Society Focal level *n*	Gross water use	Diverted water	X		
			Non-diverted water (*in situ*)	X		
			Polluted			
			Quantitative loss	X	X	X
	End users *n−i*	Net water use	Citizen water	X	X	
			Economy water	X		X
			Energy	X		X
			Evapotranspiration	X	X	
			Irrigation	X	X	
			Virtual exported	X	X	

Table 9.1, along with their classification as flow or fund. Their use is illustrated in Part III, when describing the case studies.

- *Ecosystem water recharge (EWR):* This category is defined as the water that recharges the quantity and quality of the water funds (and guarantees the stability of the appropriation). EWR is particularly relevant for the assessment of the feasibility of the metabolic pattern of society (external view). The categories of water included in the assessment of EWR are rain (and other types of precipitation) and external inflow from rivers or aquifers originating in other countries or regions (depending on the definition of the focal level). EWR is thus affected by a variety of factors, such as climate change (at level *e+2*) and international treaties that control inflow (at level *e+1*). Note that, as Mauritius is an island, inflow of water was not considered here.

- *Societal appropriation of water (SAW):* This category refers to the modification of properties of the water funds due to the societal use of water. That is, this category includes the water withdrawn and used by society and the qualitative damage inflicted by human use (e.g. nitrification or bacterial contamination). SAW is the semantic category that connects the water use by *societal* funds with the state of the *ecological* water funds (defined by considering both the supply and the sink capacity). It is where the internal and external views meet (and frequently clash). As an excess of societal water appropriation can damage the water funds from which the flow is derived, it is important to link the appropriation to the relevant water funds (i.e. lakes, rivers, aquifers or soil). For this purpose, GIS techniques are essential. The qualitative appropriation – reported in Table 9.1 as *qualitative loss* – has been measured in terms of the qualitative indicators of the state of the water funds. This analysis has been completed for the Punjab case study (see Chapter 13).
- *Gross water use (GWU):* This category refers to the flow of water that is managed by society, including the water actually reaching the end users and the losses in the distribution system; its volume corresponds to the volume of water appropriated. It is considered a flow belonging to the societal metabolism and defined at the focal level *n*. In our grammar, this flow is subdivided into water *diverted* – withdrawn from the water bodies and distributed for use somewhere else – and water *non-diverted* – when the water is used *in situ* in the water fund. This distinction is relevant for the viability check of the nexus, since the water diverted requires the existence of certain infrastructures that are not accessible for all societies.
- *Quantitative losses:* This category is considered a side process taking place within the society along the chain of extraction, (eventual) distribution, and use. It refers to the flow of water that has been diverted from the water bodies but did not reach the end user.
- *Net water use (NWU):* This category refers to the flows of water, assessed at the local and the global scales, that effectively reach the end users and provide them with a service. NWU is further subdivided according to the tasks to be accomplished (local net water uses). In our case studies, we have followed the definitions of water use of Arrojo (2006). Arrojo distinguishes between *citizen water* (the domestic use of water, or a supply of water that can be associated with the metabolism of the household) and *economy water* (the water required to produce economic value, or metabolism of the paid work). In the MuSIASEM accounting, the latter category is divided further according to the aims of the case study. For the analysis of the nexus it is essential to make a distinction between water use for *agriculture* (both *irrigation* and *evapotranspiration* from soil), water use for *energy* production (electricity generation with hydropower and cooling water) and water use for other *economic* activities (industry and services).

Where deemed important, we also include categories of virtual water flows in the grammar to quantify the role of export and import in the societal metabolic pattern (see Chapter 6). *Virtual water imports* are included in the category societal water appropriation, as they contribute to mitigate the impacts on the local water funds (Allan 1998). *Virtual water exports* are included among the end uses of society. As the water used to produce commodities destined for export is an input needed to generate added value (or foreign currency) it is included in the category economy water.

It should be noted that other categorizations of water are in use within the water community, notably the categorization of water into 'green' and 'blue' (Falkenmark 1995). These two categories of water are widely accepted and very useful for illustrative purposes or analyses of water use such as the evaluation of the water footprint (Mekonnen and Hoekstra 2010). However, they are too generic for a detailed metabolic analysis. The definition of blue water includes references to the ecosystem logic (the fraction of GWU coming from rivers and aquifers and that usually needs to be distributed) and also to the societal logic (water potentially suitable for various end uses). Hence, unless it is further divided into subcategories, the label of 'blue water' does not provide enough useful information for the purpose of our analysis. The same can be said for green water, defined as the water contained in the soil (ecosystem logic) that can be used only by plants for evapotranspiration and that can be neither distributed nor treated before use (societal logic).

A graphic representation of the water grammar is given in Figure 9.3, showing the quantification of the categories of accounting defined in Table 9.1 for the Mauritius case study. The left side of the grammar (levels $e+i$ and e) represents the external view on the water metabolic pattern and focuses on the water supply (ecosystem). The level of the water cycle and other processes taking place at this scale are beyond the scope of our analysis and are included in the grammar only for illustrative purposes. We start with the EWR at level $e+1$, divided into inflow from other ecosystems and rain and other precipitation. In order to guarantee the feasibility of the metabolic pattern of society, the EWR should be able to replenish the quantitative and qualitative loss in the water funds due to the societal appropriation of water, and to satisfy the conditions required by the ecosystems. As previously mentioned, the SAW is divided by source according to the three main water funds: surface, ground and soil water.

The right side of the grammar shows the internal view on the water metabolic pattern and focuses on water use within the socio-economic system. At the focal level n the gross water use of the society as a whole can be observed. This quantity is classified into diverted and non-diverted water flows, plus the associated qualitative changes as pollution. After accounting for the water losses in the distribution system we obtain the net water use. NWU is classified into six types of local end uses (as in Table 9.1) going to four socio-economic compartments: the household sector, energy and mining, agriculture, and the rest of the paid work. It is here, at the local level, that we can define what attributes 'water' must possess to qualify as an input flow for the funds in the socio-economic system.

The classification of the various end uses of water into societal compartments may vary with the purpose of the analysis. For example, in the diagnostic analysis of Mauritius (Figure 9.3), evapotranspiration from soil and irrigation are local

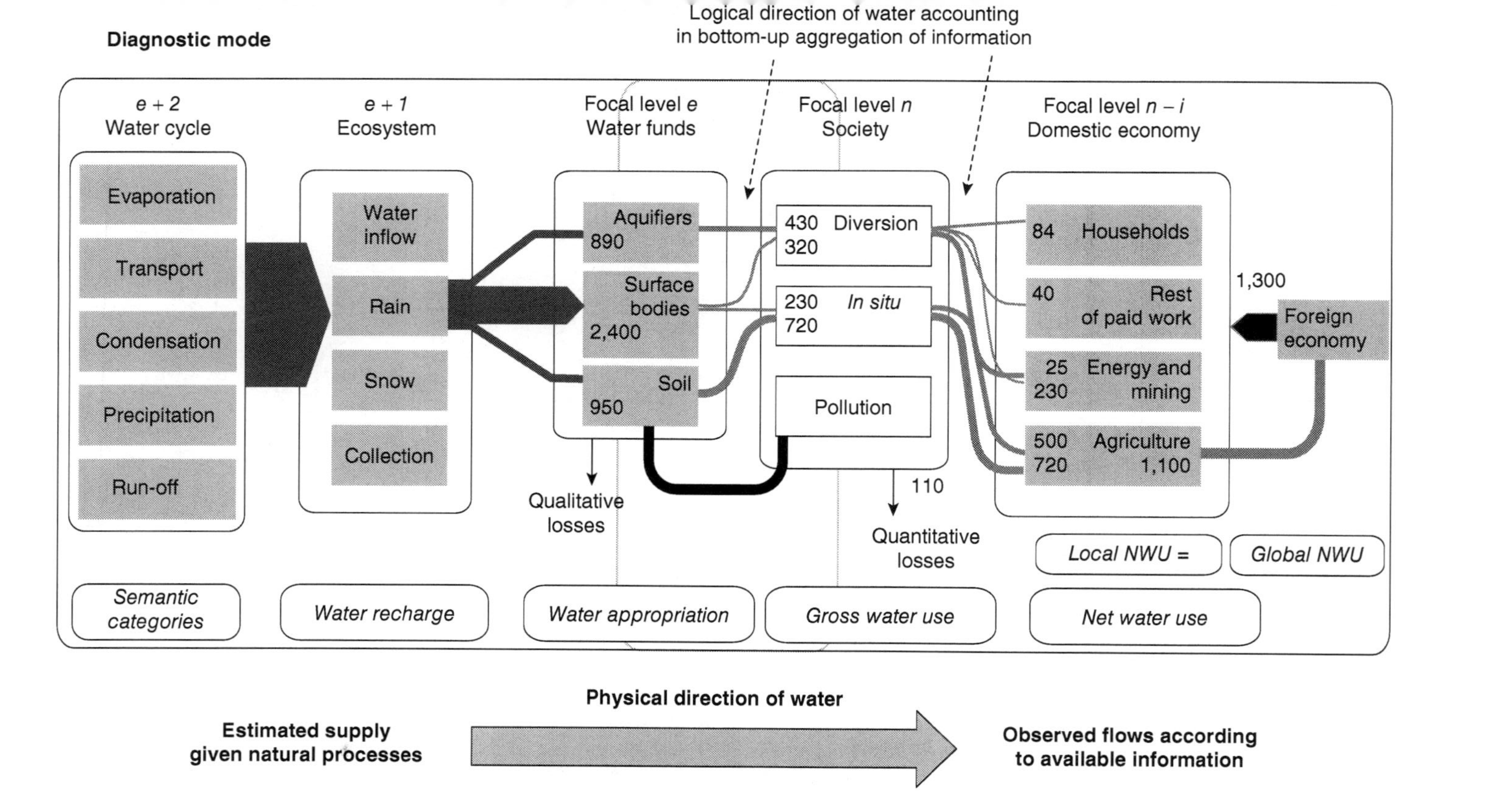

Figure 9.3 Water grammar applied to the case of Mauritius for diagnostic analysis

Note: All water quantities are reported in hm^3.

water end uses that take place only in the agricultural sector. However, the perception of these same end uses can change in scenario analysis. This is the case in one of the scenarios of the Mauritius case study (Chapter 12) in which the local production of sugarcane is used to generate biofuels. In this case, the water end uses 'evapotranspiration from soil under sugarcane' and 'irrigation of sugarcane' are allocated to the energy and mining sector, as in this scenario sugarcane is a primary energy source for the production of biofuels. This different classification of end uses is illustrated in Figure 9.4.

The difference in the logic of accounting between the diagnostic and the simulation mode is shown in Figure 9.4. In the diagnostic step (Figure 9.3) we describe *actual* physical flows of water (from left to right) across different scales, although the accounting in the internal view of the grammar starts from local observations (on the right) and is then scaled up to the focal level (bottom-up approach). In the simulation step (Figure 9.4), on the other hand, we make a comparison between the estimated (future) ecosystem water recharge (still a flow from left to right) and the projected aggregate requirement of water based on assumptions about the various local net water uses in the societal compartments. The latter projection is also generated with a bottom-up approach; it starts from the (desired) final consumption pattern, and then estimated losses are added to it, to arrive at an estimate of the societal appropriation of water, which has to be compared with the estimated ecological water recharge.

As illustrated in Figure 9.3, in the case of Mauritius, all the water required by the end uses is derived from precipitation feeding the rivers, lakes and aquifers and moisturizing the soil (as Mauritius is an island, there is no external water inflow). From these water funds, water is either diverted by the extraction and distribution functions or directly used by the end users (in the category non-diverted). Non-diverted water includes the soil water used by plants and the water needed for cooling and turbines in power generation. In Mauritius, most of the other end uses refer to distributed water. *Virtual water exports* are considered as (global) end uses. In Figure 9.3 the water accounted for in this category represents about 85 per cent of the local end use of agriculture. Virtual water imports feed into local end uses.

9.3 Formalization of the water grammar

In MuSIASEM, grammars are formalized using a combination of top-down and bottom-up approaches, using available statistics whenever possible. Usually, gross water use is built from net water use, as is shown in Figure 9.3. Therefore the accounting starts from local net uses (on the right), to which estimated losses are added. Ecosystem water recharge is built from geological and climatic data (top-down approach), as shown by the direction of the arrows. Societal appropriation of water is assessed by a combination of both approaches. Water statistics produced by national or international agencies deal with some of the semantic categories employed in MuSIASEM, like precipitation or international inflow, net water use per compartment and losses in distribution. However, data required for some other

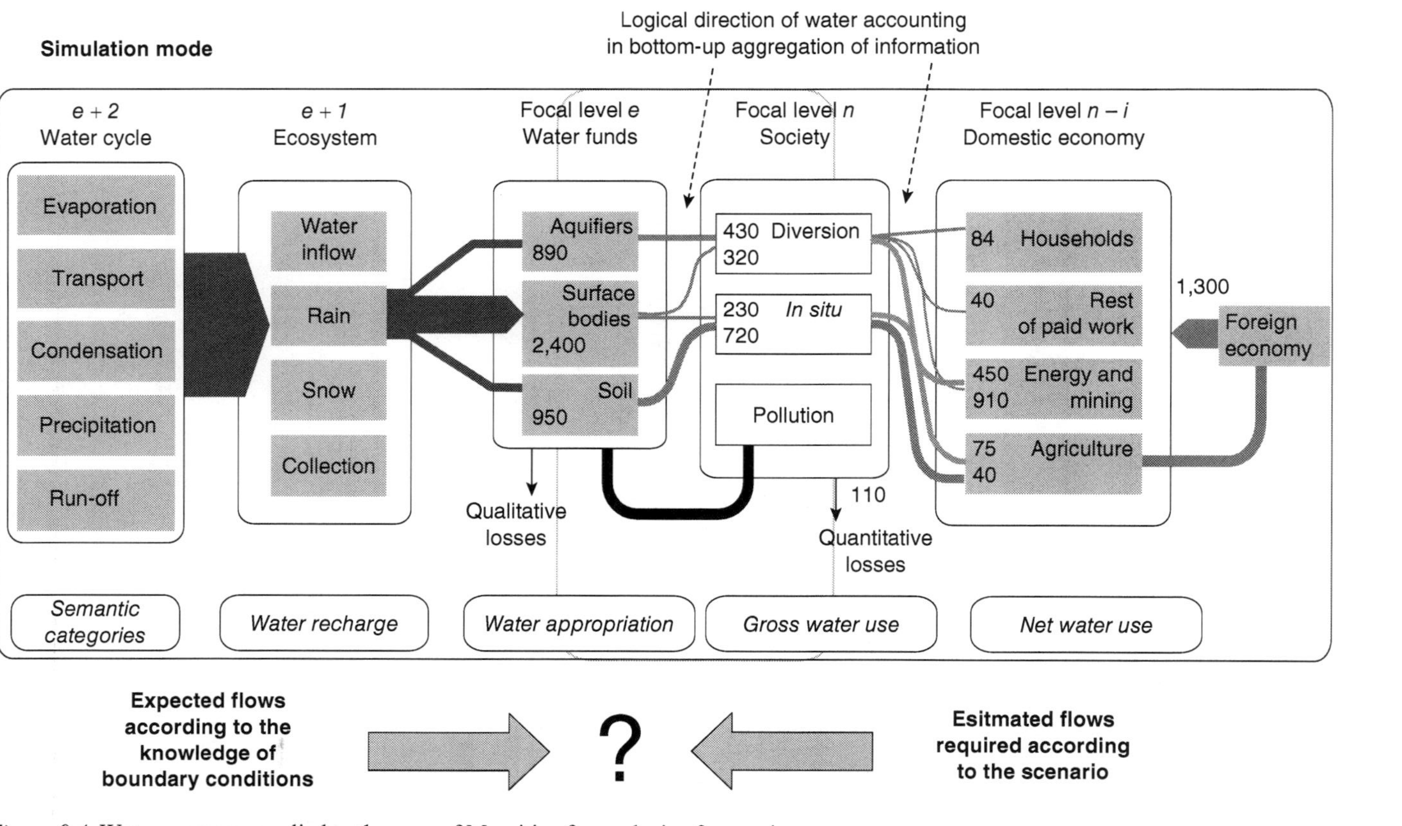

Figure 9.4 Water grammar applied to the case of Mauritius for analysis of scenarios

Note: All water quantities are reported in hm^3.

Table 9.2 Example of the formalization of semantic categories for Mauritius

MuSIASEM category	*Statistical source*
EWR	*Aquastat (FAO) and national statistics:* Surface and ground water renewable resources. Calculations of effective rain for soil moisture.
SAW	*National statistics:* Water withdrawal by source (surface, ground water). Non-consumptive uses of water for energy production by source. Soil moisture used. In Mauritius we did not assess pollution.
Gross water use	*National water company and national statistics:* Water distributed (diverted). Evapotranspiration of plants coming from rain; non-consumptive use for hydropower; and estimation of cooling (*in situ*).
Net water use	*National water company, national statistics, FAO, Water Footprint Network:* Estimations of irrigation water and evapotranspiration per type of crop. Estimations of water use per type of livestock. Data on water distribution to households and per industry. Estimations of virtual water exports embedded in sugarcane. Data on virtual water imports for all activities.

semantic categories, compartments or typologies may not be readily available, and statistical data may have to be rearranged to fit with the MuSIASEM grammar. For example, data on water withdrawal (which is in principle defined as diverted water in the grammar, belonging to the semantic category gross water use) may be used as a proxy for a rough estimation of the total net water use if this is the objective of the analysis. In that case we assume that, if the water has been extracted, it must have been used. Net use is often estimated by making inferences about expected consumption of water quantities for known metabolic characteristics (e.g. water transpiration per hectare of a known typology of crop, consumption of water per unit of production when the specific technical coefficients are known). In Table 9.2 we illustrate how we formalized the grammar represented in Figure 9.3.

As shown in Table 9.2, ecosystem water recharge can be obtained from data on the volume of renewable surface and ground water resources. The latter data are available from FAO Aquastat (e.g. for the Mauritius case) and/or regional statistics (e.g. for the Punjab case). Information on the qualitative part of the societal appropriation of water is available from data on the status of the water bodies. The quantitative part is usually available from international and national databases under the label 'water withdrawal by source'. However, the use of water for non-consumptive purposes, such as hydropower or cooling, is usually not included as withdrawal, and may have to be estimated using coefficients of water use per unit of energy carrier produced. Total societal appropriation of water includes total gross water use and the effect of environmental loading due to water waste (pollution). The total gross water use can be differentiated between diverted water (extracted from the water funds and distributed for its end use) and non-diverted water (used within the water funds). It is difficult to find data referring to this second distinction in statistics, and usually it has to be built with a bottom-up approach from data on net water uses. Net water uses are generally available from datasets on 'use by sector' in national statistics or from 'sales by user' in company statistics, as in Mauritius. Diverted water is usually well documented by the central distribution companies and available in national statistics, as are the estimated losses in the distribution network. Data on non-diverted water are generally not included in the statistics and are estimated from information on land use (e.g. irrigation) and the energy sector (cooling water, water in hydropower).

9.3.1 Assessment of water use (internal view)

The data organization underlying the grammar in Figure 9.3 is illustrated in Table 9.3 as far as the internal view of the water metabolic pattern is concerned. The structure of this type of tables (formalization of the grammar) is flexible and can be adapted to each specific case study and research question. For instance, in the Mauritius case we provide a more detailed disaggregation of societal compartments and consider more water types than for Punjab.

The bottom-up estimation is ideally based on local data and technical coefficients, rather than general statistics. As regards citizen water (household compartment), where local data are unavailable we use reference values. For the case of Punjab, a reference value of 65l per person per day has been used (Arrojo

Table 9.3 The water metabolic pattern of society (internal view) for the case of Mauritius (diagnosis): organization of data on gross and net water use

Indicator or compartment (societal function)	*GWU*	*NWU*	*Diverted*			*Non-diverted*	
			Citizen	*Economy (other)*	*Irrigation*	*EvT*	*Energy*
Whole (*n*)	**1,706**	**1,599**	**84**	**66**	**498**	**718**	**232**
% of NWU	–	100	6	4	31	45	14
% of GWU	100	94	5	4	29	42	13
HH (*n* – *1*)	98	84	84	0	0	0	0
HH–urban (*n* – *2*)	41	35	36	0	0	0	0
HH–rural (*n* – *2*)	57	49	48	0	0	0	0
PW (*n* – *1*)	1,608	1,515	0	66	498	718	232
PW–SG (*n* – *2*)	17	15	0	15	0	0	0
PW–TR (*n* – *2*)	1.72	1	0	1	0	0	0
PW–BM (*n* – *2*)	27	23	0	23	0	0	0
PW–EM (*n* – *2*)	262	258	0	26	0	0	232
PW–AG (*n* – *2*)	1,300	1,218	0	2	498	718	0

Sources: FAO Aquastat, Climwat and Cropwat databases; Mauritius National Statistics; and Central Water Authority of the Republic of Mauritius (2012).

Notes:

All data are reported in hm^3.

Virtual flows are not included.

2006). Clearly, citizen water will depend on lifestyles and available technology in the society in question. Water use for energy purposes depends on *how* the energy carriers are generated; it can be estimated from data on the primary energy sources used and the technical characteristics of the power plants. Water use in the agricultural sector for irrigation and evapotranspiration can be estimated from the unitary value of water use per type in crop production (per ha) multiplied by the area under production (in ha). We used FAO Cropwat software and the associated database Climwat for additional information on climate and soil for each crop. Given that agriculture generally represents the main water end use in society (77 per cent in Mauritius), we illustrate in Table 9.4 the procedure for assessing water use in agriculture by disaggregation of the agricultural sector into typologies of crop production. (Note that almost all the agricultural water used in Mauritius goes into sugarcane production.) By using GIS we can also relate the areas of water consumption to available water funds (see the examples in Chapter 12).

These exercises clearly show the importance of the nexus, as water use, land use (crop, animal feed, and biofuel production) and production of energy carriers are closely interrelated.

9.3.2 Linking water extraction (internal view) to water funds (external view)

The internal and external views on water metabolism meet when studying the implications of the societal appropriation of water in relation to ecological processes (see Figures 9.1, 9.2, 9.3 and 9.4). To perform a feasibility check on the

Table 9.4 Procedure for the assessment of water use in the agricultural sector (Mauritius case study)

Agriculture-related compartmentalization	*Production (ton)*	*Area harvested (ha)*	*Net water use (hm^3)*	
			Irrigation	*Evapotranspiration from soil*
Cereals, roots and pulses	24,772	1,880	0	6
Meat, milk and products	71,741	7,000	72 (economy)	0
Vegetables, fruits and products	91,561	5,683	0	22
Oil crops, oil and fats	2,083	214	0	1
Stimulants	7,380	698	0	7
Sugar crops	4,362,118	58,710	426	680
Others	2,784	310	0	1
Non-food	310	213	0	1
Total use AG	**4,562,749**	**74,707**	**498**	**718**

Sources: Elaboration of data from Chapter 12. Crop technical coefficients estimated with FAO Cropwat and data from Climwat and Mauritius national statistics. Livestock technical coefficients from Mekonnen and Hoekstra (2010).

Table 9.5 Example of data requirement and organization for a feasibility check of the societal metabolic pattern of water (Mauritius case study)

Indicator or compartment (physical supply system)	*Appropriation*	*Supply from rain*			*Appropriation as % of supply*
		To surface	*To ground*	*Total*	
Territorial system covered (*e* – *1*)	1,492	1,686	642	2,834	53
Mare aux Vacoas–Upper (*e* – *2*)	252	282	105	474	53
Mare aux Vacoas–Lower (*e* – *2*)	193	73	27	122	158
Port-Louis (*e* – *2*)	291	461	172	775	38
North (*e* – *2*)	291	213	79	358	81
South (*e* – *2*)	247	314	117	528	47
East (*e* – *2*)	229	380	142	640	36
Uncovered (*e* – *1*)	214	672	251	1,130	19
Water funds of Mauritius island (*e*)	1,706	2,358	893	3,964	43

Sources: Central Water Authority of the Republic of Mauritius (2012); FAO Aquastat.

Note: All data are expressed in hm^3.

societal metabolic pattern of water we need to examine this water appropriation further and explore the processes beyond human control that guarantee the stability of ecological funds (at a scale smaller than level *e*). In Table 9.5 we show an example of how to proceed with such a feasibility check.

For this check, the total area of Mauritius was subdivided into water supply systems (as defined by the water company), because an exact definition of the area of river basins was not available. However, according to the data source, delimitations of the water supply systems closely follow the natural limits of river basins (Central Water Authority of the Republic of Mauritius 2012). Water appropriation is then estimated for each of the supply systems and compared to the recharge of the water funds in order to check its feasibility. When considering the impact of societal metabolism on the metabolic pattern of the ecosystem, we deal with the water appropriation from specific funds that are defined following the ecosystem logic. Supply systems can be considered a proxy of ecological compartments (at level *e* – *1*, *e* – *2*). For example, looking at the water appropriation for the whole island (level *n*) in Table 9.5, there seems to be no issue with feasibility; societal water appropriation does not exceed the ecosystem water recharge at level *e*. However, when we analyse the situation at a lower hierarchical level, we see that in one of the supply systems, Mare aux Vacoas–Lower, appropriation (193 hm^3/year) exceeds recharge (122 hm^3/year). In this case, we have a lack of feasibility of the societal metabolic pattern of water at the local scale (a violation of local external constraints). If not corrected properly, this could lead to structural damage to the water funds under exploitation in one of the supply systems. Thus, when carrying out a feasibility check, the specific local-scale identity of the water fund affected by the extraction matters! This example flags the importance of linking this type of assessment to spatial analysis (see also Chapter 10).

9.3.3 Environmental loading

Environmental loading is a difficult concept to formalize in quantitative terms. The quantitative indicator 'grey water' is an attempt in this direction (Hoekstra and Chapagain 2008). It assesses the total amount of water (the size of the ecological fund) that would be required to dilute the polluted water (the size of the considered flow) to an acceptable level (in relation to the expected attributes of water inputs required by societal funds). This indicator raises two conceptual issues. First of all, it mixes the roles of water as a flow and as a fund across the ecological and societal narratives without establishing a logical relation. Second, it does not assess the damage inflicted on ecological funds, as the definition of an 'acceptable level' refers only to the expected attributes of water for human uses (e.g. drinking, irrigation). As shown in Figure 9.3, polluted water returns to the ecosystem. Generally the volume of this flow of polluted water can be quantified using existing databases. However, environmental loading cannot be characterized on the basis of the estimated quantity of water dumped into the environment only. The qualitative characterization of the pollution per unit of water volume is the main issue. This point is logically connected to the pre-analytical choice of categories of accounting used to assess societal appropriation of water.

In accord with the approach for environmental loading used in the energy grammar, we can generate an environmental impact matrix that includes (selected) attributes of waste water (e.g. heavy metals, micro-organisms, nitrogen, radioactive contamination) that are relevant for the ecological funds that must absorb and recycle this flow. We illustrate this aspect further in the case study of Punjab (Chapter 13) in relation to the damage to water funds caused by intensive agricultural production of cereals.

A summary of the dataset describing the water metabolism of Punjab is shown in Figure 9.5. The tables on the left side of the figure show data on water appropriation referring to the ecosystem or external view, whereas the tables on the right show data on net water end uses referring to the societal (or internal) view. As the metabolic pattern of water does not have a hypercycle, the total quantitative appropriation equals the total gross water use, and the latter equals the net water use plus the quantitative losses in diversion (extraction, treatment and distribution of water). In the case of Punjab the centralized water supply is not very developed, and therefore the quantitative losses are not particularly high.

The lower part of Figure 9.5 shows a breakdown of the upper aggregate values according to two different logics. The breakdown according to the internal view (lower right side) shows relevant socio-economic compartments and their water metabolic rates. In this case, we differentiate between the direct water used for economic production (the exports of cereals to the rest of India) and that used for food products consumed inside Punjab, a small fraction of the total.

External view

Appropriation	Diverted	Non-diverted	Total
Underground	12	0	12
Surface	36	0	36
Soil	0	26	26
TOTAL	48	26	74

−

Quantitative losses
0
8
0

=

Internal view

Net use	Diverted	Non-diverted	Total
Underground	12	0	12
Surface	28	0	28
Soil	0	26	26
TOTAL	40	26	66

	Appropriation	River	Aquifer
Quantitative	Recharge (km³)	21	21
	International use rights	25%	100%
	Dam reserve (km³)	11	N/A
	Blocks (no.)	N/A	138
	Extraction (km³)	15	31
	Overexploited blocks (no.)	N/A	110
Qualitative	RAMSAR in risk	3/3	N/A
	Regions over salinity	N/A	6/25
	Registries over nitrate	N/A	16/25
	Registries over metals	N/A	10/25
	Max. BOD (mgL)	50	N/A

Direct use	Diverted	Non-diverted	WMR
HH+PW* ($n-2$)	1	0	5
PW ($n-1$)	39	26	2,993
AG ($n-2$)	39	26	9,129
Rice and wheat ($n-3$)	36	23	9,064
TOTAL whole (n)	40	26	274
Imports	0	0	0

Indirect use	Diverted	Non-diverted
HH+PW* ($n-2$)	1	0
AG ($n-2$)	10	9
Rice and wheat ($n-3$)	7	6
TOTAL SA (n)	11	9
Expeditions India	28	16
Expeditions %	71%	64%

Openness
−68%
(net exporter)

Figure 9.5 Relation between the internal and the external views in Punjab

Sources: Elaboration of data from the Punjab case study (Chapter 13).

Notes: RAMSAR = the Convention on Wetlands of International Importance, called the Ramsar Convention; Max. BOD = maximum biological oxygen demand.

The breakdown of water quantities in the external view (lower left side of Figure 9.5) lists indicators of both quantitative (extraction) and qualitative (degradation) appropriation of two types of water funds (river and aquifer). It provides a good indication of the ecological status of relevant surface and ground water funds in relation to current levels of societal water appropriation.

9.4 Conclusions

The MuSIASEM system of accounting is extremely useful for the study of water metabolism, as it allows us to deal with the multi-dimensionality of water and to connect non-equivalent definitions of 'performance' across societal and ecological narratives. In particular, the water grammar makes it possible to integrate relevant information referring to the internal or societal view, in which water is defined as a set of societal flows, and the external or ecosystem view, in which water is defined as a set of ecosystem funds. In this way we can generate useful quantitative information for checking both the feasibility and the viability of the societal metabolic pattern of water.

The integrated set of semantic categories of accounting of the water grammar can be tailored to the specific characteristics of the case study so as to generate a relevant quantitative and qualitative characterization of both water appropriation (on the interface of society and ecosystem) and end uses (inside society). Depending on the case and the aims of our study, we can use different selections of compartments and different categories of accounting for the characterization of the metabolic pattern of water. In exploratory studies we may want to use generic categories, such as citizen and economy water, but a detailed disaggregation of final water uses (e.g. by crop in agriculture or by energy carrier in the energy sector) will be in place to address specific research questions. Categories of virtual water associated with trade (import/export) can be included in the analysis to deal with the openness of the societal metabolic pattern. This flexibility in the definition of the accounting scheme also allows us to regulate the required data input for the representation.

The feasibility of the water metabolic pattern of society depends on its compatibility with external constraints. These constraints are determined by the availability and integrity of water funds. The stability of the societal appropriation of water can be analysed in quantitative and qualitative terms on both the supply side (water extraction) and the sink side (water waste). In our grammar we propose the use of indicators of degradation of water resources that assess the impact of the societal metabolism (level of stress) on the actual water funds present in the socio-ecological system. This information is relevant to understanding whether the metabolic pattern of society is threatening the stability of the metabolic pattern of the embedding ecosystems. This task can be carried out only by addressing the spatial characteristics of the investigated system. The use of GIS for this purpose is detailed in Chapter 10.

10 GIS protocols for use with MuSIASEM

Richard J. Aspinall and Tarik Serrano-Tovar

Summary

This chapter presents a set of protocols for the use of GIS as part of MuSIASEM. One focus of the use of GIS is the quantitative analysis based in MuSIASEM's multi-level tables; GIS can provide input to these tables. GIS can also provide other data and insights that complement MuSIASEM, not least communication via maps, and development of alternative land uses for exploration in MuSIASEM used as a simulator. The protocols presented are intended to provide understanding and a guide to using GIS for: 1) estimating inputs to MuSIASEM's multi-level tables; 2) exploring multi-level, multi-dimensional effects and the roles of land uses and environment in different places to the metabolic performance of society; 3) using geographic data and models to support MuSIASEM's simulation mode for analysis of alternative land use patterns; and 4) imagining roles for map representations of data, results and other aspects of MuSIASEM.

10.1 Introduction

GIS provides a powerful suite of tools for management, analysis, representation and communication of geographically referenced data and other information. Not least among these tools are the abilities of GIS to:

1 manage and interrelate socio-economic and environmental data, within a common data management and analysis system, with database structure, management and analysis based on location in a common geographical referencing system;
2 subdivide regions and measure the area of land that meets selected conditions to help define land as a fund element in the MuSIASEM accounting;
3 make summaries of geographic patterns of data for selected regions and areas, measuring area of land, which is a fund element in MuSIASEM; and
4 carry out these operations at multiple geographic scales, although scales of source data are an important constraint on this.

The flexibility of data management and analysis, and the ability to link socio-economic and environmental data, with GIS, offers considerable potential for use in MuSIASEM. Socio-economic and environmental data are used throughout MuSIASEM. Land, as a fund element, measured as area, is a key component of MuSIASEM. When MuSIASEM is used in simulation mode, GIS allows alternative land use patterns to be developed for input to MuSIASEM, and linked to use of water and energy, and production of food, as well as a variety of other issues such as environmental impact assessment.

This chapter does not provide a guide to all aspects of GIS. There are many sources of further reading on database design and construction, GIS-based and spatial analysis, and other principles and issues associated with GIS (Arctur and Zeiler 2004; Longley *et al.* 2010).

In MuSIASEM, land use is a key dimension of the analysis, land representing the fund that refers to environment and ecosystem uses in the study area (Chapter 5). MuSIASEM expresses the rates of flows of food, water, energy, money and other key materials (ecosystem services, seen in MuSIASEM as ecological funds–societal flows) from the selected compartments, types or sectors of the system, across the land fund, as a series of flow/fund coefficients. However, these coefficients are not only linked with land area associated with a particular land use. GIS also allows the coefficients describing metabolic performance against land use to be represented in specific geographical locations. Therefore, depending on the availability and quality of the geographical information, it is possible to map, in detail, both the geographical extent and the location of metabolic performance for land use. This capability is not trivial, as it supports understanding, interpretation and use of the analysis in MuSIASEM. Additionally, MuSIASEM calculates flow/fund coefficients against human activity. GIS can help to interpret the relationships between flow/human activity fund and flows/land use fund, and the multi-level, multi-dimensional effect of MuSIASEM (Chapter 11).

In this chapter, the use of geographic information and GIS provides the opportunity both:

1. to obtain information about the metabolic performances of systems and places that otherwise would not be available; and
2. to simulate scenarios and their consequences, depending on simulated spatial patterns of land use.

Guidance is presented as a series of protocols. These are intended to act as a baseline guide to options for effective use and further application of GIS in relation to MuSIASEM in analysis of the nexus between food, water and energy and sustainability, especially as it relates to land systems and environmental impacts.

10.2 Uses of geographic information in MuSIASEM

10.2.1 Measurement of area

Land fund is measured as area (ha, km^2, etc.) of managed land. GIS readily provides this measurement for geographic regions from spatial data. The key to measurement of area of the land fund, however, is the definition and specification of the study region of interest and its boundary, and creation of appropriate data representing this in the GIS database. This is not trivial. Additionally, the identification and mapping of the types of land use needed for MuSIASEM are highly dependent on the context within which MuSIASEM is being used. MuSIASEM needs land use data that describe appropriate categories of land, with sufficient spatial resolution, and that are collected for an appropriate date that is compatible with other data used in MuSIASEM.

Protocol 1: The categories of land use and environmental conditions made available in the GIS must be appropriate for the analysis with MuSIASEM; they must refer to an appropriate date, and must measure categories of interest and relevance for the flows of food, water and energy, as well as human activities.

Suitable data defining boundaries of the geographic region and regions of interest must also be available.

Protocol 2: The criteria for establishing boundaries of land as a fund need to be adapted to the specific purpose and detail of the case study, and must be explicit in the analysis.

A basic distinction, central to the representation of land use in MuSIASEM, is between land that is managed and land that is not managed. This distinction is informative about the part of the ecosystem that is being used primarily for human activities (the managed land) and land that is not managed for human activities (which has relevance to the resilience of environmental systems – Chapter 5; note that land not managed for human activities may provide many ecosystem goods and services). Typically, the land that is managed defines the land as a fund. However, this may not be a simple binary distinction; land management intensity varies, and land provides different and multiple services simultaneously. For example, consider the territory of a rural village that is composed of three land uses: residential area (5 per cent), managed agricultural plots (30 per cent) and unmanaged forests (65 per cent). The decision on whether to include or exclude the forests from the land fund will have a dramatic impact on the results of the flows/hectare calculation. Although forests may not be under intensive human management, the forests may be exploited to provide resources to the community such as fuel and food, or may act as a recharge area for aquifers used for irrigation and hence influence water use. In this example, the metabolic flows of food, energy and water may differ so significantly between the agricultural and forested areas that they need to be treated as separate land compartments in MuSIASEM and flows/hectare computed for each land use separately.

Protocol 3: Multiple land use types are of interest in the calculation of land funds, in order to calculate flows/hectare for each land use; this is important for analysis of the multi-level, multi-dimensional effect, and contributions of different land uses to sustainability.

As a result of this, the main utility of GIS in relation to measurement of the land fund is not the measurement of area itself, but the ability of GIS to identify the specific land use types and compartments of interest, and to provide area measurements for each. A variety of data, rules and GIS overlay operations may be needed to identify the relevant land compartments for use in MuSIASEM.

10.2.2 Representation of metabolic systems with GIS

Beyond mapping land and measurement of area, there are many other GIS and related functions that are relevant for the analysis and representation of the metabolic performances of geographical areas (nations, states, regions, etc.). These are important because MuSIASEM provides a series of summary metrics of system metabolism, yet the food, water, energy and population systems are heterogeneous at a range of scales (Chapter 5). Use of GIS to study variability and heterogeneity across a study area offers, therefore, considerable additional insight. For example, in the same way that the average population density of a country (total population/total land) conceals patterns of high and low densities, the flow/fund ratios of MuSIASEM assess the metabolic performance of the whole system, rather than the variability in metabolism of different levels and the variable contributions of different places and land uses to the results for the whole. It is, therefore, relevant to consider the heterogeneity of the study area when analysing the societal metabolism of a system. GIS may be used to map the metabolic performances of different geographic regions within the study area, different regions being identified based on administrative or land use criteria. This is a reminder of the distribution and location of the different land uses, which allows a proper distinction and identification of different elements composing food, water and energy systems in order to assess their metabolic performance.

Protocol 4: Geographic patterns and heterogeneity contain important information that complements the insights from MuSIASEM.

10.2.3 The spatial, or architectural, structure of land use

A variety of characteristics of the spatial distribution of land uses – the architecture of land use in a landscape (B.L. Turner *et al.* 2007) – influence the performance of land and ecological systems. These include area, shape and fragmentation of parcels of individual land use types, and the configuration of land uses across a region, notably interspersion and juxtaposition. These spatial, architectural qualities of land use are most often described using methods from landscape ecology coupled with GIS (M.G. Turner 2005).

10.2.3.1 Shape and fragmentation of land uses

The summary measure 'total area' of a land use in a system is uninformative about the distribution of the land use across the study area. GIS provides a way to visualize the patterns of land uses that accompany the summary measure of land as a fund element contained in the MuSIASEM multi-level and multi-dimensional tables. Fragmentation of land use and management, through land tenure and ownership patterns or through environmental variability, may be an important influence on the potential for land use in food production, and on water use and management. Fragmentation, at fine scales, may be a limit to use of heavy machinery in agriculture, resulting in a metabolic pattern in the production of food that is very different from what it could be if the land use was less fragmented. Similarly, the distribution of water bodies across an area is of relevance to the metabolism of water used for irrigation in agriculture. Additionally, fragmentation of habitats influences species' distribution, abundance and population dynamics.

10.2.3.2 Configuration and relative position of land uses

Interactions among land uses are, in part, strongly influenced by their position relative to one another in a landscape. These interactions depend on many factors, but the relative geographic location of the different activities can be important in analysis, summary and understanding of metabolic performance. The case study of South Africa (Chapter 14) demonstrates the influences of land uses that are geographically separate. The land uses associated with energy, water and food production are not homogeneously distributed across South Africa and show relatively little overlap. The human population is located primarily in the cities, while the environmental resources that supply provisioning services (food, energy, water) to society and the associated extractive activities (agriculture, mining, water management) are located in other, largely separate, areas. In this case, energy resources must be transported and/or transmitted through the relevant infrastructures (power lines for electricity, pipelines for oil and gas, etc.). Infrastructure is also influenced by land use and the geographic configuration of the mix of biophysical constraints.

Transport networks are also important in other ways. For example, the ability of land to support activities that require heavy transport is influenced by proximity to roads as a measure of access. GIS provides a range of tools for analysis of accessibility, proximity and connections across landscapes, linking data describing transport infrastructure and networks with patterns of land use through network analysis and overlay operations.

10.2.4 Distance

The provision of food, water and energy from land and environmental systems are not dependent solely on area, as a property of land and environmental systems; they are also influenced by a variety of geographical relationships, based on distance metrics. This is partly due to the increasing costs of transportation for food, water and energy with distance. Thus, the relative distances among the different land and environmental elements contributing each of food, water and energy give additional information about constraints to the performance of particular areas within the land system. Distance is also important in evaluating the feasibility of certain systems (e.g. power transmission) for different uses, including the issues associated with use of virtual land (section 10.2.5). For example, for electricity or water, distances between the production and the consumption areas are always major constraints, requiring investment in infrastructure and entailing significant operating costs. GIS provides a range of tools for analysis of distance, both through networks and over areal extents using proximity analysis.

10.2.5 Virtual land

Virtual land is land that supports food, water and energy used by society, but that is hidden because it is located in a different region or otherwise embedded in the food, water and energy as commodities traded from one place to another. Virtual land is of growing relevance in a globalized economy (Scheidel and Sorman 2012), and is relevant to both imports and exports. It is important to consider virtual land in accounting that quantifies land use within MuSIASEM, since this provides a metric of the land fund needed for use of goods and services from outside the immediate geographical limits of the study region.

The estimation of the area of virtual land required to produce food, for example, varies for exports and imports. For exports, the land needed to produce food exports is estimated as the amount of agricultural land within the study region that is used to grow the exported crops. This portion of the land fund acts as virtual land for another region, although it is not virtual within the study region. The case studies (Chapters 12–14) use the yield (tonnes/hectare) for each crop within the relevant case study region to estimate the virtual or embodied land necessary to support exports of food.

Similarly, it is possible to estimate the virtual land for imported goods, based on estimates of the yields and quantities of imported products. In the case of imports, however, the choice of yield is important. Ideally, the yield used will be that for the specific areas where the imported products are produced, since yields vary based on the land systems (as coupled human–environment systems; see Chapter 5) in different places. However, this calculation requires knowledge of the location of production and yields for every imported good; these data may not be available. Instead, it may be sufficient to make an estimate of virtual land associated with imports using one of two methods:

1 For crops capable of being grown within the study area, the land that would be required within the study region to produce the amount of goods being imported provides an estimate of the virtual land needed to support the imports. This is an estimate of virtual land measured as the land fund that would be needed to substitute domestic production for imports.
2 For imported crops which are either not grown or not capable of being grown within the study region, the virtual land may be estimated based on international (or other regional) average yields for the product.

For food products based on animal production, the estimation of virtual land is more complex, since animals are fed grain (Chapter 7). The accounting process for virtual land for imported and exported meat products requires the land used for grain production that feeds livestock to be included. This can increase the embodied land fund, and, following Chapter 7, the land needed varies based on the type of meat (for example, 7 kg of grain to produce 1 kg of beef, or 2 kg of grain to produce 1 kg of chicken in an industrial system; Chapter 7, section 7.5.2) and the specific grain used. The contributions of livestock systems using rangeland pasture also need to be accounted for in the land fund for livestock production.

Protocol 5: Calculation of virtual land is an important part of MuSIASEM, indicating relationships and dependencies with places outside the geographical boundaries of the study region. The approaches used to compute virtual land must be made explicit.

10.3 GIS and MuSIASEM in diagnostic mode

It is possible to use the information given by the tables in MuSIASEM to estimate the characteristics of a certain geographical subdivision of the study region, through use of the geography of land characteristics in the study region in GIS. In addition, it may also be possible to calculate the density of flows if they depend on physical characteristics whose information can be obtained from maps in GIS layers. For instance, if the level of agricultural production associated with a soil type and climatic zone, or other land evaluation type, is known, then it is possible to compute a map of the rate of agricultural production per hectare as the product of the area and yield. From this, total production of the system for the specific crop can be computed as the sum of values for the area of interest. This approach has been used to compute the geographic variation and total water consumption for agriculture in Mauritius (Chapter 12), which depends on physical characteristics of the island.

Use of GIS to move between studies of the whole (region, system, etc.) and the parts (sub-regions, land uses, other functional and structural compartments) is central to the use of MuSIASEM to analyse sustainability. For example, the rate of a flow per hectare (the *density*) for each land use, combined with the distribution and extent of each land use in the study region, allows the total amount of flow at different levels of geographical aggregation in the study region to be calculated. This links the use of GIS to the multi-level, multi-dimensional effect in MuSIASEM (Chapter 11) and analysis of flows against the fund of human activity (Serrano-Tovar and Giampietro 2014).

The multi-level, multi-dimensional effect, combining human activity and land use, can be described using a hypothetical example. Two issues are fundamental:

1 the relations between the whole system and its parts, identified with functional/structural compartments, and related to funds of human activity and land use; and
2 autopoiesis and the sustainability of the system considered as a whole.

Consider agricultural production in a study region, agriculture being of different types (cereals, livestock, etc.). Land use and human activity relate to these different agricultural production types. At the level of the whole system the size of the total land fund element refers to the amount of land managed and utilized for agriculture by the population in a given year. Within this total amount of managed and utilized land, we can distinguish different categories of land use, such as agriculture, forestry and urban uses, or different types of agriculture. These categories may form the parts of the non-equivalent definition of a compartment, within the multi-scale accounting. When assessing the relations of flow elements to this set of separate land uses as individual fund elements with MuSIASEM, there is also a series of corresponding benchmarks for the density of flows per hectare (ratio flow/fund) across compartments defined at different levels. In this case, because of knowledge of farming types and techniques, we expect certain values for flow/fund ratios, for example expected yields (kg/ha) of different types of crops cultivated using different techniques and in different environmental settings. Although flows per unit of human activity and flows per unit of land use are non-equivalent, they refer to the same observed system (e.g. a type of farming system) in relation to the same set of observed flows. For homologous categories of human activity (e.g. cereal production) and land use (e.g. cereal production), the same flow (e.g. yield of cereals measured in kg) is mapped against two different fund elements: 1) human activity (measured in hours, thus: yield per hour (kg/h), as a ratio of flow/fund for human activity); and 2) land use (measured in hectares, thus: yield per hectare (kg/ha), as a ratio of flow/fund for land use). Note that in MuSIASEM both assessments are averaged over one year. This analysis implies that, for a given year, a given quantity of cereal can be related both to the corresponding amounts of human activity (measured in hours) and to land use (measured in ha) needed for its production. Hence, we can establish a relation between the size of the two fund elements, human activity and land use, belonging to the same functional/structural category (e.g. cereal production).

A second element of the coherence of the metabolic pattern is related to autopoiesis. An individual functional/structural category (e.g. cereal production) considered in isolation is not sufficient to describe the sustainability of a community. Many other functional and structural categories have to be included to express the emergent property of 'sustainability'. Indeed, for any community it is possible to identify a set of integrated functional or structural categories (used for accounting for human activity and land uses) that are required to ensure sustainability. The metabolic pattern of the given community is found in the integrated analysis of all the ratios of flow/fund calculated over all the fund elements (assessed in hours of human activity and land uses) required for the sustainability of that society.

Given these semantics of metabolic patterns and whole–part relationships (see also Chapter 3), it is possible to establish a relation between the metabolism measured against hours of human activity and against hectares of land. This value is the ratio of human activity per unit of land (which is equivalent to average population density, population measured in hours of activity, at the large scale). The metabolic pattern of a community is then used to characterize:

1 a requirement for land uses (a mix of categories and relative profile) per unit of human activity associated with that metabolic pattern – the view from the inside (human perspective); and /or
2 a requirement for human activities (a mix of categories and relative profile) which can be supported per unit of land use associated with that metabolic pattern – the view from the outside (external biophysical constraints).

These two non-equivalent accountings – the view from inside and the view from outside – refer to the same set of flows (food, water, energy, money and other key materials) used within the metabolic patterns of the whole and parts of the system.

For a case study explaining this using a fully worked example from Laos, see Serrano-Tovar and Giampietro (2014).

Protocol 6: GIS can be used to move between studies of the whole (region, system, etc.) and the parts (sub-regions, land uses, other functional and structural compartments) as part of the use of MuSIASEM to analyse sustainability.

10.4 GIS and MuSIASEM in simulation mode

The ability of GIS to present and communicate information about particular instances of the metabolic profile of the system under investigation is of considerable value. GIS is also a useful instrument for building scenarios that represent or incorporate the particular geographic possibilities of alternative land use arrangements or activities. These scenarios can also be visualized with maps. GIS can in addition be used to generate and present simulations in participatory processes that include inhabitants or other groups within the study region. Displaying the results of simulated scenarios on maps provides a check on how proposed scenarios may play out and appear differently in each sub-region of the study region.

For example, geographic information was used to simulate scenarios of land use change in Mauritius (Chapter 12):

1 to calculate the area of land suitable for an alternative pattern of agricultural production; and
2 to estimate the resulting pattern of water consumption associated with the land use scenario.

GIS was used to estimate the option space for a different mix of agricultural crops in Mauritius (see Figure 12.1). The new mix of crops was established as part of the proposed scenario, and the crops then allocated to land within Mauritius through a GIS-based overlay of data and application of land allocation rules. Data inputs were: 1) the current distribution of crops in the island; 2) a digital elevation model (DEM), providing elevation, slope and aspect; and 3) soil types. Allocation rules excluded areas of steep slopes (using the DEM) and unsuitable soils (using the soil type data) from areas already under agricultural land use (from the current distribution of crops).

The geographical pattern of water requirements for this mix of new crops was then calculated using GIS procedures (see Figure 12.2). As in the diagnostic analysis, the rate of water use per hectare (the *density*) for each new crop land use is used to simulate the resulting pattern of water consumption for the scenario, using the simulated information on the geographical locations of the new crops. In this specific example, there are considerable differences in the pattern and level of water consumption for agriculture. The GIS not only provides a visual representation of the results of the simulation, but also provides data describing the scenario to the multi-level, multi-dimensional tables of MuSIASEM for analysis of the feasibility and desirability of the scenario.

Protocol 7: Scenarios of land use change can be developed in GIS using a variety of modelling methods, and linked to MuSIASEM used in simulation mode, for evaluating alternative land use activities and their consequences.

10.5 Data issues

Ultimately, GIS and any analytical methods depend on the quality of the data that are used. This section briefly highlights some of the issues associated with data that need to be considered when using GIS with MuSIASEM.

10.5.1 Data

It is estimated that 60–85 per cent of the costs of a GIS project are associated with data capture (Longley *et al.* 2010). Data will: undoubtedly be in multiple formats, including paper; come from remote sensing, maps, or surveys and censuses; have different dates of original collection (and durations of relevance); have different projections and datums; have differing source scales; have keys that may or may not meet the needs of the analysis; and have variable levels of accessibility. There are many texts and guides to GIS that discuss data sources, capture, management and formats, and the issues involved in establishing a GIS database for use in a project (Longley *et al.* 2010).

Protocol 8: The main criteria for data to be used in MuSIASEM are that they should be:

1 applicable, having clear relevance to some aspect of the analysis to be carried out in MuSIASEM;
2 accurate, being of sufficient thematic and spatial accuracy for their use;
3 compatible, being in the same projection and with a source scale (especially if from paper maps) that is compatible with other datasets with which they will be used;
4 current, being from a source date that is applicable for the study and compatible with other data in the analysis;
5 available, being accessible for use.

Digital data are in two main formats, vector and raster. Vector format represents data in a GIS as geographically referenced points, lines and polygons. The resolution on vector maps is limited by the locational accuracy of the source data, referenced to the earth's surface, the geodetic control on data capture, and, for digitized maps, aspects of both the digitizing process and the source map. Raster format represents data in a GIS as a two-dimensional array (rows and columns) of pixels, each of which is coded with a value representing the thematic value of the data at the location referenced by the row and column. The spatial resolution of raster data depends on both the density of pixels and the source of the thematic information (for example remote sensing, or digitized map).

10.5.2 Land use and land cover

Chapter 5 describes differences between land use and land cover. The distinction between cover and use is critical for MuSIASEM; MuSIASEM is primarily focused on land use, although land cover is of relevance in mapping and analysis of environmental impacts (Chapter 4).

Land use data must be for a date that is compatible with other data used in MuSIASEM. Chapter 5 notes the difficulties of mapping land use, and that land cover, mapped using remote sensing sources, is often used as a substitute for land use. This may be appropriate, depending on the classification used in the land cover map and the structural and functional categories of land use of relevance and interest in MuSIASEM. For example, taxonomic keys to land cover classes in data derived from remote sensing often are hierarchical and the cover types capable of being reclassified into more general (higher) levels of the key using GIS. These levels (e.g. agriculture, forestry, urban) may match the needs of MuSIASEM.

Protocol 9: Land use data should:

1 use a classification taxonomy of types that can be coded to match the needs of MuSIASEM;
2 have sufficient thematic (category) and spatial (geographic) resolution to allow reliable area estimates to be made for land uses in sub-regions of interest within the study region; and
3 be available using source data with a date that is compatible with the other data in MuSIASEM.

These criteria provide a series of tests against which to evaluate any existing (secondary) land use and land cover datasets. Having criteria to test existing datasets is important, since existing data may have categories that are not relevant to the MuSIASEM analysis, may be of low accuracy, or may be out of date, given changes in land use and land cover within the study region.

It may, therefore, be necessary to generate a suitable land use (or land cover) dataset for the purposes of the study, rather than use an existing dataset. Again, the criteria in protocols 8 and 9 provide a test for generating a suitable land use or land cover dataset.

A particular issue in use of land use data in MuSIASEM is associated with the difficulty of identifying land use in urban areas, particularly for the household (HH), services and government (SG), building and manufacturing (BM) and sometimes tourism and recreation sectors, and the consequent estimate of land funds. Much of the land used for these sectors of society is in urban areas, and land use data do not disaggregate urban areas into these categories. Within larger regions (such as whole countries), urban areas generally occupy a small land area. Additionally, HH, SG and BM in many cases overlap in space, for example taking place in the same buildings or on multiple floors of buildings. These issues present challenges in estimating the land fund that should be associated with each activity. In the context of the nexus of food, water and energy, and given the relatively small footprint of urban areas compared with the extent of environments contributing food, water and energy that support human society and populations, this is perhaps of lesser importance, but it is something that should be recognized.

10.6 Conclusions

This chapter makes some observations on the coupling of MuSIASEM with geographic information and land uses, and the roles of GIS tools in data analysis in understanding the metabolic patterns of societies. GIS allows the analysis of the specific environmental and societal characteristics of regions of interest to be examined, complementing the insights from the analysis and results of the multi-dimensional and multi-level tables of MuSIASEM. The specific instances and place-based geographies of food, water and energy metabolism can be explored.

GIS allows the influences of the spatial structure and heterogeneity of the study region of interest on the metabolic performance of the diverse parts of the system to be analysed and reviewed, showing the contribution of different places to the societal whole. The distribution and the location of different land uses, activities and features used for food, water and energy production, and the distribution of communities and populations, and other human activities, show the contribution of different parts of the system to the overall metabolic performance. This in turn allows an additional and more informative understanding of the results of MuSIASEM, operating in both diagnostic and simulation modes. Most importantly, for sustainability accounting and planning, GIS makes a representation of possible outcomes for *specific instances* of the system based on the contribution of different places within the region of interest to the metabolic performance of coupled human–environment systems for food, water and energy provision.

11 The Sudoku effect within MuSIASEM

Mario Giampietro, Sandra G.F. Bukkens, Richard J. Aspinall and Jesus Ramos-Martin

Summary

This chapter illustrates the use of the Sudoku effect within the MuSIASEM toolkit. The multi-level, multi-dimensional representation of the accounting of flow and fund elements in MuSIASEM shares essential features with Sudoku. In the diagnostic step, the integrated dataset is organized in a multi-level, multi-dimensional table, similar to the Sudoku grid. This representation reveals the internal and external constraints operating on the metabolic pattern, analogous to the constraints on the numerical pattern of Sudoku, and the corresponding viability and feasibility domain. The dynamic equilibrium between the hypercyclic and dissipative macro-compartments in society expresses itself as a block constraint on the metabolic pattern. In simulation mode, MuSIASEM explores the feasibility, viability and desirability of scenarios, by comparing projected metabolic characteristics with benchmarks or observed patterns. This is illustrated for a scenario of primary energy sources of low quality.

11.1 Sudoku and its features

The game of Sudoku provides a concrete example of how to generate a complex information space by combining constraints defined at different scales. In Sudoku the objective is to fill a 9 × 9 grid with digits so that each column, each row and each of the nine 3 × 3 sub-grids (blocks) that compose the grid contain all of the digits from 1 to 9. This combination of constraints generates 'mutual information' within the information space of the Sudoku grid. As a result, each time we introduce a number in the grid we dramatically reduce the degree of freedom for the remaining numbers to be entered. In this way, the information accumulated (numbers entered) in the Sudoku reduces the option space of viable numerical patterns.

As illustrated in Figure 11.1, there are three types of Sudoku, even though most players will know only the first one:

1 *Subcritical, viable Sudoku:* If we play this Sudoku we will find that the numbers already present in the grid limit the possible patterns for the remaining numbers to a point where the Sudoku has just one solution. Under this

Subcritical, viable Sudoku

			6				3	
1		8				5		
		6					9	
	3		2	8	6			7
	8	1		3		2	6	
7			1	4	5		8	
	2					4		
		7				3		8
	5				9			

Subcritical, unviable Sudoku

1			2					
5	6	7	8	3	9	4		
	5		4	7	6			
4	7				8	9	1	3
		5	6		7			
2	4			1		5		
		3						

Supercritical Sudoku

3	4	5	6		7	1	8	
6				1		* (B)		
	1		3		5	2		7
4		3					7	
5	8							
		2				8	5	1
1			9					
2		8		5	4		9	3
9	* (A)	4	2	6		7	1	

Figure 11.1 Three different types of Sudoku: subcritical and viable, subcritical and unviable, and supercritical

Source: Shin-ichi Nakayama, Faculty of Integrated Arts and Sciences, University of Tokushima, personal communication.

Note: The supercritical Sudoku has four solutions; if A = 5 is entered, then only three solutions are left; if B = 3 is entered next, then only one solution is left.

particular condition of subcriticality, the mutual information provided by the integrated set of constraints allows us to identify the missing numbers in the given pattern. In this situation, we can say that the missing numbers are 'required' or determined by the Sudoku pattern given the characteristics of: 1) the numbers already provided (history accumulated); and 2) the set of constraints (the rules of the game).

2 *Subcritical, unviable Sudoku:* If we play this Sudoku we will find that it is simply impossible to fill all the cells of the grid. In this Sudoku, there is an incompatibility between the numbers already given and the rules of the game. Not surprisingly, this is not the typical Sudoku you buy from the news-stand. We generally only play instances of Sudoku that are purposely designed to be solvable ('viable'). If we were to entirely self-organize our Sudoku (no numbers provided), the tentative filling of the grid would require an enormous effort, especially if we have no means to detect at an early stage whether or not we are trying to solve an unsolvable Sudoku! It appears that this is exactly the predicament of sustainability science when trying to check the feasibility, viability and desirability of possible paths of development, taking into account all the elements of the nexus.
3 *Supercritical Sudoku:* If we play this Sudoku we will discover that it is not a deterministic system. Different players may get different solutions. In fact, the supercritical Sudoku shown in Figure 11.1 may yield four different solutions. However, as soon as the player enters numbers (valid information) in the Sudoku grid (accumulation of history), the required congruence over the multiple constraints increases its degree of determinedness. In the particular example shown, after two steps (e.g. A and B) the Sudoku becomes subcritical, admitting only one solution.

Sudoku is extremely useful in explaining the difference between feasibility and viability. The constraints determined by the grid format of Sudoku (e.g. 9 × 9) and the rules of the game together define the feasibility domain for the pattern of numbers that can be entered. Note that this definition of feasibility does *not* depend on the numbers entered into the Sudoku grid. As soon as numbers are entered, a new set of constraints is generated by the accumulation of history. Indeed, this input of information adds additional constraints of a new type to the original set and reduces the feasibility space into a smaller viability space. Clearly, accumulation of internal constraints may lead to lack of a viable solution (subcritical, unviable Sudoku).

11.2 Analogy between MuSIASEM and Sudoku

In this chapter we show that the MuSIASEM accounting method creates a complex information space, analogous to Sudoku, when characterizing the nexus between food, energy, water and land uses across scales and dimensions. Combining together the grammars described in Part II and applying the theoretical concepts defining the nature of the metabolic pattern presented in Part I, we obtain an integrated set of constraints over the quantitative characteristics of the metabolic pattern perceived and represented at different scales and referring to both the external view (feasibility) and the internal view (viability). The resulting complex information space, represented by the metabolic characteristics and the integrated set of constraints, shows three features that are similar to those of Sudoku:

1 An *impredicative relation* between the local metabolic characteristics (numbers within the grid) and the whole metabolic pattern (numerical pattern of the completed Sudoku). This impredicativity stems from the required congruence between the metabolic characteristics of lower-level elements (digit choice), their role or position within the nested hierarchical structure of society (number placement), and the internal and external constraints on the metabolic pattern (rules of the game).
2 Limits on the range of values that variables can take on (domain) in MuSIASEM imposed by internal and external constraints. However, as long as the system operates in a supercritical situation there is some room for manoeuvre. Different combinations are possible with the same set of constraints governing the system. As with Sudoku, we can distinguish between the feasibility domain (the set of possibilities determined by boundary conditions) and the viability domain (the set of possibilities determined by the mutual information accumulated in the system).
3 Irrelevance of the formal representation of the entries in the grid. What matters is the expected relations between the semantic categories, for they define the constraints. For example, as regards the food grammar (Chapter 7), the same set of expected relations among semantic categories (domestic supply, imports, final consumption) can be formalized in non-equivalent ways: measuring joules of nutrients or tons of food commodities. The same is true for Sudoku; it can be played with Arabic numbers (1, 2, . . . 9), Latin numbers (i, ii, . . . ix) or coloured patterns, as long as we have nine distinguishable elements.

Below we show first how to organize the integrated dataset on flow and fund elements in a multi-level, multi-dimensional table, similar to the Sudoku grid, in the diagnostic step of MuSIASEM.

11.3 MuSIASEM as a diagnostic tool

11.3.1 Multi-scale, multi-dimensional representation of the dataset

The accounting system employed by MuSIASEM results in a comprehensive dataset that allows us to characterize the metabolic pattern of society across hierarchical levels and scales. This integrated dataset makes it possible to establish an effective interface between the internal and external view. The first step is to combine and condense the information provided by the grammars outlined in Chapters 6–10 so as to depict an integrated profile of allocation of the various flows and fund elements across the societal compartments (see, for example, Table 12.7). This will immediately give us valuable 'diagnostic' information on the metabolic characteristics (rates, densities and intensities of energy, food and water flows) and the size of compartments (in terms of hours of human activity, hectares of managed land, watts of power capacity) at different organizational scales:

- *At the level of society as a whole (n)*, we have the overall metabolic characteristics of the socio-economic system under analysis, including the overall endowment of fund elements (total human activity, total power capacity, total managed land) and the overall throughput of the various flows (total energy throughput, total food throughput, total water throughput, gross domestic product).
- *At the level of socio-economic compartments (n−i)*, we have: information on the profile of allocation of production factors; requirement of inputs; and rate of waste generation. At this level we also deal with the presence and efficiency of hypercycles. The reproduction of the metabolic pattern implies the simultaneous stabilization of several autocatalytic loops in which flows are consumed to generate themselves and fund elements are allocated to reproduce themselves. This set of internal constraints is illustrated in Figure 11.2

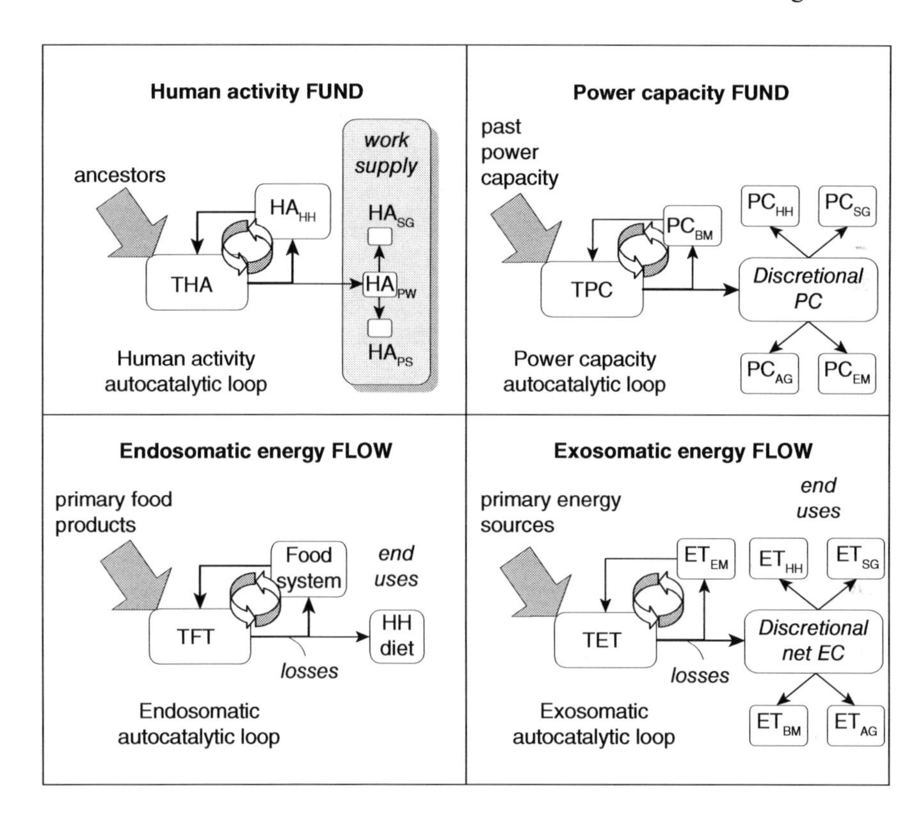

Figure 11.2 The four autocatalytic loops governing the characteristics of the metabolic pattern of modern society (constraints on the viability domain)

for endosomatic energy (food) and exosomatic energy flows and for the funds human activity and power capacity. In modern society, the viability of the exosomatic energy loop is of particular importance in determining the characteristics of the metabolic pattern.

- *At the level of the end uses (local level)*, we have information on the use of production factors (flow and fund elements), conversion efficiency, and biophysical and economic cost for the specific processes or tasks (e.g. energy technologies, agricultural practices) taking place in the various socio-economic compartments.

Thus, in this way we can express the sizes of the various compartments and end uses in terms of allocation of human activity, technological capital and managed land (fund elements), and characterize the use of the flows of food, energy, water and money (flow elements) in terms of total requirement, proportion of domestic consumption, losses, degree of self-sufficiency, imports and exports. A series of flow/fund ratios characterize the rate (per hour of human activity), density (per hectare of managed land) and intensity (per watt of power capacity) of the flows across the different organizational scales (the whole society and each one of the lower-level compartments and/or end uses).

When observing the established metabolic pattern in this way, we can use the metabolic characteristics (flow/fund ratios) as descriptions of the identity of the lower-level elements. As described in the next section, these ratios can then be compared against reference values describing 'typical' socio-economic systems.

11.3.2 Benchmarking

Benchmarking is an important feature of MuSIASEM. Earlier work on MuSIASEM (Giampietro *et al.* 2012) has shown that marked differences exist among the metabolic characteristics of different types of socio-economic systems: post-industrial versus developing societies, closed versus open markets, densely populated versus sparsely populated systems, and so on. On the basis of these observations, typologies of metabolic patterns have been set up, which can be used for benchmarking. For example, densely populated countries exhibit intense use of energy per hectare in agriculture (fertilizer and irrigation); wealthy countries invest in considerable machinery per agricultural worker (high power capacity per hour in agriculture); socio-economic systems facing water shortage show a lower proportion of total water consumption in agriculture (Giampietro 1997b; Arizpe-Ramos *et al.* 2011). Depending on the focus of the study, we can use specific benchmarks to classify metabolic patterns and compare observed metabolic characteristics with expected values. Benchmarks for flow densities are particularly useful for an analysis of external constraints and environmental impact. This makes MuSIASEM a powerful *diagnostic tool*.

Benchmarks can also be employed to predict selected metabolic characteristics of socio-economic systems belonging to a known typology of metabolic pattern.

For example, a developed society with abundant production factors per capita will invariably have a large share of its power capacity and human activity invested in the dissipative compartment, including the household and government and service sectors (see Table 8.1). Transition economies will be found to invest their limited production factors mainly in primary and secondary production activities (AG, EM and BM), while poor developing societies will allocate their scarce resources mainly to the agricultural sector.

As regards lower-level compartments, we can predict that the energy and mining sector of any post-industrial society dependent on fossil energy imports will utilize a negligible proportion of the total human activity, but a larger share of the total power capacity. Such an energy sector will invariably exhibit a huge exosomatic metabolic rate per hour of labour (see Table 8.1). For example, in Spain we find that all energy consumed per capita in a year is supplied with only eight hours of work in the EM sector. Thanks to an enormous investment of power capacity, one hour of labour in the Spanish EM sector stabilizes a total energy throughput in the society of no less than 20GJ of GER!

We can expect a similar metabolic feature for the agricultural sector of developed countries: a low investment of human labour requiring heavy injection of fossil energy and power capacity. For example, we find that the present per capita food consumption in Spain is made possible with only 48 hours of work per capita per year. According to Pimentel and Pimentel (1996), the difference in biophysical productivity of labour engaged with corn production between mechanized agriculture in the United States and traditional agriculture based on manual labour may be as much as 700 times!

11.4 MuSIASEM as a simulation tool

11.4.1 Using the Sudoku effect in MuSIASEM

As a simulation tool, MuSIASEM provides a feasibility, viability and desirability check of proposed scenarios. The feasibility check concerns the compatibility of the societal metabolism with boundary conditions and requires an examination of the external constraints. This aspect has been discussed in Chapters 7, 8 and 9, when presenting the grammars of food, energy and water, and their ability to address the analysis of external constraints. In this chapter, we focus on the analysis of the viability and desirability (internal constraints) of proposed scenarios using the Sudoku effect in MuSIASEM.

In order to better focus on the mechanism of the Sudoku effect in MuSIASEM, we start out with a simplified example describing the metabolic pattern of energy of Spain (2004). A more complex case, including all elements of the nexus, is described in Chapter 12 in relation to the Mauritius case study. As with the diagnostic analysis, a correct organization of the data over different hierarchical levels of analysis is imperative. An example of a useful representation of data revealing the Sudoku effect in MuSIASEM is illustrated in Figure 11.3 (a simplified version of Table 8.1).

SPAIN 2004	Production factors Flow and fund elements (expressed per capita/year)			Metablic characteristics Flow/fund ratios		
	Energy throughput (GJ-GER)	Human activity (hours)	Power capactity (kW)	Exosomatic metabolic rate (MJ/h)	Power capactity intensity (MJ/kW)	
Whole society	141	8,760	21	16	6.7	Level n
Household sector	37	7,825	14	5	2.6	Level $n-1$
Service and government	43	598	5	70	8.6	Level $n-2$
Building and manufacturing	43	280	1.3	159	33	Level $n-3$
Agriculture	4.3	48	0.3	90	14	Level $n-4$
Energy and mining	12	8	0.4	1,537	31	Level $n-4$

Figure 11.3 Multi-level table describing the end uses of energy consumption in Spain (2004)

Data source: See Table 8.1 (minor differences in the numbers are due to rounding).

Note: Values of flow and fund elements are expressed on a per capita per year basis.

As can be seen from Figure 11.3, our simplified example focuses only on the nexus between the three quantities written in the multi-level table: energy (a flow element), power capacity (technological capital: a fund element) and human activity (a fund element). We summed together the power capacity referring to different types of energy carriers (electricity, heat and fuels), since here this element is considered as a structural fund (a quantity of exosomatic devices). The use of these three production factors is shown simultaneously across different hierarchical levels of analysis ($n, n-1, \ldots n-4$), in such a way that the compartments shown respect the condition of closure (see Chapter 2 and Figure 2.1). The first row refers to society as a whole at the focal level n. It describes the overall societal average (SA) per capita use of the three production factors (energy, power capacity and human activity) on a year basis. This is the routine approach for assessing the metabolic pattern of a country: a description based on the adoption of only one scale at a time. Moving down the rows in Figure 11.3, we see what happens if we move the analysis to lower-level compartments. We have the household sector (HH), described at level $n-1$, the service and government sector (SG), described at level $n-2$, and finally the three productive sectors: building and manufacturing (BM), also known as the secondary production sector, at level $n-3$, and the agricultural sector (AG) and energy and mining sector (EM) at level $n-4$ (these sectors together form the primary production sectors at level $n-3$). We can now see *how* the three production factors are used *within* society, and discover that the various socio-economic compartments use production factors in different proportions to guarantee the expression of their functions. As discussed earlier, this pattern of allocation is at the basis of the possibility of defining typologies of metabolic patterns for different countries. Note also that the choice of definition of the set of compartments is flexible, as it can be tailored to the characteristics of the system studied. Compartments may be aggregated or further disaggregated depending on the relevant issue to be dealt with, *provided that the closure requirement is observed.*

The way data are organized across hierarchical levels (rows) and dimensions (columns) is extremely important, because it immediately reveals two types of constraints on the socio-economic functioning:

1 The production factors can, to a certain extent, complement each other. So within each row (each socio-economic compartment) a decrease in use of one of the production factors can be compensated to a certain extent by an increased use of another. However, the combination of production factors must be such that each compartment (or end use) can effectively fulfil its tasks. This can be considered a horizontal constraint.
2 The endowment of production factors in a given society is limited. Therefore, for each production factor (each column), it holds true that, if one compartment increases its share of use, other compartments must reduce theirs to keep the total (sum) constant. This is a vertical constraint. Note that it is essential that the data representation observes closure to allow summing over the compartments.

These two types of forced relations, together with the block constraint introduced in section 11.4.4, represent the Sudoku effect in MuSIASEM. This effect is generated by the mutual information associated with impredicative relations between the metabolic characteristics of elements defined across levels (compartments) and dimensions (distinct production factors) within the same metabolic pattern. The characteristics of the parts do affect the characteristics of the whole and vice versa.

Below we examine the three types of constraints revealed by the MuSIASEM toolkit in detail.

11.4.2 Vertical constraints: competition for limited resources

The requirement of closure entails that the sum of the compartmental sizes for any fund or flow element must equal the overall size of that element for the whole of society. In Figure 11.3 this shows as a vertical constraint: the sum of rows 2 to 6 must equal the value in row 1 (society as a whole) for all the columns of flow and fund elements. In fact, looking at the three production factors, we have the following forced relations:

- The total energy throughput (TET) in society (148GJ p.c./yr) is equal to the sum of the energy throughputs of the individual compartments (GER_i).
- The total human activity (THA) in society (8,760h p.c./yr) equals the sum of the hours of human activity allocated to the various compartments (HA_i).
- The total power capacity (TPC), defined as the technological capital enabling the use of exosomatic energy, in society (23.8kW p.c./yr) equals the sum of the kW of power capacity used by the lower-level compartments (PC_i).

In practical terms this means that the various compartments of society compete for the given amount of flow and fund elements. For this reason, any proposed change in the profile of distribution of fund and flow elements over the set of compartments must somehow be compensated by a change in the total amount or by an adjustment in the corresponding flow/fund ratios in order to keep congruence among the data in the grid and hence maintain functionality of the socio-economic compartments. However, this would require a change in the 'identity' (lower-level metabolic characteristics) of the fund elements processing flows at the local scale (in the data array describing end uses).

11.4.3 Horizontal constraints: substitution of production factors

Looking at the rows in Figure 11.3, we see the use of production factors associated with specific end uses or functional compartments. From this information (the value of the flow element exosomatic energy and the fund elements human activity and power capacity), one can calculate two crucial metabolic characteristics (flow/fund ratios) for each end use (shown in the two columns on the right):

- the exosomatic metabolic rate (EMR_i in MJ/h) – defined as the amount of exosomatic energy used per hour of human activity allocated to compartment or end use *i*;
- the energy intensity of the power capacity (IC_i in MJ/kW) over the year – defined as the energy throughput per year per kW of power capacity allocated to compartment or end use *i*.

It is important to recall here that the metabolic characteristics of end uses are process-specific and can only be defined using bottom-up data based on the observation of these local processes (see Chapters 7 and 8). In contrast, the characterization of society as a whole is based on top-down data that refer to a much larger scale (the one used by economic analysis for countries) and, therefore, these per capita values tend to hide the existence of large differences in the metabolic characteristics of lower-level elements. For example, as shown in Figure 11.3, the average rate of energy throughput in the Spanish society (17MJ/h) is markedly different from the energy throughput in the energy and mining sector (1.5×10^3 MJ/h). This high energy throughput results from the low value of labour input in the energy and mining sector (eight hours of labour per capita per year). Another interesting observation is that the majority of power capacity in Spain (and most other developed societies) is invested in the household sector (almost 75 per cent!), where the energy intensity (depending on the utilization factor) is extremely low (2.2MJ/kW). Whereas the bigger power plants in the EM sector serve millions of people and operate 80 per cent of the time (7,000 hours per year), private cars in HH are used for only a few hundred hours by only a few individuals. In this way, modern households minimize the requirement of human activity for domestic chores at the cost of allocating a large share of society's power capacity to activities with a low utilization factor.

In conclusion, the breakdown of quantitative information given in Table 11.3 specifies for each row the required mix of fund and flow elements, and the resulting required metabolic characteristics, to carry out the task implied by the end use. In this way we can check the plausibility of scenarios by checking for each specific end use or functional compartment the congruence of the proposed metabolic characteristics with known reference values.

11.4.4 Block constraints: expected performance of macro-compartments

Apart from the two types of constraints described above, there are additional limitations on the configuration of societal metabolism, which are reflected in a limited degree of freedom for the values taken on by the flow and fund elements shown in Figure 11.3. These limitations are closely related to the viability of the overall societal metabolism and concern the strength of the exosomatic hypercycle (see Figure 11.2) and the bioeconomic pressure (the social expectation about the allocation of production factors to the HH and SG sectors, discussed in Chapters 6 and 8).

The strength of the exosomatic hypercycle (SEH) is a measure of the amount of fund and flow elements that have to be allocated to the primary (AG and EM) and secondary (BM) sectors in order to stabilize the whole metabolic pattern in terms of supply of food, energy and power capacity (including infrastructures). It reflects the biophysical productivity of the primary and secondary production sectors (BM, AG and EM, corresponding to rows 4–6 in Figure 11.3; see also Figure 2.1). Thus we have that the allocation of flow and fund elements to the hypercyclic compartment (lower rows of the multi-level table) must be congruent with the expected allocation of fund and flow elements to the dissipative compartment (HH and SG sectors: rows 2 and 3, respectively). The stronger the SEH, the smaller is the proportion of production factors claimed by the hypercyclic compartment and the larger is the share of production factors available for the dissipative compartment. Post-industrial societies exist by virtue of a strong exosomatic hypercycle.

The bioeconomic pressure (BEP) concerns the expected characteristics of the dissipative macro-compartment composed of the household, and service and government sectors (HH and SG) (corresponding to rows 2–3 in Figure 11.3; see also

Figure 2.1). BEP is a measure of the material standard of living and hence of the *desirability* of the metabolic pattern (Pastore *et al.* 2000; Giampietro *et al.* 2012). The stronger is the bioeconomic pressure in society, the larger the share of production factors that ought to be allocated to the dissipative macro-compartment.

Obviously, the expected metabolic characteristics of these two macro-compartments (for the metabolic pattern to be viable and desirable) must be congruent with all the other metabolic characteristics. Thus, in scenario analyses, the hypothesized changes in the characteristics of the socio-economic compartments must not only be congruent with the vertical and horizontal constraints, but also guarantee the viability and desirability of the metabolic pattern as a whole. The addition of the latter block (macro-compartment) constraint makes the Sudoku metaphor complete!

The macro-compartment constraint implies the existence of strong non-linearity in the configuration of the metabolic pattern (Giampietro *et al.* 2012). When looking at the integrated set of functional relations between the individual compartments and the hypercyclic and dissipative macro-compartments, it becomes clear that the stabilization of the metabolic pattern is a complex phenomenon involving a series of autocatalytic loops (Figure 11.2): human reproduction depends on food production, which in turn depends on the production of technical inputs, which in turn depends on the delivery of effective services, which in turn depends on the reproduction of educated humans at the household level, and so on. Unless one is able to address this complex set of autocatalytic relations it is impossible to make any informed assessments about the feasibility, viability and desirability of proposed metabolic patterns involving a different allocation of flow and fund elements across the metabolic pattern. This is why the MuSIASEM toolkit is needed to combine the information organized in different grammars.

Thus, given 1) the observed characteristics of the metabolic pattern (information gathered in the diagnostic step) and/or benchmarks for the relevant typology of metabolic pattern, and 2) projected changes in metabolic characteristics under different scenarios, one can check the congruence of these two pieces of information in relation to the integrated set of constraints determining the feasibility, viability and desirability of the overall metabolic pattern. A detailed example analysing scenarios of land uses in Mauritius, based on the application of the MuSIASEM approach, is described in Chapter 12.

11.4.5 The link between the quality of energy sources (EROI) and SEH

The Sudoku effect is also useful in examining the link between the concept of energy return on investment (EROI), presented in Chapter 8 and referring to the quality of primary energy sources, and the strength of the exosomatic hypercycle, determining the viability and desirability of the metabolic pattern – see Figure 8.4. A metabolic pattern based on the exploitation of primary energy sources of 'low quality' (having a low EROI) entails that a relatively large share of the gross supply of energy carriers must be allocated to the energy and mining sector for the very production of energy carriers. This large investment of energy carriers in the hypercycle will inevitably be accompanied by a large share of the other production factors (power capacity and human labour) to produce and reproduce the technical capital and infrastructure of the EM sector. This will result in a concomitant decrease in the share of production factors (including energy carriers) allocated to the other productive sectors – AG and BM – and hence compromise the viability and desirability of the metabolic pattern. We provide a brief example.

Assume a scenario for Spain replacing all of the energy presently provided by fossil fuel with biofuel from crops. Looking at the characteristics of the production process of biofuel from crops we find an output/input ratio of thermal energy carriers of 1.3/1 (Giampietro and Mayumi 2009). This means that the net supply of 1J of thermal energy carrier to society requires the generation of 4J of thermal energy carriers, 3J of those gathered in the exploitation of this PES having to be reinvested in the internal loop! Under this scenario, the resulting net supply of energy carriers per hour of labour in the EM sector is 100 times lower than the value achieved when exploiting fossil energy PES (Giampietro and Mayumi 2009). Therefore, large-scale production of biofuels from crops as a primary energy source would tremendously increase the demand for both human activity (from the amount available in HA_{PW}) and power capacity in the EM sector. This high demand for production factors would undermine the strength of the exosomatic hypercycle and compromise the viability and desirability of the metabolic pattern (in relation to the internal view). In addition, the low output/input ratio of energy carriers for the production of biofuel from crops would increase the requirement for land and other natural resources (e.g. water) and therefore make the metabolic pattern unfeasible when considering compatibility with external constraints.

Using the Sudoku effect to frame the analysis of the metabolic pattern, it thus becomes evident that the development of society to its present post-industrial state was made possible by the exploitation of easily accessible primary energy resources, that is, fossil energy. The analogy with Sudoku can be applied more generally to an analysis of the evolution of complex systems. For example, human societies tend to senescence following excessive accumulation of 'non-negotiable' identities of their components (too many internal constraints in the form of mandatory end uses in HH and SG). This compromises the rearrangement (adaptability) of the identity of the whole in the face of significant changes in boundary conditions, with the result that a collapse and complete readjustment of the identity of the system are required before reaching another phase of smooth evolution (e.g. Tainter 1988, 2003). A similar notion has been suggested in economics, that is, the concept of creative destruction (Schumpeter 1942), and in evolutionary biology, that is, the theory of punctuated equilibrium (Gould and Eldredge 1977). In all these cases, an excessive accumulation of 'history' within the system causes the system (Sudoku) to become first subcritical then unviable.

11.4.6 The Sudoku effect to check the robustness of scenarios

In conclusion, the quantitative analysis of scenarios in MuSIASEM uses the Sudoku effect to check for congruence among: 1) the vertical constraints, that is, the distribution of the limited endowment of production factors over the various compartments or end uses represented by the rows; 2) the horizontal constraints, that is, the metabolic characteristics of the compartments or end uses must guarantee the expected functionality (the observable external referents) of specific end uses; and 3) the block constraints, that is, the performance of the hypercyclic and dissipative macro-compartments must guarantee a satisfactory performance of society as a whole.

Given a typical demographic structure and dependency ratio (determining the division of human activity between HH and PW at level $n-1$), a post-industrial economy generally has less than 1,000h per capita per year available in the paid work sector (Giampietro *et al.* 2012). Given also the enormous requirement for human activity in the service and government sector of post-industrial societies (600–700h per capita per year; Giampietro *et al.* 2012), we simply cannot expect to have a viable metabolic system when a significant share of the remaining supply of working hours (300–400h per capita per year) must be invested in the energy or agricultural sector. In fact, the EM and AG sectors, along with building and manufacturing, have to *compete* for these working hours. This is why MuSIASEM, and in particular the MuSIASEM Sudoku analysis, can be used as a *simulation tool*. Again, observing the system from different perspectives (across different dimensions and different scales) increases the robustness of scenario analysis and simulations by providing a triangulation of information from different sources: top-down, bottom-up, expert judgement, and common sense.

Part III

Case studies

12 The Republic of Mauritius

Tarik Serrano-Tovar, Juan José Cadillo-Benalcazar, François Diaz-Maurin, Zora Kovacic, Cristina Madrid-Lopez, Mario Giampietro, Richard J. Aspinall, Jesus Ramos-Martin and Sandra G.F. Bukkens

Summary

This chapter provides a detailed example of an application of the MuSIASEM toolkit using Mauritius as a case study. It shows the application of both the diagnostic mode, characterizing in quantitative terms the actual metabolic pattern across scales and dimensions, and the simulation mode, checking the feasibility, viability and desirability of possible scenarios, in relation to the nexus, integrating the quantitative information in MuSIASEM with a spatial analysis of metabolized flows in GIS. The case study illustrates the type of insights that the Sudoku effect within MuSIASEM can provide when discussing policies for development of a given socio-ecological complex.

12.1 Introduction

12.1.1 Background

Since independence in 1968, Mauritius has developed its economy by strongly expanding its financial and tourism sectors. In this process agriculture has remained locked into sugarcane plantations, producing sugar for export. In 2010, 78 per cent of the agricultural land and 65 per cent of the water used in the agriculture of Mauritius were used for this single task. More recently, this allocation of available production factors to sugar is questioned, since sugar exports contribute only 2.5 per cent of Mauritius's gross value added, while the country imports most of its consumed food (84 per cent in energetic terms) and energy (80 per cent). Moreover, the ACP sugar protocol programme (a form of support from the European Union to the African, Caribbean and Pacific group of states) has been ended, and the prices of sugar are no longer guaranteed.

12.1.2 Objectives

In this case study we apply the MuSIASEM toolkit to characterize the existing metabolic pattern in relation to the use of production factors, technical coefficients and external constraints given by the availability of natural resources, and to check the feasibility, viability and desirability of possible changes to the agricultural sector of Mauritius, as an alternative to the existing specialization in sugar exports.

In technical terms we use the MuSIASEM toolkit in diagnostic mode to analyse the existing pattern of energy, water, food and monetary flows in relation to the requirements of human activity, power capacity and land use, considering the implications on imports and exports. Then we use MuSIASEM in simulation mode to check the viability and feasibility of two policy options:

1. Using sugar currently exported for internal production of biofuels (scenario 1). This local production of energy carriers would have the goal of reducing the dependency on energy imports.
2. Moving to an alternative pattern of agricultural land use on the island in order to increase local food production, thus reducing the dependency on food imports (scenario 2), looking for potentially feasible and viable solutions through the Sudoku effect.

12.2 MuSIASEM as a diagnostic tool: multi-scale integrated characterization of the existing situation

12.2.1 Land use

Table 12.1 shows the main land uses for Mauritius. Data on urban land use (land use referring to all socio-economic sectors other than agriculture) are not commonly found in land use statistics, and were obtained from remote sensing sources (Chung Tze Cheong *et al.* 2011). It is important to recognize the difficulties of using remote sensing to discriminate between land uses corresponding to the MuSIASEM categories, that is, residential (household sector), energy and mining, manufacturing, and service and government (i.e. the land occupied by various buildings and other infrastructure associated with these sectors). Because of these difficulties we adopted a generic category (PW*) for accounting and spatial

Table 12.1 Land uses of Mauritius (2010)

Category	*Land use (ha)*
Country area	204,000
Land area	203,000
Agricultural area	98,000
Agricultural area irrigated	21,000
Arable land	87,000
Permanent crops	4,000
Permanent meadows and pastures	7,000
Forest area	34,980
Other land	70,020
Inland water	1,000
Irrigated land	21,500
Urban	28,070

Sources: Chung Tze Cheong *et al.* (2011) for urban land use; FAOSTAT databases for all other land uses.

Table 12.2 Harvested land of the main groups of agricultural production of Mauritius (2010)

Indicator	*Harvested land (ha)*	*Harvested land (%)*
Cereals and roots	1,881	2.5
Pasture	7,000	9.4
Fruits and vegetables	5,683	7.6
Oils	214	0.3
Stimulants	698	0.9
Others	310	0.4
Sugarcane	58,709	79
Total AG production	74,495	100%

Sources: FAOSTAT for pasture; Ministry of Finance and Economic Development of the Republic of Mauritius (2012a) for all crops.

analysis that includes the land uses referring to all economic sectors other than agriculture and the household sector.

Harvested land for the main categories of agricultural uses for 2010 is detailed in Table 12.2. Note that the sum over the categories of harvested land equals the total agricultural land in production (closure), as the total excludes the agricultural land that is not harvested.

As shown in Table 12.1, half of the surface area of Mauritius is used for agricultural production. Urban areas cover 15 per cent of the island. Although sugarcane land has slightly decreased in area lately, it remains by far the most important agricultural crop (Table 12.2). The four major sugarcane varieties grown are R570, M3035/66, M695/69 and 1658/78 (Chung Tze Cheong *et al.* 2011). The area cultivated by other agricultural crops (potatoes, vegetables and fruits, tea and tobacco) accounts for less than 12 per cent of the cultivated area. Pastures cover around 10 per cent of the land under production. A map of agricultural land use obtained from Chung Tze Cheong *et al.* (2011) is shown in Figure 12.1a.

As the volcanic geology of Mauritius has similarities to that of the Hawaiian islands, the soils are classified using the soil classification system of Hawaii; this is based on age of rocks and rainfall. The soils map for the island is shown in Figure 12.1c. Two main types of soil are relevant for agriculture in Mauritius: mature latosols and immature latosolic soils.

In relation to imports, we estimate the virtual land associated with imports according to the following protocol:

1 If the imported food is already being produced in Mauritius, we use the land requirement per tonne that is associated with the imported product on the island; these values are from the yields of crops or the land requirement associated with animal products (pasture plus the conversion of feed into animal biomass).
2 If the imported food is not produced in the island, then we use a benchmark estimate of land requirement per tonne of product, using the value of hectares/tonne of food product for the country that provides the largest share of the imported product.

12.2.2 The use of geographic information

Geographic information on Mauritius is shown in Figure 12.1. The maps in Figure 12.1 were used for two purposes:

1 for the calculation of water consumption in agriculture, in relation to different crops cultivated in different climatic zones (e.g. in scenario 2.1); and
2 for the calculation of land suitable for an alternative pattern of agricultural production (e.g. scenario 2.1).

Geographic information makes it possible to check the option space for a different mix of agricultural crops. For this purpose, we had to establish relationships that describe the current distribution of crops in the island (Figure 12.1a), and eliminate the areas with slopes that are too steep (Figure 12.1b) and/or with inappropriate soil types for the cultivation of the specific crops included in the cropping mix (Figure 12.1c). The result of this analysis is illustrated in Figure 12.1d, from which one can define a spatial location of an alternative crop mix – the map on the right of Figure 12.1.

As illustrated in Chapter 10, geographic information makes it possible to carry out an analysis of flow/fund ratios in spatial terms (considering land as a fund element), such as yields per hectare or, as illustrated in Figure 12.2, crop water requirement per hectare. These ratios can be calculated for categories of land uses

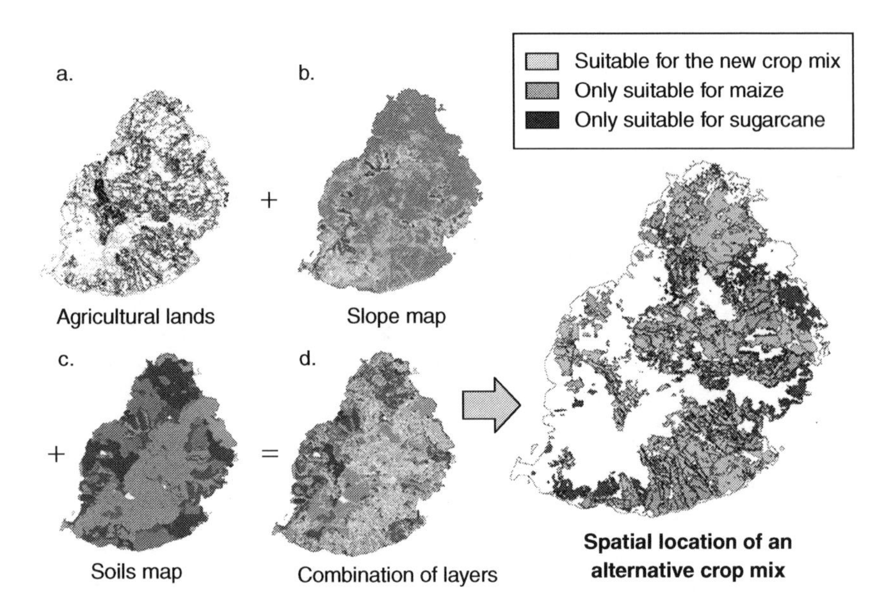

Figure 12.1 Suitability of land for an alternative crop mix in Mauritius

Sources: Own elaboration based on: Directorate of Overseas Surveys (1957); Shuttle Radar Topographic Mapping Mission (2000); Ministry of Housing and Lands of Mauritius (2003); Chung Tze Cheong *et al.* (2011); GADM (2012).

Table 12.3 Flows of major food commodities in the Republic of Mauritius (2010)

Category	*Production (tonnes)*	*Imports (tonnes)*	*Changes in stock (tonnes)*	*Export (tonnes)*	*Re-export (tonnes)*	*Domestic supply (tonnes)*
Cereals, pulses and roots	26,312	379,688	1,233	43,393	43,393	361,374
Meat, milk and products, fish	71,439	147,336	−2,946	99,157	99,088	122,564
Vegetables, fruits and products	110,460	52,900	0	1,957	780	161,403
Oil crops, oil and fats	5,484	33,188	−30	674	674	38,028
Stimulants	1,477	2,426	0	80	80	3,823
Sugar crops	452,473	26,945	7,526	435,105	26,945	36,787
Others	2,784	32,401	938	1,811	1,811	32,437
Total	670,428	674,884	6,720	582,177	172,771	756,415

Sources: Ministry of Finance and Economic Development of the Republic of Mauritius (2012a, 2012b).

defined at the local scale (i.e. land uses referring to the production of individual crops), and then scaled up to the hierarchical level of the agricultural sector as a whole, as average flow densities. Using the MuSIASEM mechanism (with weighted averages measured over higher-level components made up of lower-level components), this information can then be further scaled up to arrive at the national level. In the final aggregation, the density of flows in rural land uses has to be integrated (using a weighted sum) with the density of flows in urban land uses (Chapter 4, section 4.5).

12.2.3 The metabolic pattern of food

An overview of the flows of major food commodities in Mauritius is illustrated in Table 12.3. Note that for analytic purposes some commodities have been grouped (pulses and roots have been summed with cereals). Some processed commodities (e.g. alcoholic beverages) have been considered as primary commodities equivalent (required for their production).

A dual reading of food flows, in terms of nutrient carriers and food commodities, is shown in Table 12.4. The columns in this table show flows of food energy (in PJ) for categories of nutrient carriers. The nutrient carriers selected in this case study include the macro-nutrients, carbohydrates, proteins and fats, required by the endosomatic metabolism (see Chapter 7). The rows in Table 12.4 show flows of food energy for categories of 'primary nutrient sources' (food commodities).

In Table 12.5 we show the degree of self-sufficiency (openness of the food system) for various categories of food commodities. It is evident from these data that Mauritius heavily relies on imports for its food supply. The degree of food self-sufficiency is low.

Table 12.4 Accounting of flows of food in terms of nutrient carriers and primary nutrient sources for the Republic of Mauritius (2010)

Category	*Carbohydrates (PJ/year)*	*Proteins (PJ/year)*	*Fats (PJ/year)*	*Total food energy (PJ/year)*
Cereals, pulses and roots	4.08	0.50	0.28	4.86
Animal products (including fish)	0.12	0.36	0.39	0.86
Vegetables and fruits	0.18	0.02	0.01	0.21
Oil crops, oil and nuts	0.01	0.01	1.22	1.24
Stimulants, sugar crops	0.80	0.02	0.04	0.86
Total	5.19	0.90	1.94	8.03

Sources: Ministry of Finance and Economic Development of the Republic of Mauritius (2012a, 2012b).

12.2.4 The analysis of water metabolism

Using the grammar described in Chapter 9 we can characterize the metabolic pattern of water use for Mauritius. In this case study, we focus on water flows in the agricultural sector, because this sector accounts for 76 per cent of the societal appropriation of water on the island (Table 12.7). Water use in agriculture is important not only because of its sheer volume, but also because of the key role it plays in establishing a nexus between land use, food production and energy in relation to environmental impacts.

We consider two main categories of water use in the agricultural sector:

1 *Irrigation:* This concerns water that is distributed and therefore extracted from the funds (diverted water). This water use requires investment of production factors and therefore always has an economic cost.
2 *Soil water use:* This concerns water that is taken directly from ecological funds and which does not require investment in treatment and distribution (not diverted water). Given that soil water use is defined as the actual fraction of soil moisture evapotranspirated by crops, no losses in distribution occur and therefore soil water use is, by definition, equal to soil water appropriation.

Table 12.5 Contribution of local production and imports to the gross supply of food for the Republic of Mauritius (2010)

Categories	*Local supply %*	*Imports %*
Cereals, pulses and roots	2	98
Meat, milk and products, fish	43	57
Vegetables, fruits and products	56	44
Oil crops, oil and fats	10	90
Stimulants	7	93
Sugar crops	100	0
Others	9	91

Sources: Ministry of Finance and Economic Development of the Republic of Mauritius (2012a, 2012b).

Table 12.6 Irrigation and soil water use in agriculture for Mauritius (2010)

	Production (10^3 ton)	*Area harvested (10^3 ha)*	*Irrigation water use (hm³)*	*Soil water use (hm³)*
Cereals, roots and pulses	25	1.9	0	6
Meat, milk and products	72	7.0	72	0
Vegetables, fruits and products	92	5.7	0	22
Oil crops, oil and fats	2.1	0.21	0	1
Stimulants	7.4	0.70	0	7
Sugar crops (export!)	4,362	59	426	680
Others	2.8	0.31	0	1
Non-food	0.3	0.21	0	1
Total AG	4,563	75	498	718

Sources: FAO Cropwat and Climwat databases; Central Water Authority of the Republic of Mauritius (2012).

In Table 12.6 we show irrigation and soil water use by agricultural land uses.

In order to construct a map of crop water requirements (CWR), we estimated for each of the crops considered the requirements of diverted (irrigation) and non-diverted (soil) water flows, using FAO's Cropwat 8.0 (Penman–Monteith method) with climatic data from FAO's Climwat database and soil information from the soil map of Mauritius (Figure 12.1). The irrigation flow was corrected using statistical information on water supply from the Central Water Authority of the Republic of Mauritius (2012). These maps serve to improve the accuracy of the spatial analysis in a situation of marked local differences in climatic conditions.

The meteorological stations used to gather weather and climatic data about different zones within the island are: Vacoas for the super-humid climate zone (Station 1), Flacq for the humid climate zone (Station 2) and Pamplemousses for the sub-humid climate zone (Station 3). The cropland under each climatic zone was assumed to mirror the distribution of the area of the climatic zones. In this way, climatic, soil and crop data were combined to obtain an estimate of *effective rain* and from there the *crop water requirement*. The comparison of these two pieces of information makes it possible to calculate the amount of water needed for irrigation when the effective rainfall is lower than the CWR.

In relation to the water needed in animal production, we followed the procedure described in Hoekstra and Chapagain (2008). For this case, coefficients of water use per capita of cattle are multiplied by the number of head of cattle. Water requirements (WR) per head of cattle were obtained from Mekonnen and Hoekstra (2010) and include feed and maintenance water requirements.

The resulting spatial pattern of the present crop water requirements in Mauritius is illustrated in the left graph of Figure 12.2.

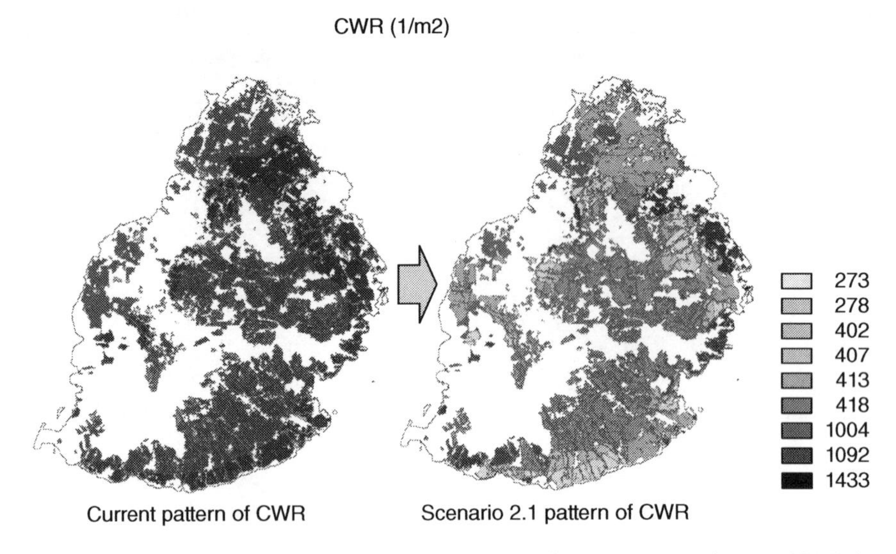

Figure 12.2 Estimated changes in the spatial pattern of crop water requirement (CWR in l/m^2) following projected changes in crop mix in Mauritius

Sources: Elaboration of data from Directorate of Overseas Surveys (1967); Chung Tze Cheong *et al.* (2011); Central Water Authority of the Republic of Mauritius (2012); GADM (2012).

The differences between diverted and non-diverted water use in the agriculture are important. With the present agricultural production pattern, the most important share of water use (700 hm^3, about 60 per cent) belongs to the non-diverted category, that is, soil water, with the sole exception of sugarcane, which has a high irrigation requirement. As also shown in Table 12.6, at present irrigation is mainly used in sugarcane cultivation (426 hm^3) and animal production (72 hm^3).

To estimate virtual water exports we applied the same method as described above. To estimate imported virtual water embodied in imported crops also produced within Mauritius, we used the local CWRs previously calculated and applied them to the virtual amount of land required for the production of the imported crops. To calculate imported virtual water embodied in imported crops not produced within the island, we estimated the CWRs, assuming that the imported crops were produced under the conditions prevailing in the major exporting countries.

12.2.5 Putting the pieces together: the multi-level, multi-dimensional representation of the metabolic pattern of Mauritius

At this point it is possible to provide an overview of the metabolic pattern of food, energy and water of Mauritius looking simultaneously at the internal view (how the flows are used inside the society) and the external view (how the flows are made available to society via local production and imports). This integrated characterization is shown in Table 12.7. It allows us to explore the nexus between food, energy and water, by establishing a link between the two non-equivalent representations linking quantitative assessments across levels and dimensions, and including imports and exports.

Note that the multi-scale integrated characterization of the metabolic pattern of Mauritius illustrated in Table 12.7 is based on simple numbers. These numbers present the information generated by the relative grammars presented in chapters 6-9 in a very condensed form and are useful only for flagging the existence of internal constraints (congruence among flows and fund-flow ratios) within the metabolic pattern.

The data in Table 12.7 are represented in rows organized in three blocks:

1 The upper block represents the internal view and focuses on which compartment is consuming which flows, using which funds (the different end uses of the flows in the compartments).
2 The lower part represents the external view and focuses on the supply through either the domestic production or the imports compartment.
3 The middle row represents the throughputs for the society as a whole and interfaces the two views.

Columns represent biophysical flows (food, energy, water), fund elements (human activity, power capacity, managed land) and monetary flows (gross value added). The rows in the upper block represent the socio-economic compartments: HH, SG, BM, AG and EM (already described in Part I and Part II), as well as compartments producing exports. Exports have been singled out to analyse the openness of the socio-economic system. The inclusion of exports among the compartments (end uses) still respects the condition of closure, as exports imply the use of a certain share of the domestic flows and funds (production factors) to generate products and services (for non-domestic consumption). For this reason, the accounting of production factors in the production of exports has to be disaggregated from the accounting of production factors in the sector generating the export. For example, the export sector has been further divided into agricultural exports (EXP_{AG} – obviously the production factors used here are not accounted for in the AG compartment) and other exported products and services (EXP_{PW*} – the production factors used here are not accounted for in PW*). As mentioned earlier, other ways of aggregating or disaggregating compartments are possible and are adopted in the other case studies.

The lower block of data in Table 12.7 focuses on the supply of the various flow and fund elements. We distinguish only two compartments (two rows) here: the domestic supply and imports. For the sake of clarity we did not include the assessments of *virtual* imports, which in any case can be calculated using the approach presented earlier; for example, the virtual water associated with food imports is 770 hm^3, and the virtual land associated with food imports is 210,000 ha.

Imports generate a biophysical supply of metabolized flows without requiring the use of production factors (but requiring the availability of economic surplus for paying for them), whereas export 'uses' production factors (fund and flows, such as labour, capital, land, energy and water) to generate products that are not

Table 12.7 Multi-level and multi-dimensional representation of the metabolic pattern of Mauritius (2010)

		Flow elements			*Fund elements*			*Gross value added (million us$) [or gdp]*
		Food (PJ)	*Energy (PJ-GER)*	*Water (hm^3 appropriation)*	*HA (million hr)*	*LU (10^{3}ha)*	*PC (GW)*	
End uses	HH	5.9	16	98	10,000	28	4.5	N/A
	PW*	0.8	37	44	600		1.4	8,000
	AG	1.3	negl.	190	39	21	negl.	220
	EM	N/A	2.2	260	8	negl.	0.03	180
	Exports PW*	N/A	N/A	3	590	N/A	N/A	50% GDP
	Exports AG	negl.	0.36	1,100	39	54	0.02	2.5% GDP
	Whole	8	56	1,700	11,300	100	6	9,800 (GDP)
Sources	Imports	6.7	49	N/A	N/A	N/A	N/A	63% of GDP
	Domestic supply	1.3	7	1,700	11,300	100	6	9,800

Sources: Elaboration of data from MREPU (2010) for energy and power capacity; FAO Cropwat and Climwat databases, Hoekstra and Chapagain (2008), Mekonnen and Hoekstra (2010), Statistics Mauritius (2011) and Central Water Authority of the Republic of Mauritius (2012) for water; Ministry of Finance and Economic Development of the Republic of Mauritius (2012a, 2012b) and FAO (2013a) for food; FAOSTAT for land use; Ministry of Finance and Economic Development of the Republic of Mauritius (2010, 2012c, 2012d, 2012e, 2012f) for human activity and monetary flows.

consumed within the producing society. On the other hand, exports make it possible to generate economic revenues for domestic consumption expenditures which can be used for the imports of other goods or services (if the revenues are used for this purpose!). To better explore the trade-offs of exports in biophysical terms, we separated the exports into 'agricultural exports' and 'exports generated by the rest of the paid work sector'. Agricultural exports imply two specific features: 1) they require an enormous amount of water and land (when compared with the exports of the rest of the economy); 2) they generate a lower economic return per unit of production factor (low economic productivity), especially in relation to the requirement of labour.

The last column on the right of the multi-level table can be used as a bridge between the biophysical reading and the economic reading. In fact, by comparing the monetary flows associated with the activities of the various compartments to the quantity of production factors one can establish a connection with the economic reading of the metabolic pattern. Particularly important is the analysis of the gross value added divided by the hours of labour in the various economic sectors considered in the analysis (economic labour productivity – ELP; see also Chapter 6). Looking at these values we immediately see the marked difference between the agricultural sector (ELP_{AG} is less than 6USD/h) and the rest of the economy (ELP_{PW*} is almost 14USD/h). This difference can explain the scarce allocation of the fund element human activity to the category paid work in agriculture, and is an important factor in the discussion of possible scenarios related to the agricultural sector.

In conclusion, the multi-level table illustrated in Table 12.7 integrates different quantitative assessments referring to different levels of analysis and different views of the metabolic pattern. However, the epistemological challenges implied by complexity entail that these numbers must always be used together with the complementing quantitative information gathered in the different grammars used to generate such a multi-level table.

Finally, the analysis of the nexus is also directly related to the spatial distribution of land uses, a dimension that is not reflected by the numbers in Table 12.7. Therefore, the quantitative information described in multi-level tables has to be embedded into a more complex system of accounting capable of interfacing with GIS, as illustrated in the examples of Figures 12.1 and 12.2. This interface makes it possible to perform simultaneously: 1) a spatial analysis of the quantitative flows in relation to both the requirement of society (determined by the size of the activity of the resident population) and the supply (determined by the size of the production factors spatially based plus imports); and 2) an analysis based on the pace and the density of the flows in relation to profiles of investments of production factors.

12.3 MuSIASEM as a simulation tool: multi-scale integrated characterization of scenarios

In this section we check the feasibility and viability of three alternative scenarios to exemplify the use of MuSIASEM as a simulation tool, by carrying out a quantitative analysis based on the framework of multi-level integrated characterization, and taking advantage of the Sudoku effect, generated by the MuSIASEM toolkit.

12.3.1 Scenario 1: using the present sugarcane output for local ethanol production

The first scenario considered is: to use all present sugarcane exports for the production of local biofuels (ethanol from sugarcane). This scenario does not require many additional calculations within MuSIASEM. It simply implies that all of the production factors presently allocated to the row labelled 'agricultural export' are moved to the row labelled 'energy and mining sector', to produce energy carriers for local use. This move concerns both the fund elements (the area planted to sugarcane for export purposes plus the power capacity and human labour involved in its production) and the flow elements (water, energy and food). This movement does not apply to the quantities of value added. It affects only the biophysical accounting.

We did not carry out a detailed analysis of the technical coefficients of a hypothetical implementation of this scenario in the Mauritius islands. The desirability of this scenario already seems to be a major problem when considering existing experience with sugarcane as an alternative energy source. Using standard data on productivity of ethanol production from Brazil (Giampietro and Mayumi 2009), we estimate that the net supply of energy carriers to society from the local production of biofuels in Mauritius would be quite limited, only 8PJ, thus reducing the energy imports by 16 per cent, but still requiring 65 per cent of the water use and 72 per cent of the agricultural land (which, additionally, would not reduce the heavy dependency on imports for food security).

Two aspects of this scenario, economic viability and ecological compatibility, are worrying, and they can be discussed using the insight provided by the grammars without getting into detailed, local-scale, quantitative analysis.

In economic terms the production of biofuel from sugarcane is negatively affected by the large internal loop of energy and other production factors required in the generation of the net supply of energy carriers. This process can be carried out with either:

1 A small investment of labour and an enormous investment of other production factors. This makes the net supply 'not viable' in economic terms, and dependent on subsidies (as in the USA or in the EU in the production of ethanol from crops). Moreover, this lack of economic viability will remain even in the case of an increase in the price of oil, since production factors will increase in opportunity cost even more than the increases in the price of oil (Giampietro and Mayumi 2009).
2 A large investment of labour to make up for the limited investment of other production factors. This makes the net supply of ethanol 'not viable' in biophysical terms, when dealing with situations in which abundant and cheap labour is not available, as is the case in Mauritius.

In ecological terms it is well known that the two steps of 'production of sugar' and 'production of ethanol' from sugarcane generate an enormous environmental loading (e.g. in terms of biochemical oxygen demand – BOD) because of the effluents from sugar-mills and distilleries (Giampietro and Mayumi 2009). Either the effluents are treated (requiring significant investments of production factors, such as labour to recycle the vinasse in the production and to protect the soil) and this increases the cost of the net supply of ethanol, or the heavy loads of BOD become a threat to the environment. This would be a particularly disturbing side-effect in a country like Mauritius with a growing tourist industry.

In conclusion, we used MuSIASEM here as a quick appraisal method to find that this scenario is undesirable and most likely unviable and infeasible without getting into a detailed analysis at the local scale.

12.3.2 Scenario 2.1: replacing sugarcane with food crop cultivation to improve food self-sufficiency by using all the land currently in sugarcane production

The simulation for this scenario has the goal of checking the feasibility (congruence with external constraints) and viability (congruence with internal constraints) of a scenario in which Mauritius shifts the land used for existing agricultural production of sugarcane monoculture to food and feed crop cultivation. This would have the goal of increasing the level of food self-sufficiency.

In Figure 12.3 we describe the expected set of relations over flows of food energy in the different compartments of the metabolic pattern of Mauritius for scenario 2.1, assuming that all the land available for agricultural production in Mauritius is used for domestic food crop production. For this characterization we use the grammar illustrated in Chapter 7 (in Figures 7.2 and 7.3). Presenting the scenario in this way, it is possible to check the assumptions regarding the technical coefficients and other hypotheses used in the simulation:

- *External constraint (constraints for suitable land for changing to food crops):* A large-scale move from existing sugarcane plantations to food crop production for internal consumption is subject to geographic constraints, including soil type, slope, and hydrological characteristics. We use the existing crop characteristics and take account of the land suitability to analyse the expansion of their distribution across the area currently planted to sugarcane. Using GIS, we estimate the food crops can only be expanded over 64.6 per cent of the agricultural area (Figure 12.1). Such a change in cropping pattern would leave Mauritius still in a situation of dependence on food imports. Examining existing benchmarks, we cannot expect an internal supply larger than 35 per cent of actual gross requirement of food.
- *Internal constraint (labour shortage):* The results of this simulation show that this scenario is not viable because of shortage of labour. When we try to allocate the required production factors (including labour) to the agricultural sector, the Sudoku effect in MuSIASEM's tables cannot be solved in

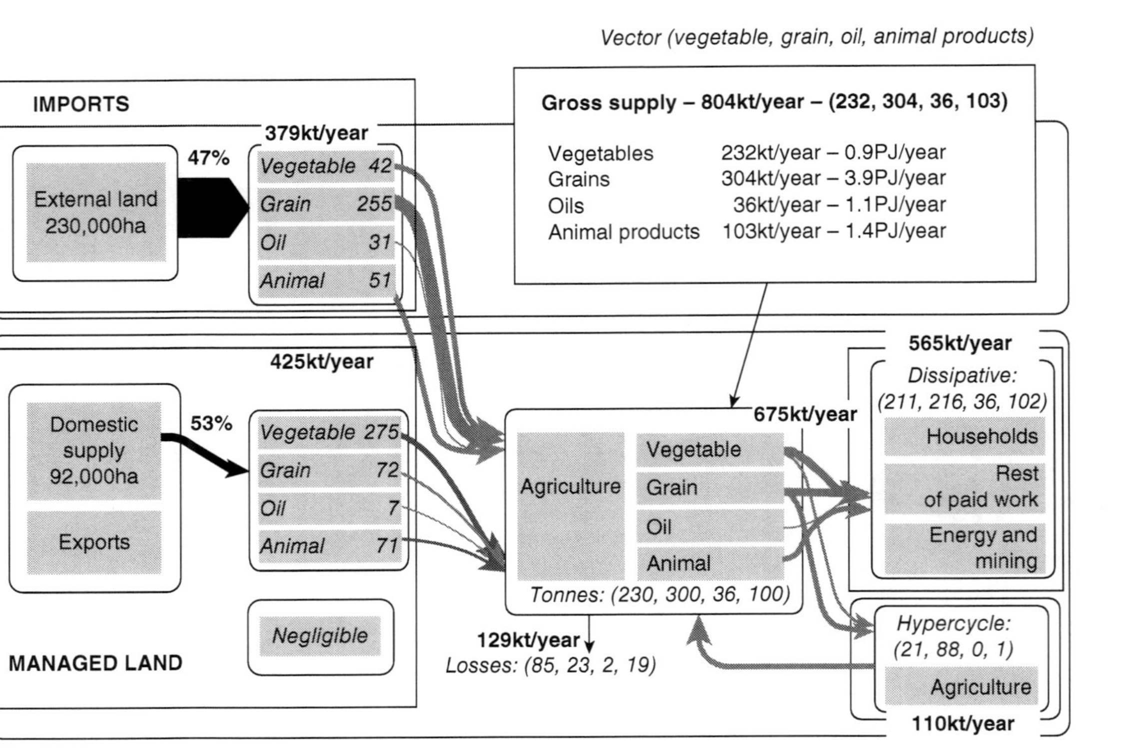

Figure 12.3 Representation of the expected relations over quantities of flows within the metabolic pattern assuming a change in the area of production (scenario 2.1)

Sources: Elaboration based on data from Ministry of Finance and Economic Development of the Republic of Mauritius (2012a).

relation to the fund element human activity. We assume, in first approximation, an expansion of the present mix of crops to be grown according to geographical constraints (such as climatic zones, slopes and soil). The result is that, with the expansion of this crop mix, the labour requirement per hectare for its cultivation would be much larger than for a land use based on sugarcane cultivation. Sugarcane requires much less labour per hectare per year. Therefore, a switch to food crops would imply an increase in the labour requirement in the agricultural sector, a result that is incongruent with the existing profile of allocation of labour in society. Implementing this scenario would demand a major readjustment of the allocation profile of labour over the different economic sectors. Moreover, the economic labour productivity (ELP) of agriculture in Mauritius does not encourage such readjustment. As discussed when commenting on the economic information of Table 12.7, the ELP of agriculture is the lowest of all economic sectors in Mauritius (as in all modern economies). Therefore, a reallocation of the work force in favour of agriculture not only is very unlikely (since workers get better-paid jobs in the other sectors) but would also lead to a reduction in the overall value added generated in Mauritius.

12.3.3 Scenario 2.2: replacing sugarcane with food crop cultivation to improve food self-sufficiency by using all available human activity now invested in the two sectors: agriculture internal supply and agricultural exports

After acknowledging that the land currently under sugarcane production cannot be *completely* converted to produce local food supply because of labour shortage, we explore a scenario in which all available work supply currently engaged with agriculture (AG plus $Export_{AG}$ sectors; 78 million hours in total) is allocated to the cultivation of food crops (rather than sugarcane).

In Figure 12.4 we describe the expected set of relations over flows of food energy in the different compartments of the metabolic pattern of Mauritius in scenario 2.2. Local food production is limited by the available labour in the agricultural sector (after moving all the labour currently used in sugarcane production to food production). For this characterization we use the grammar illustrated in Chapter 7 (in Figures 7.2 and 7.3).

By adopting the average requirement of labour per hectare into the mix of local crop production we calculate that only 39,000 hectares of agricultural land could be cultivated in this way. This means that, because of internal constraints, only 52 per cent of the agricultural land presently in production could be used, without changing the profile of distribution of human activity within the paid work sector. This is a clear example of an internal constraint (shortage of labour) that would prevent making full use of available resources. This situation could be improved by increasing the biophysical labour productivity (food output/hour of labour) through use of machinery; however, this would increase the cost of production, by requiring a larger investment of inputs per hectare (machinery and other inputs),

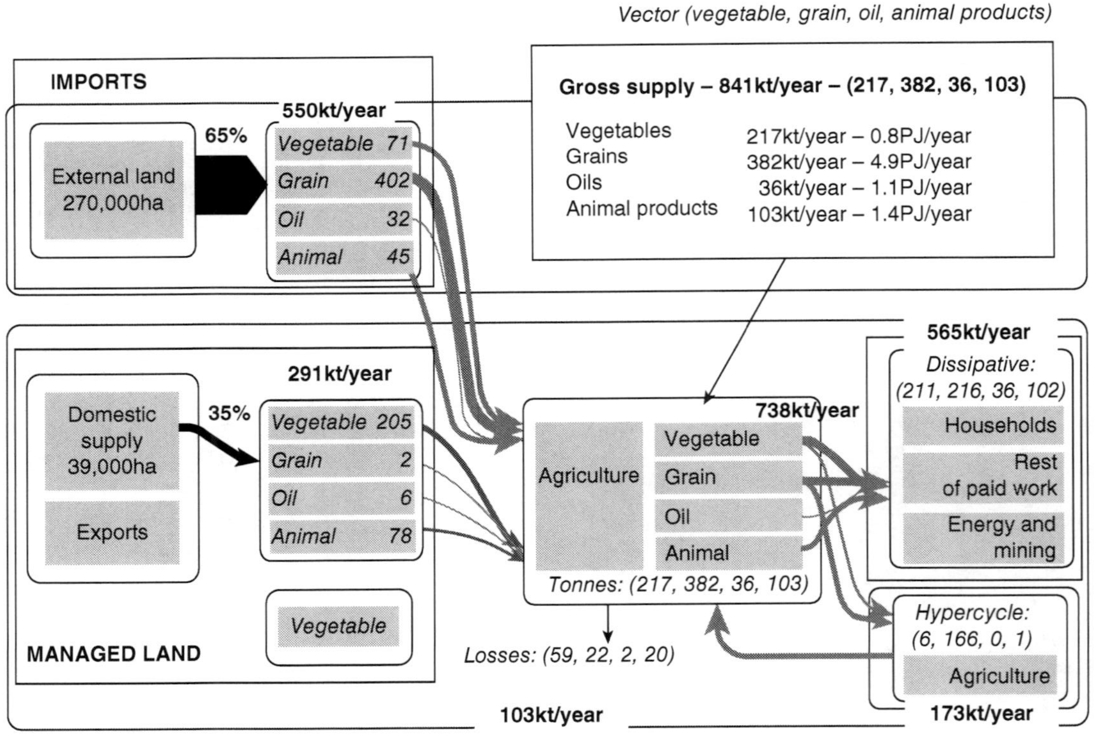

Figure 12.4 Representation of the expected relations over quantities of flows within the metabolic pattern imposing a constraint on labour supply (scenario 2.2)

Sources: Elaboration of data from Ministry of Finance and Economic Development of the Republic of Mauritius (2012a).

which could also have a negative impact through the environmental loading associated with this activity. When considering the economic viability of this option, as noted earlier, the major problem is associated with the low economic labour productivity of the agricultural sector, which also explains the shortage of labour in this sector. In relation to this, if the internal food supply could be sold to tourists and residents at high prices it would perhaps be easier to find local workers willing to move into agriculture (without considering the option of immigrating agricultural workers). This would require development of marketing strategies to valorize the market value of local products (e.g. traditional delicacies, special local recipes, organic products, etc.). Achieving economic viability for the internal production of crops is essential to justify its adoption in the first place. Clearly, in this theoretical exercise it is not appropriate to elaborate more to detail practical options.

12.4 Lessons learned from this case study

Using the MuSIASEM toolkit it is possible to carry out an integrated characterization of the metabolic pattern of a socio-ecological complex across different dimensions and scales, including analysis of land use and possible land use change. This integrated characterization makes it possible to explore the nexus between food, energy, water and land use in quantitative terms by using variables capable of addressing the effect of socio-economic processes and the effect of ecological processes on feasibility, viability and desirability.

The diagnostic–simulation toolkit can be used to help an informed discussion on the performance of the system. This provides the possibility of generating indicators 'à la carte', referring to different dimensions of analysis by comparing intensive and extensive variables that describe the specific metabolic characteristics of specific compartments. The case study illustrates clearly that this type of analysis cannot be done from the desk of an office, and without the active involvement of social actors in deciding the semantics of the grammars or the robustness of the data to be used in the formalization of the grammars. This confirms the statements made earlier about the nature of the work presented in this book: the results of our analysis have the goal of illustrating the potential of the MuSIASEM approach; they cannot and should not be used as reliable scientific information about the specific situation in Mauritius, because they have been generated without the active involvement of local actors. The production and use of quantitative analysis for decision making require a process able to check the quality of 'knowledge claims' about both diagnostic and simulation modes. Without this quality check, 'scientific results' are not robust enough to be used as input for policy.

Given that this is an illustrative example, the quantitative results of this case study, in our view, clearly indicate that the MuSIASEM approach can increase the robustness of the quantitative analysis of the nexus of food, water, energy and land use, because it generates an information space that is complex. In particular, two innovative characteristics are very important for the quality of this information space:

1 Quantitative assessments are not just single numbers coming from either a measurement or a calculation based on a given narrative about the number. Rather they are determined by a given set of expected relations between a variety of different observable attributes of the investigated systems; these can only be observed and represented at different scales and in relation to different dimensions and narratives; however, they have to result in being consistent with each other. This intrinsic complexity of the information space guarantees that the overall quantitative representation can be double-checked looking for incongruent estimates or wrong assumptions using many different external referents.
2 The quantitative assessments and their relations, as defined in the grammars, are perfectly transparent. This implies that social actors can provide their own individual feedback about any of the choices made in the application of the toolkit. That is, they can check the quality of the pre-analytical choices about the semantic of the grammars (choice of relevant narratives), and the analytical choices about the formalization of the grammars (choice of data and models). This second characteristic is especially important when applying the MuSIASEM toolkit to the characterization and discussion of scenarios.

Finally, the MuSIASEM approach makes it possible to identify three different classes of constraints determining feasibility and viability: 1) constraints that are given and very unlikely to change in the future, for example laws of thermodynamics, characteristics of fund elements difficult to change (biophysical characteristics of human beings), and characteristics of biogeochemical cycles; 2) constraints that are given but that can be changed in the future, for example technical coefficients describing the performance of technology, and characteristics of fund elements that can change at a slow speed (demographic changes, structural changes of the economy); and 3) constraints that are given but that can be changed easily, for example laws and regulations, prices, and the preferences of people for specific goods and services. When discussing possible future scenarios, and when dealing with a 'not viable' Sudoku in MuSIASEM, it is important to recognize the lack of feasibility and viability for solutions and thus to look for a different solution, which can be expressed through knowledge of which numbers, of the ones already in the MuSIASEM tables, can be easily changed and which numbers cannot be changed at all.

13 Punjab state, India

Cristina Madrid-Lopez, Juan José Cadillo-Benalcazar, François Diaz-Maurin, Zora Kovacic, Tarik Serrano-Tovar, Tiziano Gomiero, Mario Giampietro, Richard J. Aspinall, Jesus Ramos-Martin and Sandra G.F. Bukkens

Summary

In this chapter we use MuSIASEM to explore the metabolic pattern of rural Punjab, with a special focus on the economic viability and ecological feasibility of the specialization of its economy in food grain production. We show how remittances from abroad and subsidies from the central government tied to the National Food Security Bill maintain a relatively high per capita income and keep the metabolic pattern of the rural economy of Punjab viable. Relating monetary flows to water and soil use patterns, we find that the present system of subsidies for electricity and the minimum support price programme regulated by the central government are responsible for the progressive overdraft of aquifers and soil degradation.

13.1 Punjab state: the granary of India

In this chapter we employ MuSIASEM to study the link between the socio-economic context of agricultural production in Punjab and the state of its environment. As illustrated in Part II of this book, MuSIASEM connects, in theoretical and quantitative terms, societal dynamics to their environmental impact across different levels of analysis. In the case of Punjab, four distinct levels are relevant: rural households, Punjab (state level), the Republic of India (national level) and the international markets. As regards the environmental impact, we focus on the overdraft of water for irrigation, which has been for years the most dominant environmental problem in the area (Dhawan 1993).

The broader *region* of Punjab is located within the Indus river basin. Its name is related to water abundance and literally means 'the five rivers'. In 1947, with the Partition of India, the region was split between India and Pakistan. In this case study, we exclusively focus on the Indian state, to which we refer from now on as simply 'Punjab'.

13.1.1 Socio-economic context of Punjab's agricultural production

Punjab, like the other Indian states, is subject to country-level regulations regarding resources management, energy subsidies, food distribution policies and

Table 13.1 Socio-economic variables for Punjab, India, selected Indian states with similar GDP per capita, and countries with a similar contribution of agriculture to GDP (2010)

Country	*Agriculture, value added (% of GDP)*	*GDP (current 10^9 USD)*	*GDP per capita (current USD)*	*Life expectancy at birth (years)*	*Population (10^6 people)*
Benin	32	6.6	690	58	9
Rwanda	32	5.6	520	62	11
Togo	31	3.2	500	55	6
Malawi	30	5.4	360	53	15
India	18	1,400	880	65	1,200
Uttarakhand	10	12	**1,200**	–	10
Punjab	**31**	**42**	**1,500**	**72**	**28**
Kerala	16	51	**1,600**	74	33

Data sources: IAMR (2011); GoP (2012b); GoI (2013b); GoK (2013); GoU (2013); WB (2013).

Note: All data refer to 2010.

international trade. However, looking at the socio-economic characteristics, Punjab presents a peculiarity compared with the other Indian states with similar GDP per capita and countries with similar agricultural contribution to GDP: the Punjabi GDP per capita is relatively high, about 1,100USD (nominal, in 2010), in spite of having a large contribution to the GDP from the agricultural sector (31 per cent) (see Table 13.1).

Owing to Punjab's location in important river valleys, its soils are extremely fertile. This has motivated Indian public investment in farming in the state. Agricultural production has been actively promoted ever since the green revolution in the 1970s, and this has resulted in a strong specialization in cereals, particularly rice and wheat, as shown in Figure 13.1. The Food Corporations Act 1964 of India through the Food Corporation of India has established a national food distribution policy that induces Punjab to cede a significant part to the central pool of food grains. In 2010 Punjab provided about 45 per cent of the wheat and 25 per cent of the rice entering India's central pool, corresponding to the procurement by the central government of about 70 per cent and 80 per cent of Punjab's total production of wheat and rice respectively (GoP 2012b). The food flow to the central Indian pool of food grains is actively encouraged by the minimum support price programme and by energy and trade policies.

The Government of India establishes the minimum support price (MSP) for procurement of food grains so as to ensure the livelihood of farmers. The price is estimated each year on the basis of the evolution of the cost of inputs which is different in each state. Punjab has the highest MSP for rice of all Indian states; providing a high percentage of the central pool, it has acquired strong negotiation power. In practice, costs of agricultural production in Punjab are fairly low,

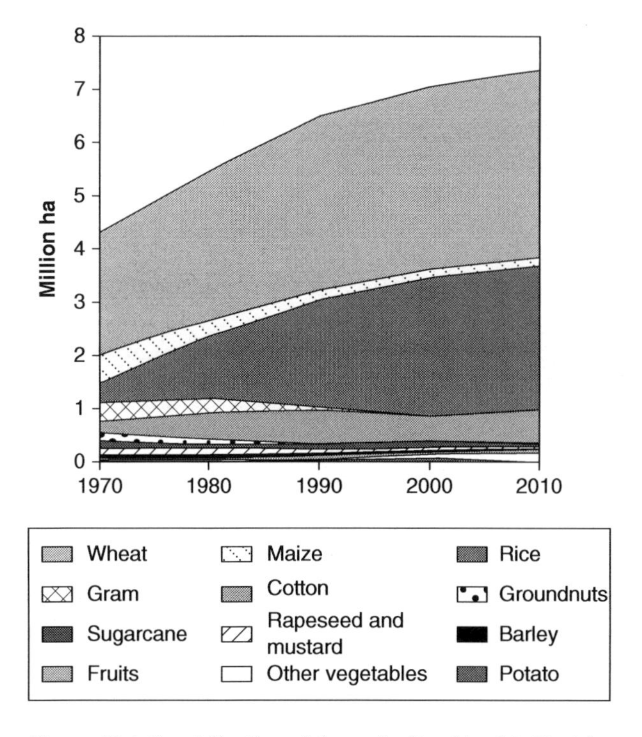

Figure 13.1 Specialization of the agricultural land in Punjab

Data source: GoP (2012b).

Notes:
Area cultivated to the various crops in millions of hectares (ha).
Owing to double-cropping the sum of the areas cultivated to the various crops exceeds the total agricultural land area of Punjab.

because the farms are frequently family-run, and energy for irrigation is highly subsidized. Indeed, as part of the energy planning, the Government of India provides high subsidies on electricity for ground water pumping in Punjab, despite India's burgeoning energy deficit – our estimation is that 95 per cent of its gross energy requirement is imported – and the rising awareness about the need for a more careful use of energy resources (GoI 2006). India's ability to provide reliable and adequate energy supplies for other sectors of the economy is heavily dependent on how efficiently water for crop production is managed (Kumar *et al.* 2013). The relatively high MSP in Punjab ensures that labour does not leave the agricultural sector for more profitable sectors by keeping the economic labour productivity in agriculture at an artificially high level (IFPRI 2007). Indeed, critical voices have suggested that the MSP provides a wicked market stability in the region that prevents the diversification not only of the economic structure but also of the agricultural activities (Bhullar and Sidhu 2007).

13.1.2 Environmental problems in Punjab

Intensive agricultural production in Punjab has resulted in severe environmental impacts: not surprisingly, as about 87 per cent of the total state surface is devoted to agriculture, most of it under irrigation and fertilization. Intensely irrigated agricultural production presently covers about 85 per cent of the land (against 2 per cent of rain-fed agriculture). Out of this surface, about two-thirds are irrigated with ground water withdrawn from the aquifers and one-third with surface water provided by governmental canals (GoP 2012b). Currently most of the water for irrigation is withdrawn from aquifers with the support of electric pumps, a tendency that has grown over time, as shown in Figure 13.2. As a consequence, ground water exploitation has surpassed the natural recharge, reaching an over-exploitation of 150 per cent of renewable ground water resources, lowering the level of the water table every year and further increasing the electricity needed for irrigation.

Intensive agriculture in Punjab has also depleted its rich soils of nutrients. Figure 13.2 shows the evolution of fertilizer use in the state over the last 40 years. The soils of 16 out of 22 districts have run out of nitrogen, and ten districts now have only a medium level of phosphorus (IISS 2010). Increased fertilizer use is closely linked to the price control and subsidies implemented by the Indian Fertilizer (Control) Order of 1985. Increased fertilizer use is making Punjabi agriculture more dependent on fertilizer imported from elsewhere.

13.2 Diagnostic step: checking the severity of internal and external constraints

The above background information portrays a state whose natural resources are being depleted in order to sustain the strategy of national food security imposed

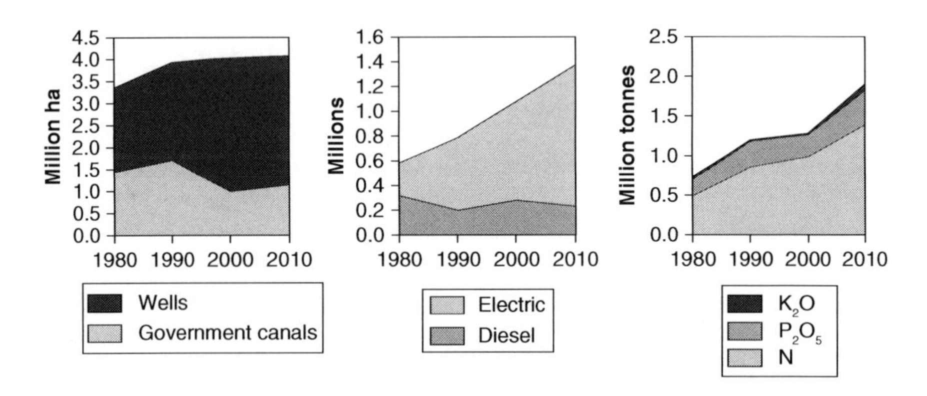

Figure 13.2 Evolution of the irrigated surface (in millions of hectares) in Punjab by water source (left), the number of wells (in millions) per energy carrier (centre), and use of fertilizer (in millions of tonnes) by fertilizer type (right)

Data source: GoP (2012b).

by the central government of India. In this section, we use MuSIASEM to establish a formal link between the socio-economic and ecological processes described at the upper societal levels of analysis (India and international markets) and those described at the local scale (Punjab and rural households). This analysis enables us to explore the viability (internal constraints) and the feasibility (external constraints) of the metabolic patterns of water, energy and land use in Punjab.

13.2.1 Metabolic description of Punjab

The interrelation of the various levels of analysis considered in this case study is shown in Figure 13.3. In this multi-level analysis we consider Punjab as level n, India as level $n+1$ and the international markets as level $n+2$. In accord with the other case studies, at level $n-1$ we consider the household (HH) and paid work (PW) sectors, while at level $n-2$ we differentiate only between the agricultural sector (AG) and the rest of the paid work sector (PW*). The ecosystem levels (e) have been adapted to the case study. We are using here the definition of levels explained in Chapter 9 (Figure 9.2). We have included at level e the water funds that are included within the geographical area of the state. The upper levels of ecosystems and the water cycle processes are considered at levels $e+1$ and $e+2$ respectively (see section 9.2). They have not been studied in depth, because changes in climate and international water treaties were beyond the scope of this study. Level $e-1$ defines the funds included within each river basin for the rivers Beas, Sutlej and Ghaggar. Subdivisions at level $e-2$ have not been considered.

A first look at the funds human activity and land (Figure 13.3, left side) at the focal level n (Punjab) and below shows that about one-third (30 per cent) of the paid work is devoted to agriculture, a higher share than in the other case studies (7.6 per cent for Mauritius in Chapter 12 and 5.2 per cent for South Africa in Chapter 14). Regarding land, most of the Punjabi area is devoted to agriculture (89 per cent), leaving a mere 11 per cent of the surface classified as non-managed land. Most of the total land (70 per cent) is under cultivation of rice and wheat.

The right-hand graph in Figure 13.3 reports the flows metabolized in Punjab, including food, exosomatic energy, water and GDP. For each flow (at level n) we show the percentages that are imported, produced and consumed within Punjab, and exported. Punjab exports 80 per cent of the food produced to the rest of India mainly through its contribution to the central pool of food. This means that the societal function of food production is to support not only the Punjabi system, but also the whole of India. Within the metabolic narrative we can say that Punjab is a functional organ of India producing cereals for the rest of the country. This specialization is directly connected to the use of energy: 10 per cent of the energy of Punjab is devoted to the pumping of water for irrigation. Virtual exports of water, mostly embodied in food grain procurements, also shown in Figure 13.3, account for as much as 65 per cent of the water used within the region. As we will see later, this water comes from both diverted (distributed and non-distributed) and non-diverted (soil moisture) sources. Regarding monetary flows, exports abroad amount to 5.2 billion USD.

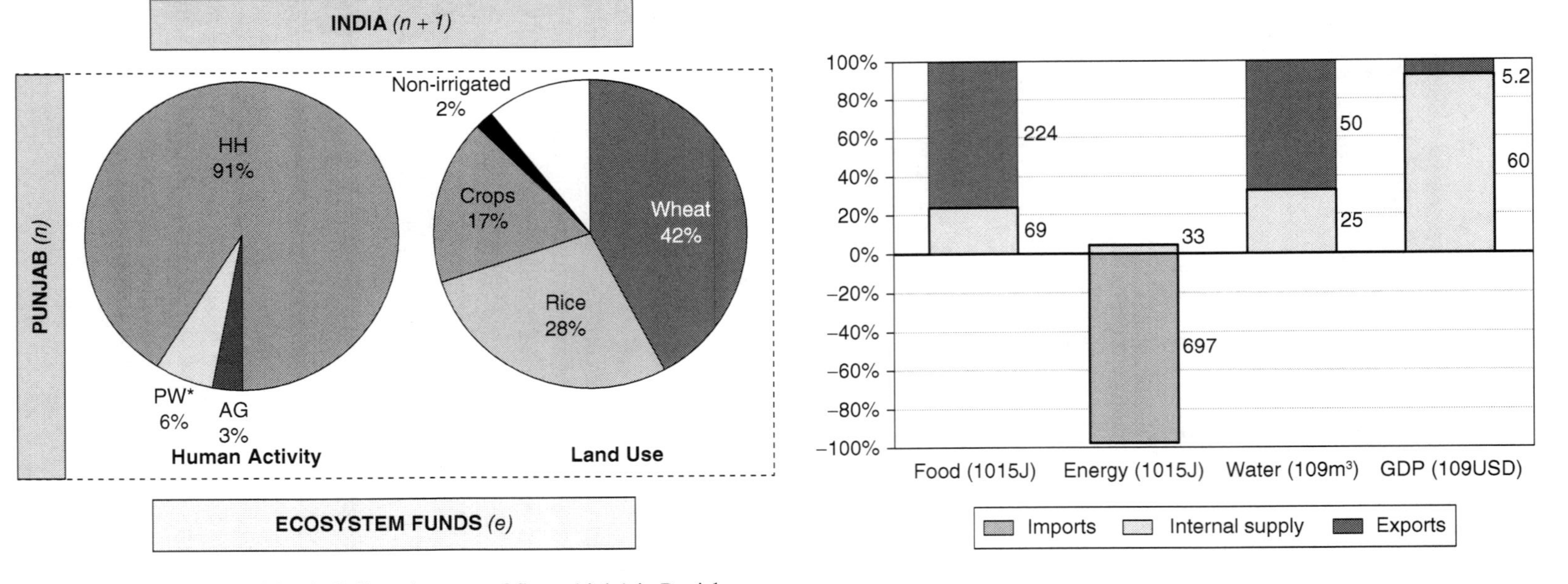

Figure 13.3 Allocation of funds (left) and source of flows (right) in Punjab

Data sources: Singh and Mittal (1992); FAO (2001, 2003, 2012a, 2012b); IEA (2005); Goel and Bhaskaran (2006); GoI (2006, 2011a, 2011b, 2011c, 2011d, 2012a, 2012b, 2013a, 2013b); IFPRI (2007); PSTC (2010–11); Sidhu and Singh (2010); EAGP (2011a, 2011b); GoP (2011a, 2011b, 2012a, 2012b, 2012c); Gustavsson *et al.* (2011); Sorman (2011); Diaz-Maurin and Giampietro (2013); ILO (2013); RBI (2013).

Note: Abbreviations used: HH = household sector, AG = agricultural sector, PW* = off-farm paid work.

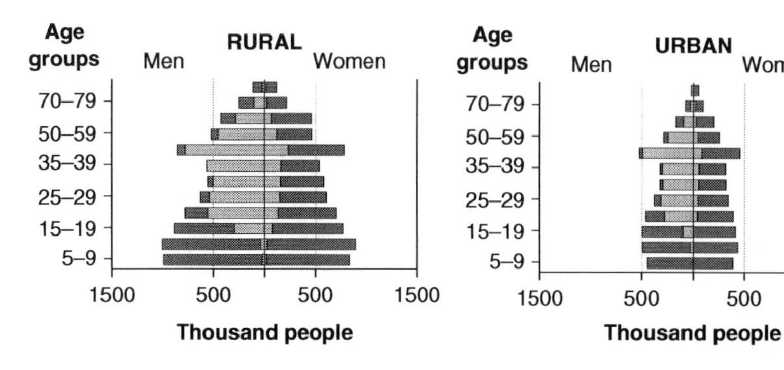

Figure 13.4 Age and gender structure of the rural (left) and urban (right) population of Punjab

Source: GoP (2012b).

Note: The working population is represented in light grey.

13.2.2 The viability of the metabolic pattern of rural Punjab

The population pyramid for rural and urban Punjab, indicating the working population, is shown in Figure 13.4. Note that working population includes only registered or paid work; unpaid household and farm work is not accounted for here. The urban population (37 per cent) is about half the rural population (63 per cent). Registered work is mainly performed by men in both rural and urban areas. In rural areas, the working age is lower.

We have mentioned before that Punjab presents simultaneously a high percentage of state GDP from agriculture and a high per capita GDP, a combination that is not found in other Indian states or other countries. Also, the larger part of the land is devoted to irrigation farming, which is largely maintained by unpaid human activity (family). To better understand this situation we detail the relation between monetary flows, food grain production and human activity in Figure 13.5. This graph focuses on Punjab (level *n*) and its interactions with the upper societal levels (*n*+*i*) and the interface with the ecosystem level (*e*). Monetary flows are represented by dark grey arrows, food grain flows are represented by light grey arrows, dotted arrows represent the allocation of the fund human activity, and traced arrows show the connection with the ecosystem. At the top we have the interface with the market, including export/import of food grains and monetary flows, and at the bottom we have the water funds observed in the region. Note that food grain production for export is mainly destined to India (87 per cent); only a small share is sold on international markets (13 per cent).

Most of the human activity (220×10^9 hours) is allocated to the household (HH) compartment to maintain the fund human activity. The rest of the human activity is dedicated to the production of food and other agricultural products and to other paid work (PW*), mostly within the service and government sector. In this context, the MuSIASEM accounting system makes it possible to individuate

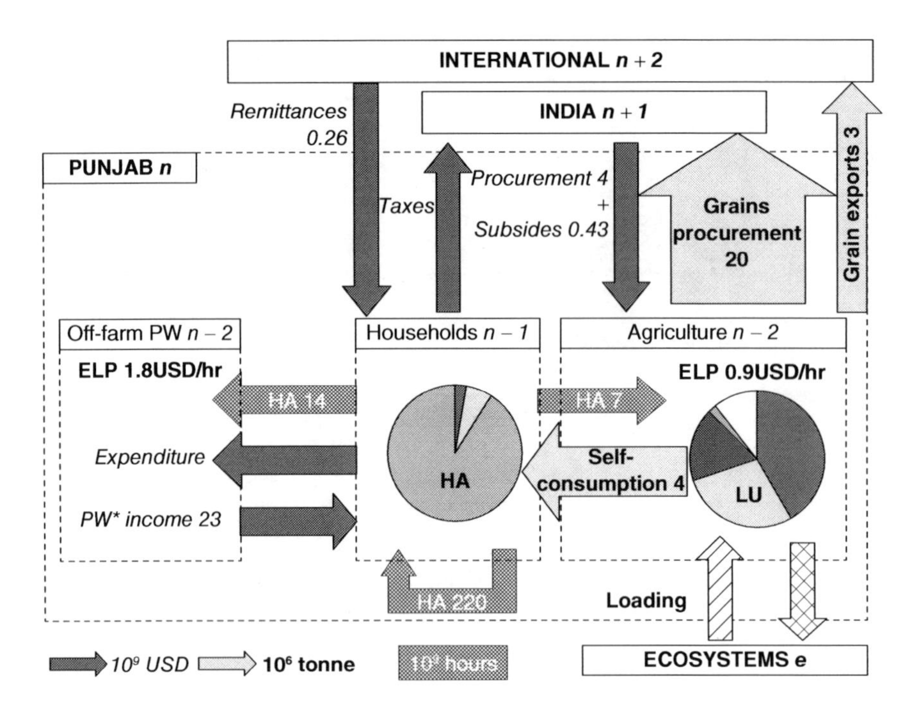

Figure 13.5 Assessment of the viability of the metabolic pattern of Punjab in relation to the funds human activity and land and flows of food grains and money

Data sources: FAO (2001, 2003); Goel and Bhaskaran (2006); IFPRI (2007); Sidhu and Singh (2010); EAGP (2011a, 2011b); GoI (2011a, 2011b, 2011c, 2011d, 2012a, 2013b); GoP (2011a, 2011b, 2012b, 2012c); Gustavsson *et al.* (2011); ILO (2013); RBI (2013).

Note: Abbreviations used: HA = human activity; LU = land use; PW* = off-farm paid work; ELP = economic labour productivity).

a peculiarity in the metabolic pattern of households in Punjab. Given the fact that in Punjab a large share of the work is engaged with agricultural activities, it is unclear how it is possible that the state of Punjab enjoys a relatively high income per capita compared to other Indian states. This apparently anomalous situation can be explained by the existence of other sources of income entering the local economy. Indeed, three main monetary flows enter the Punjab economy: 1) central grain procurement payments through the MSP programme; 2) subsidies on electricity from the government of India; and 3) remittances from abroad.

The livelihood of rural households is mainly determined by the flow of money entering from agricultural activities. With a monetary flow of 4 billion USD entering into the sector of grain production through the central procurement of 20 million tonnes of grain and 7 billion labour hours in agriculture (Figure 13.5), we obtain a rough estimate of the monetary flow from the central grain procurement per hour of labour in agriculture of 0.9USD/hour. As may be expected, this is less than the economic labour productivity of the off-farm sector in Punjab, which is

1.8USD/h. This low level of economic productivity of labour explains why subsidies are essential for making the pumping of underground water for irrigation economically feasible for farmers and why remittances are essential for maintaining the economic viability of rural households.

Indeed, the role of remittances is especially relevant, as they accounted for more than 10 per cent of the GDP of Punjab in the period 2000–08 (RBI 2013), twice as high as for India as a whole. Thus, paradoxically, remittances to Punjab are currently instrumental in the viability of the metabolic pattern of the rural Punjabi population (considering the household level, $n-1$), and hence for the viability of the entire Punjabi socio-economic system (at level n) and, indirectly, for the food security of India as a whole (at level $n+1$). Unfortunately, the flow of remittances shows a negative trend (it dropped to 8 per cent of the GDP of Punjab in 2010), probably owing to the economic crisis in the countries of origin. If this negative trend continues, a difficult situation in Punjab (and in India!) may arise in the near future.

With the subsidies for electricity the government of India aims not only to ensure the livelihood of rural households but also to encourage intensification of agricultural production. Indeed, subsidies for electricity are a key factor in maintaining high yields (biophysical productivity) in grain production. Looking at a historical series of surface and underground water consumption data for Punjab (Figure 13.6), it is evident that availability of water is not the only factor determining the extent of its use for irrigation. As illustrated by Figure 13.6, when heavy monsoons made available plenty of water in the region (1990) the overall sources and extent of irrigation did not change significantly. On the other hand, the introduction of subsidies for the use of electricity for irrigation (1996/97), alleviating the internal constraint represented by the excessive cost of electricity,

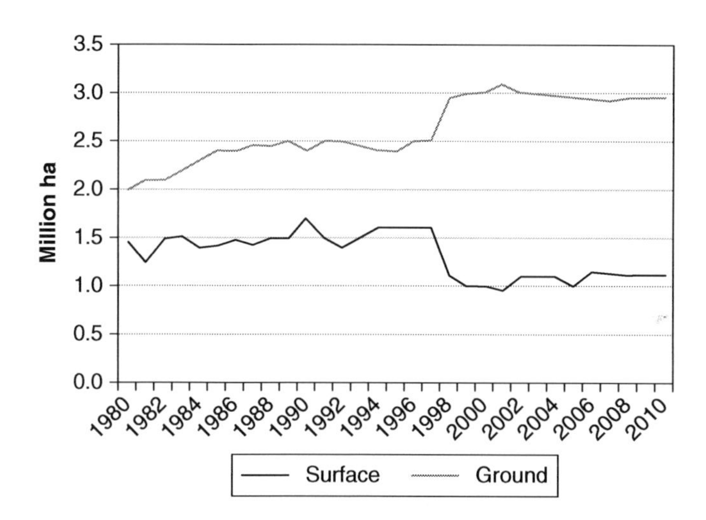

Figure 13.6 Evolution of the area of irrigated land (surface and ground water; in millions of hectares) before and after the implementation of electricity subsidies (1997)

Data sources: GoP (2012b).

generated an immediate shift from surface water to underground water utilization by farmers. Evidently pumping underground water with electricity is much more convenient for them than using surface water.

Unfortunately, these subsidies also have negative side-effects, such as an increase in the impact on aquifers and the quality of soil of Punjab (e.g. Bhullar and Sidhu 2007). This relation is discussed in depth in section 13.2.3.

From this viability analysis, it is clear that the specialization of Punjab's economy in the production of wheat and rice is a consequence of the national food security policy of the Indian government and not of the economic return that this activity provides to the state. This national policy causes a lock-in of the system, preventing the economy of Punjabis from diversifying not only its economic activities (outside agriculture) but also the types of crops cultivated (within the agricultural sector).

13.2.3 The feasibility of the metabolic pattern of rural Punjab

In subsection 13.2.2 we saw that the monetary flows entering Punjab from India and from abroad are essential for maintaining the system as economically and socially viable, but at the same time they are promoting a progressive environmental degradation in a region that has a small margin for self-management of its natural funds, especially water. Owing to institutional settings (international treaties with Pakistan and government decisions affecting Rajasthan and Haryana) a large amount of surface water is diverted from Punjab's rivers. As a consequence, irrigation (diverted water) pumped from the aquifers is offered as the main solution and is encouraged with subsidies from the central government. However, the resulting progressive intensification of agricultural production has resulted in a severe impact on environmental funds. This direct link between the societal and the ecosystem level through changes in the metabolic characteristics of land use (LU) is illustrated in Figure 13.7.

To assess the level of environmental stress due to agricultural production in Punjab we can use the concept of 'societal appropriation', indicating the impact generated on ecological funds by human activity (discussed in Chapter 9). This concept can be applied to both water and soil funds. An assessment of societal appropriation of water (SAW) and societal appropriation of soil (SAS) is shown in Figure 13.7. In relation to SAW, the gross water use equals 150 per cent of the water fund recharge. More specifically, about 75 per cent of the aquifer blocks (*e–1*) are considered as overdrafted (GWU > EWR), and about 60 per cent of the surface water monitoring stations report high levels of heavy metals and biological contamination.

In relation to SAS, irrigated agriculture is the main factor responsible for the degradation of the soils. The lack of control over water use (regulated mainly through electricity prices) has frequently resulted in overwatering. Owing to nutrients leaching and continuous over-exploitation, the soil is constantly exposed to nutrient loss. Figure 13.7 shows that as a result of intensive agriculture more than 60 per cent of the Punjab districts have nitrogen-impoverished soils and that the percentage of salt- and fluoride-impacted soils is already significant.

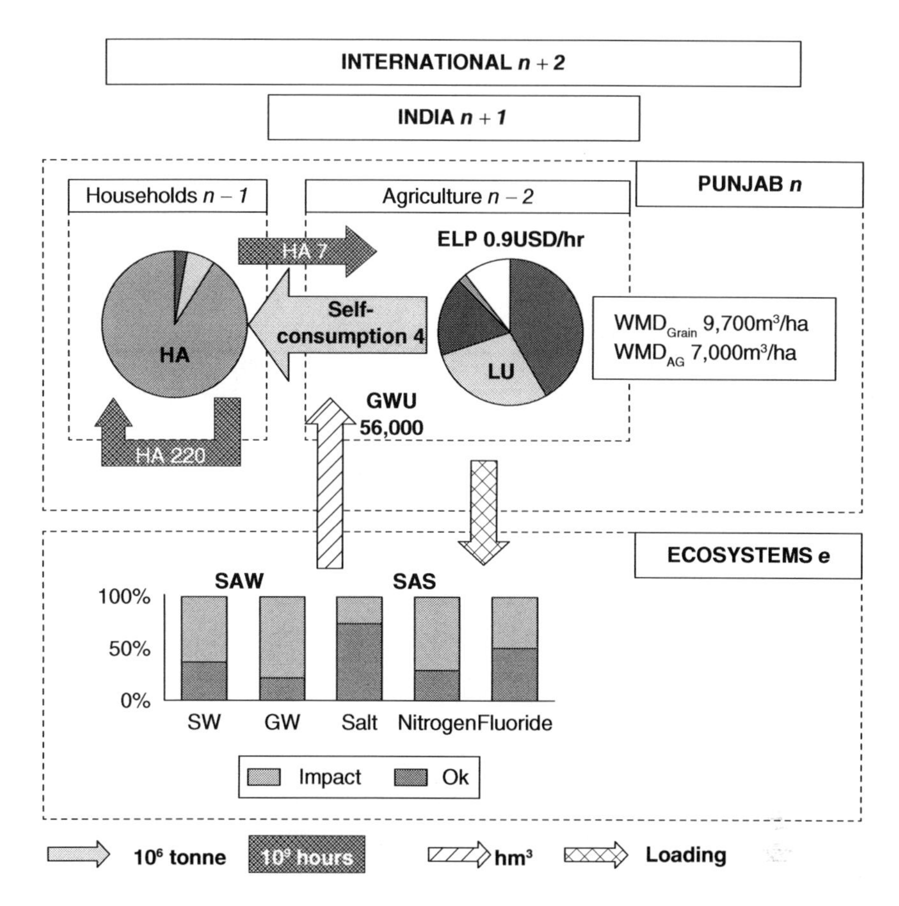

Figure 13.7 Societal appropriation of water (SAW) shown as a percentage of healthy water bodies (surface (SW) and aquifers (GW)) and societal appropriation of soil (SAS) expressed as a percentage of districts with high levels of salt and fluoride, and with nitrogen presence in soil lower than 50 per cent of the natural

Data sources: Dhawan (1993); Bhullar and Sidhu (2007); IFPRI (2007); GoI (2011b, 2011c); GoP (2011a, 2012a, 2012b); FAO (2012a, 2012b); ILO (2013).

Notes:
Water metabolic density (WMD) refers to gross water use (GWU) per unit of land use (LU).
All data refer to 2010 or the closest year available.

13.3 Analysis of trends at the interface between India, Punjab and local ecosystems

Looking at the factors affecting the viability of the metabolic pattern of India as a whole (national level, *n+1*) we find worrying trends. It is reasonable to expect in the future a constant increase in the international price of energy (energy is needed at the local scale for irrigation and at the local and national scale for making fertilizers) and, as a consequence, in the international grain prices. An increase in international prices will make it more difficult for India to import grains from abroad, and hence the central government is likely to press for further intensification of grain production in Punjab. These developments may force the central government to 1) augment subsidies or 2) adopt higher procurement prices, in order to prevent Punjab from exporting its food production abroad. Otherwise the economic situation would stress rural households and increase social tensions in the state of Punjab.

Looking at the effects that these trends will have on Punjab at the state level (*n*) we obtain an equally worrying picture. The population of Punjab is still growing, while foreign remittances are shrinking. The policy of heavy subsidies to electricity use in rural areas will have to be reconsidered sooner or later because of its high cost and negative side-effects (Bhullar and Sidhu 2007). This means that we should also expect a future decrease for this second source of economic assistance to the local economy. This new situation would pose a serious threat to rural livelihoods. As a matter of fact, even to maintain current levels of agricultural production, more electricity will have to be consumed in the immediate future to pump water from lowering water tables. This additional consumption of electricity, if not compensated for by subsidies, will further decrease the already low economic labour productivity of agriculture in Punjab, at the very same moment at which quite strong institutional settings prevent diversification of its economic activities.

Finally, when considering the ecological compatibility of the metabolic pattern of rural Punjab in relation to the preservation of local ecological funds (ecological level *e*), the situation seems to be even more scaring. So far the socio-economic tensions within Punjab and between Punjab and India have been externalized to local ecosystems in the form of an increasing over-exploitation of aquifers and soil degradation. The big question is for how long these tensions within the societal metabolic pattern – expected to grow further in the future – can be mitigated by a further increase of the environmental load to local ecosystems (stressing its stability) before a dramatic negative feedback will cause the entire agro-ecosystem to collapse.

13.4 Conclusions

As shown by the case study of Punjab state, the MuSIASEM toolkit allows us to carry out an effective integrated characterization of the metabolic pattern of a socio-ecological complex across different dimensions and scales. Relevant interrelations between food, energy and water can be identified and explained in relation to institutional settings. This case study has also shown that it is possible to identify relevant characteristics (prices, subsidies, remittances) of socio-economic processes in relation to the viability and the feasibility of the metabolic pattern at different levels of analysis (the agricultural sector, the aquifers, the whole state, the international market). In the same way, the integrated analysis across scales and dimensions makes it possible to identify 'special' features of the investigated system based on a comparison with expected characteristics of metabolic elements.

Finally, we want to flag, again, that the results presented in this case study only have the goal of illustrating the possible applications of the MuSIASEM toolkit. In this exercise we individuated possible relevant narratives about the sustainability of the state of Punjab. This study has been performed from behind our desk. We are well aware that these narratives require a reality check by experts of the area and local actors. However, we hope that this case has demonstrated that one of the strengths of MuSIASEM is precisely the possibility of individuating narratives about the sustainability of a metabolic pattern from the integrated analysis of different types and sources of data. Academics have been said to 'torture the data until they confess', but, as with MuSIASEM the data refer to an integrated set of different external referents, they are more prone to say something independent of what the tormentor wants to hear!

14 The Republic of South Africa

François Diaz-Maurin, Juan José Cadillo-Benalcazar, Zora Kovacic, Cristina Madrid-Lopez, Tarik Serrano-Tovar, Mario Giampietro, Richard J. Aspinall, Jesus Ramos-Martin and Sandra G.F. Bukkens

Summary

This chapter shows how MuSIASEM can be employed to generate an integrated assessment of the feasibility, viability and desirability of alternative energy sources, and more in general to characterize scenarios of alternative exosomatic metabolic patterns of society. The analysis focuses both on the potential contribution (quantity) and convenience (quality) of two potential alternative primary energy sources for the production of electricity in South Africa: concentrated solar power and woody biomass. The chapter illustrates how to integrate technical and spatial analyses into the multi-level system of accounting.

14.1 Background and objectives

The objective of this case study was to check how MuSIASEM can be employed to generate an integrated assessment of the potential contribution (quantity) and convenience (quality) of concentrated solar power (CSP) and woody biomass as alternative sources for the production of electricity in South Africa. We used published studies as input for our analysis to define plausible hypotheses about technical coefficients and logistic aspects – e.g. plausible locations – of the adoption of CSP and woody biomass as primary energy sources (PES), in order to illustrate the possibility of integrating technical and spatial analyses in a multi-level system of accounting.

14.2 Diagnostic analysis of the South African energy sector

The multi-scale multi-dimensional table that presents the dimensions typically considered in the nexus assessment is shown in Table 14.1. It includes the flow elements food, energy, water and value added, and the fund elements human activity, power capacity and managed land. The values for the flow and fund elements shown in Table 14.1 have been generated with the grammars described in Chapters 6, 7, 8 and 9. The procedures of accounting followed for energy and power capacity are presented in section 14.3 of this chapter.

Table 14.1 Multi-scale, multi-dimensional table of the metabolic pattern of South Africa

Consumption side	*Flow elements*				*Fund elements*		
	Food (PJ-NFS)	*Energy (PJ-GER)*	*Water (10^3 hm^3-GWR)*	*Value added (10^9 USD)*	*Human activity (10^9 h)*	*Power capacity (GW)*	*Managed land (10^6 ha)*
Whole society (*n*)	**330**	**6,500**	**41**	**330**	**450**	**750**	**100**
Dissipative compartment ($n-1$)	230	6,400	39	290	450	750	100
Hypercycle ($n-1$)	N/A	110	0.89	37	0.46	2.7	negl.
Losses (*n*)	**100**	**240**	**0.79**	**N/A**	**N/A**	**N/A**	**N/A**
Exports (*n*)	**−61**	**−1,400**	**−9.0**	**76**	**N/A**	**N/A**	**N/A**
Supply side							
Imports	62	1,600	11	−76	N/A	N/A	N/A
EM sector	N/A	6,500	N/A	N/A	N/A	N/A	N/A

Sources: WB (2009) and OECD/IEA (2011) for energy and power capacity; SSA (2001, 2009a, 2009b, 2012a, 2012b) for human activity; SSA (2012c) for water; SARB (2010), CIA (2012) and SSA (2012d, 2012e, 2012f) for value added; von Blottnitz (2006) and FAO (2013b) for managed land.

Notes:

Data refer to 2010, except for energy and power capacity data, which refer to 2009.

Numbers may not add up because of rounding.

As this case study focuses on the assessment of the quality of PES and the process of production of energy carriers (EC), we single out the energy and mining (EM) sector as the hypercyclic compartment of society responsible for the production of energy carriers. To this purpose we use the energy grammar outlined in Chapter 8. The relevant categories of accounting in this case study are illustrated in the graph of the energy grammar shown in Figure 14.1, and include:

- *In the internal view (demand side):* The requirement of energy carriers in society is defined as the sum of the net supply/consumption of energy carriers (NSEC), the exports and the losses. In the diagnostic mode, NSEC coincides with the observed consumption of energy carriers in the various societal compartments (indicated in the data array of end uses). NSEC is divided into a purely dissipative part (energy used to express functions outside the energy sector) and the hypercyclic part (energy used within the energy sector).
- *In the external view (supply side):* The requirement of gross supply/consumption of EC defined in the inside view is translated into a requirement of domestic primary energy sources and imports. This requires the analysis of two potential sources of energy carriers: 1) the EM sector or hypercyclic part (production of energy carriers from domestic supply and/or imports of primary energy sources); and 2) direct imports of energy carriers.

The information required to build an interface between these two views is provided in Table 14.2. It concerns the use of production factors within the South African energy and mining sector and the set of available domestic primary energy sources exploited.

Using the energy grammar (Figure 14.1) it becomes possible to link supply and demand sides by tracking the various energy forms and their relative relations. In particular:

- *On the supply side:* The flows of energy identified as 'supply' (last two rows of Table 14.1) correspond to the gross energy requirement (GER) on the left side of Figure 14.1 (6,500PJ-GER and 1,600PJ-GER, for local supply of PES and imports, respectively). We are using here the partial substitution method to assess this quantity (as explained in Chapter 8).
- *On the demand side:* The flows of energy carriers consumed within the different functional compartments are expressed in terms of requirement of end uses (REU) for which thermal energy and mechanical energy are not equivalent. For this reason, each number shown on the 'consumption' side (the upper part of Table 14.1) corresponds to the GER-equivalent obtained by multiplying REU by the GER/GSEC ratios (1.0 and 2.6, for thermal and mechanical energy, respectively) that account for the energy used in the energy and mining sector for the conversion of thermal energy into electricity (this approach is illustrated in Figure 8.3). Thus, GER/GSEC ratios characterize the way energy carriers are generated, which depends on the specific country and, to a lesser extent, the year of analysis. Given a chosen formalization of the energy grammar it becomes possible to provide more details on the characteristics

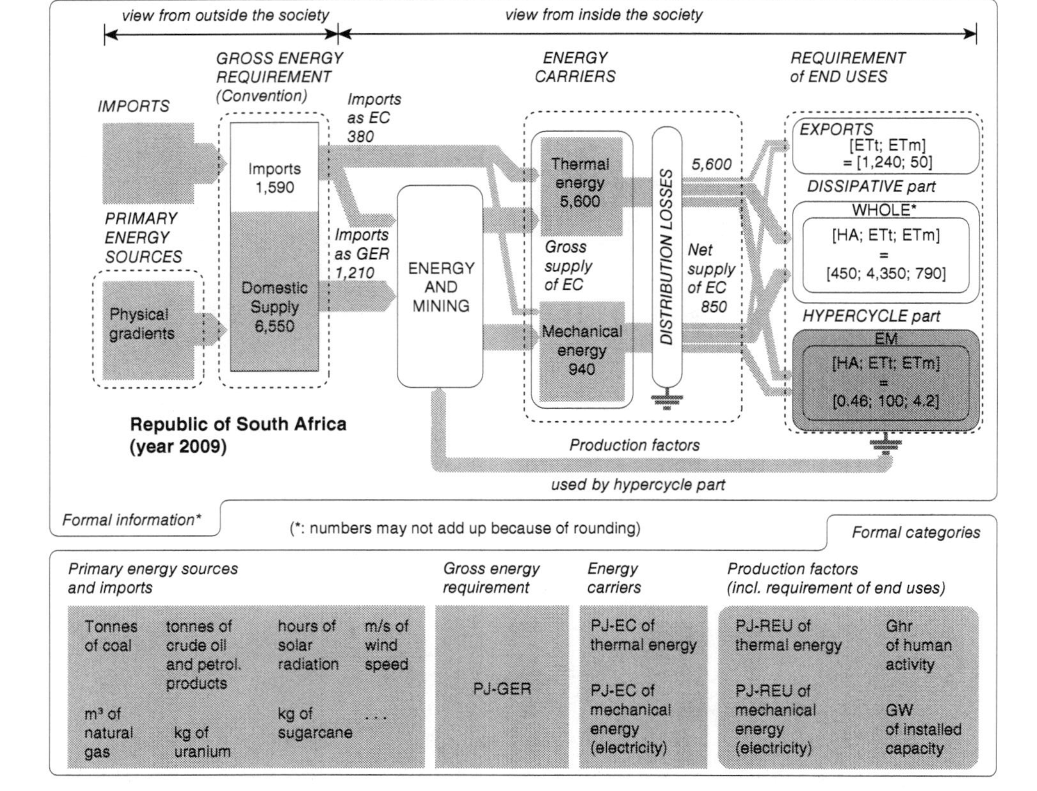

Figure 14.1 The energy grammar characterizing the exosomatic metabolic pattern of South Africa

Sources: Elaboration of data from WB (2009) and OECD/IEA (2011).

Note: All data refer to 2009.

Table 14.2 Profile of investment of production factors (human activity, energy throughput, power capacity) in the exploitation of different primary energy sources in the South African energy sector (2009)

EM sector	*Consumption of production factors*					*Supply of energy carriers*	
	HA (10^6 h)	*ET-t (PJ-EC)*	*ET-m (PJ-EC)*	*PC-t (MW)*	*PC-m (MW)*	*NSEC-t (PJ-EC)*	*NSEC-m (PJ-EC)*
EM (*n*−2)	**460**	**100**	**4.2**	**2,600**	**130**	**5,600**	**850**
Local supply of PES (n−3)	***430***	***100***	***4.2***	***2,600***	***130***	***4,200***	***800***
Fossil fuels (n−4)	150	37	2.6	370	84	3,600	750
Nuclear (n−4)	12	3.2	1.5	32	48	–	42
Biofuels (n−4)	270	60	negl.	2,200	negl.	600	3.4
Others (n−4)	negl.	negl.	negl.	negl.	negl.	negl.	5.9
Imports as GER (n−3)	***35***	***0.85***	***0.03***	***9.2***	***0.8***	***1,200***	***7.2***
Fossil fuels (n−4)	35	0.85	0.03	9.2	0.8	1,200	7.2
Imports as EC (n−3)	***negl.***	***negl.***	***negl.***	***negl.***	***negl.***	***260***	***40***
Fossil fuels (n−4)	negl.	negl.	negl.	negl.	negl.	260	negl.
Electricity (n−4)	negl.	negl.	negl.	negl.	negl.	–	40

Sources: See Table 14.1.

Note: HA = human activity; ET = energy throughput; PC = power capacity; NSEC = net supply of energy carriers; ‘t’ = thermal energy; ‘m’ = mechanical energy.

of end uses, without losing the distinction between energy carriers of different type. In fact, we can use a data array that contains information on the production factors (shown in Table 14.2): human activity (HA); two different energy throughputs (ET-t and ET-m, carriers of thermal and mechanical energy respectively); and two different assessments of power capacity (PC-t and PC-m, for dissipation of thermal and mechanical energy respectively).

As done with the analysis of food in Mauritius, the change of perspective, from the external to the internal view (e.g. Figure 7.1), implies switching from a quantitative representation of flows based on aggregate values to a quantitative representation of flows based on data arrays. Thus, whereas gross energy requirements are expressed in GER-thermal joules (e.g. tons of oil equivalent), a description of the use of energy carriers inside society demands the use of data arrays describing the different typologies of energy carriers: J of thermal energy (fuels and process heat) and J of mechanical energy (electricity).

In the PES/EC supply representation shown in Table 14.2, we assess: 1) the relative contribution of each primary energy source in terms of total net supply of energy carriers (the columns NSEC-t and NSEC-m on the right); and 2) the relative consumption of energy carriers (the columns ET-t and ET-m) in the EM sector. In this way, it becomes possible to establish a relation between the overall characteristics of the EM sector, using a vector (at level $n-2$), and the characteristics of its subparts using a multi-level table (at levels $n-3$ and $n-4$). In particular, we distinguish three main categories of accounting at level $n-3$: 1) local (domestic) supply of primary energy sources; 2) imports as GER-thermal, which correspond to imported primary energy sources used for making energy carriers (e.g. coal or fuel to power plants or refineries); and 3) imports as EC, which correspond to the import of energy products that are used directly as energy carriers (e.g. petroleum products or electricity with no conversion losses).

Table 14.2 is useful for identifying the profile of production factors required for the exploitation of different types of primary energy sources. By aggregating these data we can define the overall investment of production factors (fund and flow elements) in the energy and mining sector (EM) to generate the internal gross supply of energy carriers of society. On the basis of this representation of energy flows, we can generate the following two indicators:

1 Potential supply from a given primary energy source (external view): This indicator performs a check on the severity of external constraints. It allows us to assess the maximum size (in extensive terms) of the net supply of energy carriers (NSEC) that can be provided by a given PES in relation to its specific external constraints (limited availability of favourable physical gradients).
2 The contribution of each primary energy source to the energy return on investment (EROI) of the energy and mining sector (internal view): This indicator is defined as the amount of energy carriers that is generated by the exploitation of a mix of primary energy sources divided by the amount of energy carriers

that must be invested in such exploitation (see also Chapter 8). In this representation the energy return is represented by the GSEC of the whole society (the output of the EM sector) and the energy investment is represented by the energy carriers consumed in the EM. The return on investment is determined by the amount of internal energy delivered by the primary energy source exploited. The resulting quantitative representation of EROI is a multi-level table, as illustrated in Table 14.3. As shown in Table 14.3, imported energy carriers boost the overall output of the EM sector but do not require investments in the EM sector (no conversion losses). They therefore improve the EROI of the EM sector. However, the solution of energy imports implies an economic cost, and therefore a requirement of production factors to generate the relative monetary flow (unless the imports are obtained by making debt).

The multi-level characterization of the EROI makes it possible to assess both the external constraints, by addressing the non-linear relation between the requirement of PES (physical gradients beyond human control) and the supply of EC, and the internal constraints, by making it possible to characterize the requirement of production factors in the EM sector and in the rest of the society. Therefore, the implementation of the EROI rationale within the MuSIASEM approach is particularly useful in scenario analysis, as will be shown in section 14.4.

14.3 The implementation of the protocol of energy accounting used in this case study

In this section, we show in detail the processes used to generate the quantitative assessment of the energy grammar presented in Figure 14.1. First, we provide the entry points for the typologies of data used. Then we provide the logical framework of the energy analysis by means of a set of steps presenting how the outputs are generated. The logical framework explains the formalization of the analysis, and especially how to deal with non-equivalent forms of energy in an integrated analysis. We use the South Africa case as an example, but the same data entry points and logic apply to the cases of Mauritius (Chapter 12) and Punjab (Chapter 13).

14.3.1 Data entry points

Three data entry points are identified in the energy analysis, which correspond to the only data that can be measured.

At the level of end uses, for the whole system (country) and each of its compartments:

1 *Energy statistics on imports and domestic supply of energy products.* These data are used in the energy grammar in relation to the different energy products from imports and from local supply. They are expressed in biophysical units (tonnes, m^3, etc.) or in thermal equivalent units (e.g. toe).

2 *Energy statistics on electricity generation and consumption by activity.* These data are used in the energy grammar in relation to the local production of electricity per energy system as well as the electricity consumption per sector (agriculture, transport, construction, manufacturing, services, household, etc.). They are expressed in watt-hour (Wh).

At the level of energy systems:

3 *Technical coefficients on energy systems.* These data provide the input for the assessment of production factors required (consumption of energy carriers, human labour, land, etc.) and the net supply of energy carrier provided by the most significant energy technologies employed in the system. This information typically includes:

- i net supply of energy carriers;
- ii average size of plants (unit's power capacity);
- iii operation load (number of hours of use per year, as defined in Chapter 8, section 8.5);
- iv capacity load (fraction of the total unit's capacity actually used, averaged over the year, as defined in Chapter 8, section 8.5);
- v internal consumption of energy carriers (electricity and fuels);
- vi requirements of labour, land and water (either aggregate or per plant);
- vii significant types and quantities of waste or pollution generated;
- viii facilities' lifetime and construction time.

14.3.2 Logical framework

The logical framework adopted in the diagnostic analysis consists of a succession of logical steps dealing with different forms of energy:

- *Step 1: PES/imports category split*

  Step 1 distinguishes three categories of energy products: 1) imports in the form of primary energy sources (expressed in GER) that are used for generating electricity; 2) imports in the form of EC that are directly consumed in the different sectors of society (end uses); and 3) domestic primary energy sources (supplied locally). In addition, exports of EC are also identified so as to equilibrate the energy balances.

- *Step 2: GER (convention) and EC split*

  Step 2 evaluates the GER of each of the energy products and establishes the distribution among the different EC generated. To this purpose, we track which of the energy products (PES, imports) are used to generate what energy carriers (thermal, mechanical). In dealing with non-equivalent forms of energy (GER/PES and EC-thermal and EC-electrical), the formal evaluation of GER is based on a convention about the equivalence between quantities expressed in GER-thermal referring to flows of energy carriers. Using the partial substitution method described in Chapter 8, we can assume:

GER-thermal/EC-thermal = 1.0

GER-thermal /EC-electric = 2.6 (1/0.385)

Note that, in strict terms, these GER/EC ratios can be calculated only after having characterized the end uses. However, the latter characterization in turn would require the use of GER/EC equivalent ratios (impredicativity of energy analysis). Therefore, in this initial step, we are using standard values (1.0/1.0 and 2.6/1.0) only to have a first division of the total flow of EC between thermal and mechanical EC. For the final characterization of the metabolic pattern, obtained in step 7, we use a more refined assessment of the ratios GER/EC (calculated for each specific country and each specific year after looking at the profile of end uses).

- *Step 3: GSEC and losses*

  Step 3 evaluates the gross supply of energy carriers (GSEC), split into thermal or mechanical, as well as the losses of distribution for each energy product. Distribution losses are assumed to be negligible for thermal energy. This step allows us to calculate the net supply of energy carriers (NSEC) generated by each PES and import category.

- *Step 4: characterization of the hypercycle*

  Step 4 characterizes the internal investment of energy carriers (conversion losses, as thermal energy and mechanical energy) and other production factors (power capacity, human activity, land use, water throughput) in the hypercyclic part (EM sector) of the system.

- *Step 5: NSEC–end uses bifurcation*

  Step 5 quantifies the end uses corresponding to each PES and import category based on the estimate of NSEC derived from steps 3 and 4. When focusing on energy supply issues, the end uses can be divided into dissipative, hypercyclic (consumed in the EM sector) and export.

- *Step 6: characterization of REUD*

  Step 6 characterizes the requirements of end uses in the dissipative compartment (REUD) of the system, which correspond to the consumption of energy carriers (thermal and mechanical) and of other production factors (e.g. power capacity, human activity, land use, water throughput) for the functions expressed in this macro-compartment.

- *Step 7: GER (iterative) for PES/import categories*

  Step 7 is the formal assessment of the total GER of each PES/import category using the iterated values for the GER/EC ratios. In this step, the standard values indicated in step 2 (1.0 for thermal and 2.6 for mechanical/electrical) have to be corrected, in case the specific value of GER/EC ratios calculated for a particular country and a particular year from the profile of end uses is significantly different from these benchmarks (see Diaz-Maurin 2013, chap. 3). In the case of South Africa in 2009, the difference was negligible, and we maintained the original benchmarks.

- *Step 8: diagnostics of the exosomatic metabolism*

  Step 8 is the formal characterization of the diagnostics of the energetic metabolism of the system. This step summarizes information about the energetic metabolism for the purpose of having an informed discussion about the other dimensions of the nexus (money, food, water, land). Four key pieces of information obtained in this step are:

  i quantification of the non-linear relation between final energy end use and primary energy source requirement due to the internal autocatalytic loop of energy carriers (hypercycle);
  ii characterization of the various flows at different levels using different categories of accounting for distinct forms of energy (mechanical and thermal);
  iii specification of the requirement of production factors in both the energy and mining sector and the other sectors of the economy;
  iv definition of a set of technical coefficients for the various PES that, when adopting the rationale of the energy return on investment (EROI), make it possible to assess the quality of energy sources in relation to the expected characteristics of the energy and mining sector of the given society.

Once the diagnostic characterization has been performed it becomes possible to apply the MuSIASEM accounting system to a simulation analysis, focusing here on the impact on the existing exosomatic metabolic pattern of introducing alternative energy sources (e.g. CSP and woody biomass).

14.4 Integrated assessment of the potential of CSP and woody biomass for electricity production

In this assessment we use the MuSIASEM toolkit in a simulation mode to characterize two options for generating electricity with alternative primary energy sources in South Africa: concentrated solar power and woody biomass. These sources are currently not used in South Africa to generate electricity.

1 *Concentrated solar power:* power tower systems similar to the one considered for the 50MW Bokpoort CSP power plant in South Africa under the UN's CDM programme (UNFCCC 2012). For this scenario, we used data referring to the similar 20MW Gemasolar plant in Spain with molten salt storage and wet cooling (Torresol Energy 2011), as well as data from the literature on the CSP potential in South Africa (Fluri 2009) and on the requirement of production factors for this type of plant (Larrain and Escobar 2012).

2 *Woody biomass for electricity production:* dry woodchips production from forestry residue in South Africa. For this scenario, we used data from the literature (Pimentel *et al.* 2002) and from the Centre for Renewable and Sustainable Energy Studies of Stellenbosch University (CRSES 2013).

14.4.1 Present contributions of primary energy sources to the EROI of the EM sector and to the SEH of the whole society

In order to assess the performance of these two alternative PES, we start by characterizing the present contribution to the EROI of the current mix of PES used in the EM sector of South Africa, including in this analysis the effect of imports. In this way we will have a set of benchmarks against which to assess the effect of the adoption of new alternative PES. The resulting overview is given in Table 14.3.

The scheme used in Table 14.3 follows the logic of accounting presented in Figures 8.2 and 8.4. For example, the ratio between the output (750PJ-EC) and input (2.6PJ-EC) of energy carrier electric for fossil fuels, equalling 288:1, refers only to the actual flows of energy carriers consumed by the various facilities (mines, refineries and power plants) making up these energy systems for their own operation (described by four standard unit operations: mining, refining, generating power and handling waste/pollution; see Diaz-Maurin and Giampietro 2013). This ratio does not include the energy involved in the conversion of fossil energy into electricity. The amount of energy dissipated in the power plant is accounted for as output thermal in the output/input describing the PES energy (e.g. for electricity generated with fossil fuels this quantity would be equal to 2.61/1 GER/EC × 750 PJ-EC = 1,960 PJ-PES). This explains also the sign of infinity that would be obtained if one considered the output/input of energy carriers of the process of importing fossil fuels (indicating that the output/input is extremely large!). What matters for our assessment is the set of four ratios determined by the overall performance of the EM sector in terms of: 1) 'PES energy out' and 'physical gradients in' (calculated twice for thermal and mechanical energy); and 2) 'joules of EC out' and 'joules of EC in' (calculated twice for thermal and electric energy). When carrying out this analysis one discovers that the mix of PES used in South Africa corrected by the effect of the imports implies an output/input of 205:1 for electricity and 56:1 for thermal energy carriers (heat and fuels). Note that this characterization of the EROI based on two output/input ratios for thermal and electric energy carriers can only be applied to the level of the whole EM sector. In fact, it is an emergent property of the whole EM sector, reflecting: 1) the characteristics of individual processes of exploitation of PES; and 2) the relative contribution of the various PES to the overall domestic generation of GSEC.

Starting from this analysis of energy flows within EM we can now evaluate the implications of these values in relation to external and internal constraints. To this purpose, we put in evidence the relation between the use of production factors by the EM sector and the use of production factors by the rest (dissipative compartment) of society. This is illustrated in Table 14.4.

Table 14.3 Present contribution of the various PES to the EROI of the EM sector of South Africa and the effect of imports

PES/imports categories			*Primary energy sources*		*Energy carriers*	
			Thermal PJ-PES	*Mechanical PJ-PES*	*Thermal PJ-EC*	*Electricity PJ-EC*
Local supply of PES	Fossil fuels	Output	5,558	N/A	3,600	750
		Input	tonnes of coal, tonnes of oil, m^3 of gas	N/A	37	2.6
	Nuclear	Output	126	N/A	N/A	42
		Input	tonnes of uranium	N/A	3	1.5
	Biofuels	Output	609	N/A	600	3.4
		Input	ha of crops	N/A	60	negl.
	Wind, hydro, PV, others	Output	N/A	7.1	negl.	5.9
		Input	N/A	m/s blowing wind, W/m^2 solar radiation, water kinetic energy	negl.	negl.
Imports as GER	Fossil fuels	Output	19	N/A	1,200	7.2
		Input	N/A	N/A	1	0.03
Imports as EC	Fossil fuels	Output	N/A	N/A	260	negl.
		Input	N/A	N/A	negl.	negl.
	Electricity	Output	N/A	N/A	N/A	40
		Input	N/A	N/A	negl.	negl.
					Output/input EC-thermal 56:1	**Output/input EC-electric 205:1**

Source: Elaboration of the data of Tables 14.1 and 14.2.

Table 14.4 Moving from the characteristics of the EROI of the EM sector to the characteristics of the SEH of the whole society

Diagnostic analysis	*Flow elements*			*Fund elements*			
	ET-thermal (PJ-EC/y)	*ET-electric (PJ-EC/y)*	*Water (hm^3/y)*	*HA (10^9 h/y)*	*LU (10^6 ha)*	*PC-thermal (GW-REU/y)*	*PC- electric (GW-REU/y)*
Whole (*n*)	4,352	794	41,000	454	100	345	403
Dissipative part (*n−1*)	4,234	789	39,000	453	100	342	403
Hypercycle (EM sector only!) (*n−1*)	117	5	890	0.46	negl.	2.6	0.13
Strength of exosomatic hypercycle (SEH) = whole/ hypercycle	37	155	46	979	N/A	132	3,029

Table 14.4 shows the use of production factors by 1) the whole society (top row); 2) the dissipative compartment; and 3) the EM compartment. With this information we can describe the strength of the exosomatic hypercycle (when considering only the metabolism of exosomatic energy) using a data array – the bottom row – in which each element is the ratio between the total amount of production factor used by society and the amount of production factors consumed in the EM sector. For example, the first element of this data array indicates that the society as a whole uses 37 times more thermal energy carriers than the EM sector; the second element indicates that the society is using 155 times more electricity than the EM sector; when considering human activity the society as a whole uses 979 times more human activity than the EM sector. In this way, we obtain a set of 'expected' characteristics of the performance of the energy sector based on the present (observed) situation.

14.4.2 The simulation step: analysing the potential contributions of concentrated solar power and electricity from biomass

We first define the set of characteristics of these two new alternative energy sources in relation to the potential contribution they could give to the EROI of the EM sector of South Africa. This analysis, based on the scheme illustrated in Chapter 8 (Figure 8.4), is shown in Table 14.5.

For each of the two PES we individuate a set of the technical coefficients determining the contribution to the EROI of the specific exploitation. These characteristics are defined per 'unit of plant size'. That is, we can calculate a series of 'output' flows and 'input' flows, observed at the local scale (at the plant level) used to characterize the process of exploitation per typology of plant. Following the scheme given in Figure 8.4, this characterization is obtained by defining: 1) two ratios of inputs and outputs referring to the interface of external view and internal view – the amount of physical gradients required as input and the associated quantity of energy generated by the PES (in relation to thermal and mechanical energy); 2) two ratios of inputs and outputs referring to the internal view only – the amount of energy carriers generated by the exploitation and

Table 14.5 Estimated contribution of CSP and woody biomass (per hectare of plant) to the EROI of the EM sector of South Africa

PES/imports categories		*Primary energy sources*		*Energy carriers*	
		Thermal GJ-PES	*Mechanical*	*Thermal GJ-EC*	*Electricity GJ-EC*
Woody biomass (from residues)	Output	45	N/A	0	15
	Input	1 ha	N/A	1.2	negl.
CSP (100MW)	Output	1,800	N/A	0	780
	Input	1 ha	N/A	140	20

consumed because of the exploitation for the operation of the power plants (in relation to thermal and electric energy). These assessments refer to a unitary size of plant, in this case per hectare of plant (alternatively, these coefficients could have been assessed per unit of power capacity).

Owing to the nature of the exercise (just to illustrate the application of the methodology) and to the fact that detailed information on the performance of these PES in South Africa is not available, we estimated these values using a set of technical coefficients taken from the literature:

1 For CSP the assumptions (after Larrain and Escobar 2012) are: size of power plant 100MW; area of plant 180ha (1.8ha per MW of power capacity); and average solar radiation 2,700kWh/m^2/year. The outputs are: 3,230TJ thermal (provided by solar radiation); and 1,400TJ electricity (produced by the plant). The inputs of EC refer only to operation and maintenance (per year) and the construction of the plant (discounted over a lifespan of 30 years).
2 For woody biomass the assumptions (after Pimentel *et al.* 2002) are: the amount of biomass per hectare is 3t (with a thermal content 15GJ/t). The outputs are: 45GJ thermal (provided by biomass); and 15GJ electricity (conversion thermal to electricity 3/1). The input of thermal EC refers only to the collection of biomass – 1.2GJ of fuel per ha.

The information in Table 14.5 allows us to define a relation between the requirement of the production factor (in this case the land area for gathering sufficient solar energy to produce the output of 'process heat') and the resulting net supply of energy carrier (electricity) to society for the type of power plant considered. In this way, we can characterize the two alternative energy sources in relation to external constraints: the spatial constraints on potential sites. At the same time we can assess the requirement of production factors used in the exploitation process. This characterization of the technical performance of power plants, referring to the local scale, can be 'scaled up'. In order to do so, we have to use a quantitative definition of how many plants exploiting this particular PES will be operational in the future.

As regards CSP, the spatial constraints or exclusion criteria are determined by Fluri (2009):

1 the availability of direct normal solar irradiation (DNI greater than 7.0kWh/m^2);
2 the slope (less than 2 per cent);
3 the distance to the existing transmission grid (less than 20km).

A spatial analysis of these external constraints and the resulting potential net supply of electricity for South Africa are illustrated in Figure 14.2.

As regards woody biomass, spatial constraints or exclusion criteria are determined by CRSES (2013):

1 availability of biomass resources (forests, excluding protected areas);
2 the biomass land productivity;
3 logistics for transportation.

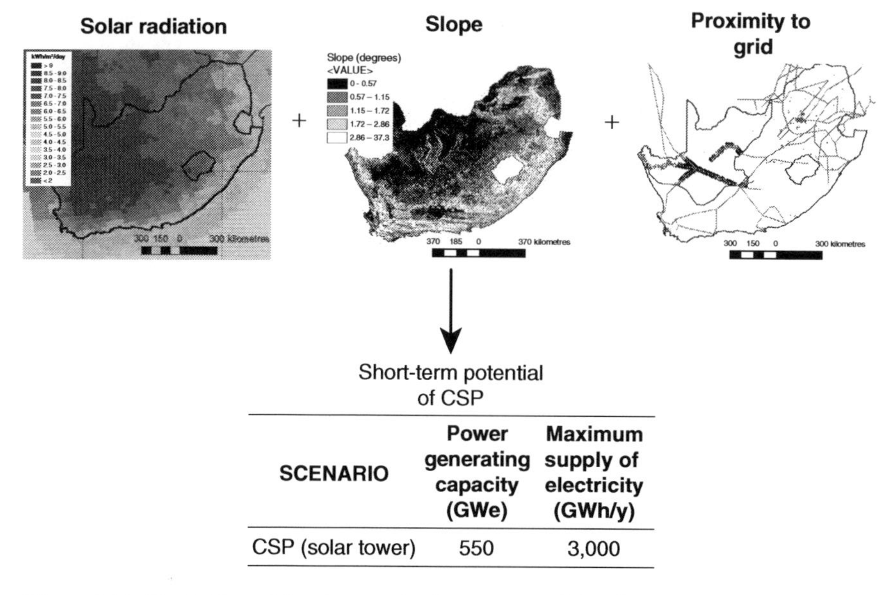

SCENARIO	Power generating capacity (GWe)	Maximum supply of electricity (GWh/y)
CSP (solar tower)	550	3,000

Figure 14.2 Illustration of the characterization process of the short-term potential of CSP electricity production in relation to external constraints

Source: Elaboration of data from Fluri (2009).

A spatial analysis of these external constraints and the resulting potential net supply of electricity for South Africa are illustrated in Figure 14.3.

The data in Figures 14.2 and 14.3 show that the short-term potential of electricity production from CSP and woody biomass in South Africa is significantly limited by external constraints. Given these technical coefficients and suitable locations, these two PES could supply only 1.2 per cent and 2.3 per cent respectively of the total amount of electricity produced in South Africa in 2009.

After defining the maximum supply that these two PES could provide (under the criteria defining external constraint), we calculated the requirement of production factors that would have to be invested in the energy and mining sector to generate this amount of electricity, that is, to increase the actual supply of 3.5 per cent. This information is given in Table 14.6.

Finally, in Table 14.7 we illustrate the effect of the addition to the actual mix of PES of CSP and woody biomass for electricity production on the metabolic pattern of exosomatic energy of South Africa.

We see that in this scenario the strength of the exosomatic hypercycle has been negatively affected by the addition of CSP and woody biomass to the existing mix of primary energy sources. When considering the big picture, exploitation of the 'maximum short-term potential' of CSP and woody biomass, equal to 3,000GWh (an increase of 1.2 per cent of total electricity production) and 5,900GWh (an increase of 2.3 per cent of total electricity production) respectively, causes changes in the EM sector (an increase in the requirement of production factors)

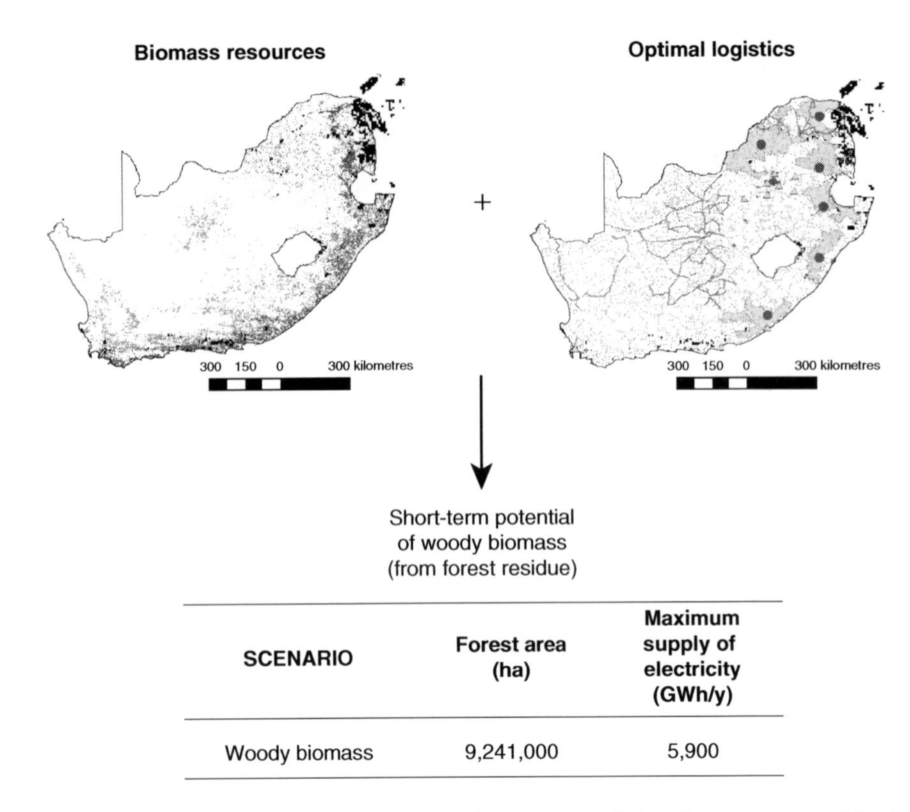

SCENARIO	Forest area (ha)	Maximum supply of electricity (GWh/y)
Woody biomass	9,241,000	5,900

Figure 14.3 Illustration of the characterization process of the short-term potential of woody biomass electricity production in relation to external constraints

Source: Elaboration of data from CRSES (2013).

that will significantly diminish the strength of the exosomatic hypercycle. Indeed, the adoption of these two alternative energy sources, when compared with fossil energy and imports, would imply an increase in the demand for production factors much larger than the increase in the supply of energy carriers they provide. The implications of this effect in terms of desirability have been discussed in Chapter 11.

14.5 Lessons learned from this case study

This case study shows that the MuSIASEM toolkit can be tailored to specific issues when focusing on just one dimension – in this case energy – whereas it keeps information on other relevant dimensions that could be expanded 'à la carte' depending on the purpose of the study. In this case we used a set of criteria defining external constraints not including water availability, soil characteristics and critical environmental loads, but these criteria could be easily included in the

Table 14.6 Profile of investment of production factors and resulting supply of energy carriers for the exploitation of CSP and woody biomass in the South African energy sector

New PES categories	*Consumption of production factors*							*Supply of energy carriers*	
	Energy throughput thermal (PJ-EC/y)	*Energy throughput electric (PJ-EC/y)*	*Water (hm^3/y)*	*Labour (10^6 h/y)*	*Managed land (ha)*	*Power capacity thermal (MW)*[a]	*Power capacity electric (MW)*[b]	*NSEC thermal (PJ-EC)*	*NSEC electric (PJ-EC)*
CSP (solar tower)	0.7 (0.6%)	0.1 (1.6%)	9.1 (1%)	2.7 (0.6%)	5,100 (negl.)[c]	10 (0.4%)	4 (2.6%)	–	10 (1.2%)
Woody biomass for electricity (from forest residue)	11 (10%)	1.1 (22%)	N/A (–)	120 (26%)	9,271,000 (9%)[c]	148 (6%)	47 (36%)	–	19 (2.3%)

Sources: Elaboration of data from Protermosolar (2011), Torresol Energy (2011), Larrain and Escobar (2012) and IRENA (2013) for CSP; and Pimentel *et al.* (2002), Fluri (2009), FSA (2010) and CRSES (2013) for woody biomass.

Notes:
Values between parentheses are the corresponding fraction from the overall EM sector (current), except as otherwise indicated.
a Assuming 25% efficiency and 60% utilization factor (see Chapter 8).
b Assuming 80% efficiency and 60% utilization factor (see Chapter 8).
c As a fraction of the whole society.

Table 14.7 Changes in the characteristics of the SEH of South Africa determined by a change in the characteristics of the EROI of the EM sector

Simulation analysis	*Flow elements*			*Fund elements*			
	ET-thermal (PJ-EC/y)	*ET-electric (PJ-EC/y)*	*Water (hm^3/y)*	*HA (Ghr/y)*	*LU (10^6 ha)*	*PC-thermal (GW-REU/y)*	*PC-electric (GW-REU/y)*
Whole (n)	4,364	796	41,000	454	100	345	403
Dissipative part ($n-1$)	4,234	789	39,000	453	91	342	403
Hypercycle (EM sector only!) ($n-1$)	129	6	900	0.59	9	2.8	0.18
Strength of exosomatic hypercycle (SEH) = whole/hypercycle	34 (−9%)	125 (−19%)	46 (−1%)	774 (−21%)	11 (N/A)	125 (−6%)	2191 (−28%)

Source: Elaboration of data from Tables 14.4 and 14.6.

analysis following the same procedure. Again we warn the reader that this exercise has been done with the sole goal of illustrating the approach and by no means should this set of data be considered as a reliable quantitative assessment referring to the potential application of these technologies in South Africa. In a real application, all the assumptions and the technical coefficients used in the analysis should be double-checked with local experts and local actors. However, this was not the goal of this case study. This case study had the goal of illustrating that the proposed method of accounting relies on relatively simple and easily accessible datasets – in this case national statistics about energy supply and demand provided by the International Energy Agency and World Bank – and technical coefficients available in the literature. The flexibility of the method makes it possible to provide a rapid appraisal in relation to internal and external constraints across scales and dimensions of analysis so as to highlight possible trade-offs when changing the mix of primary energy sources in different scenarios.

Acknowledgement

We would like to thank Alan C. Brent and Johann Görgens from the Centre for Renewable and Sustainable Energy Studies (CRSES) for providing data on CSP and woody biomass, Willem Nel from Sustainable Concepts for his advice on energy statistics in South Africa, and Eduardo García Iglesias from Protermosolar for providing information on CSP in Spain.

15 Resource accounting for sustainability assessment

Mario Giampietro, Richard J. Aspinall, Jesus Ramos-Martin and Sandra G.F. Bukkens

Summary

This chapter revisits the themes of the book in the context of the Routledge Explorations in Sustainability and Governance series, of which this text is the first. The development of this multi-scale, multi-dimensional accounting framework for analysis of the nexus of food, energy and water uses theory and lessons from complexity science to address a globally significant challenge for analysis in sustainability. In our view, making the approach operational represents a step toward the development of a quantitative post-Cartesian science that can directly address some of the most complex issues of sustainability and change that are currently faced.

15.1 Introduction

This book has introduced a quantitative, multi-scale, multi-dimensional and multi-domain approach, based on accounting resources as funds and flows, for diagnostic analysis and simulation of the food, energy and water nexus. The approach integrates flows of food, energy and water with funds of human population, land use and power capacity; financial wealth and environmental impacts are also considered. The approach is accounting based in examining flows of food, energy and water as input–outputs, and funds of human, natural and technological capital. The methodologies and techniques used are founded in concepts from complex systems theory (Chapter 2), systems perspectives on societal and ecosystem metabolism (Chapter 3), the flow-fund model of bioeconomics (Chapter 4), and the structures and functions of coupled human–environment systems (Chapter 5) organized, irreducibly, at multiple scales. The approach also draws heavily on insights from interdisciplinary thinking, experience and practice. The analytical approach is formally implemented using a series of transparent grammars (Chapters 7–9), GIS techniques (Chapter 10), and a structured and explicit suite of interconnections and interdependencies across scales and domains, which are expressed through a Sudoku effect provided by a variety of fund-based boundary constraints, requirements for coherence and congruence between and within scales, and explicit multiple interactions (Chapter 11).

In this chapter, we consider the framework and method provided by MuSIASEM as an approach to resource accounting for sustainability assessment. This is discussed in the contexts of 1) the distinctive characteristics and challenging demands of sustainability science, and 2) scientific approaches to sustainability, which are the purpose of the Routledge Explorations in Sustainability and Governance book series, of which this text is the first.

15.2 MuSIASEM and sustainability science

The nature, information needs, and policy and management challenges of sustainability represent a class of questions and problems that conventional scientific approaches based on reductionism, and on separated disciplinary structures and knowledge, struggle to address. Sustainability challenges, and the policy imperatives for sustainable development, can be recognized by a set of distinctive characteristics that prescribe the approaches needed for their resolution (Clayton and Radcliffe 1996; Kates *et al.* 2001; Martens 2006; Bettencourt and Kaur 2011; Quental *et al.* 2011):

1. holistic, requiring consideration of the whole system, as well as its parts;
2. complex, with non-linear dynamics, and exhibiting emergent properties and adaptation;
3. irreducible, focusing on the operation and function of the whole system, and not capable of analysis by considering sub-elements or subparts of the system;
4. contingent;
5. integrative, requiring multiple perspectives from theoretical and applied sciences, as well as including participation from a wide range of actors;
6. multi-scale, often being hierarchically multi-level, and spanning spatial (global–regional–local) and temporal (intergenerational) scales;
7. multi-dimensional, involving multiple domains (including, at least, economic, environmental and socio-cultural);
8. normative;
9. subjective;
10. spanning scientific theory, practice and policy;
11. ambiguous; and
12. open to multiple interpretations.

In response, a general 'sustainability science' has grown to address problems with these characteristics (Kates *et al.* 2001; Bettencourt and Kaur 2011; Kates 2011).

The nexus provides a fundamentally important area for the extension and application of sustainability science. The coupled problems of the food, water and energy nexus, and its coupling to projected global population growth and environmental changes, display all the distinctive characteristics of sustainability science. They are also central to scientific and policy debates over sustainability and future human security at global, regional, national and local scales (Beddington 2010; Godfray *et al.* 2010; Foley *et al.* 2011).

In this context, MuSIASEM provides an important advance in quantitative assessment in sustainability science. MuSIASEM uses an accounting model of flows and funds, within the formalized understanding of dynamics that is provided by the perspectives of 1) system metabolism and 2) grammars of component system function and interactions, to generate information that analyses the viability, feasibility and desirability of both the existing system metabolism and proposed scenarios, for a specific multi-scale coupled system. Coupling flows of food, energy and water to funds of human activity, land use and power capacity, with links to environmental impact and economic wealth, at multiple scales, addresses many of the characteristics of sustainability problems that are listed above. Using MuSIASEM within participatory approaches, as we advocate, increases its utility from science, and potentially takes it directly into policy and practice, encouraging discussion, debate and decision making as the data and materials used in MuSIASEM are collected by the relevant communities.

The benefits of MuSIASEM to policy and practice arise from:

1 the strong theoretical scientific base in complexity science and bioeconomics;
2 the use of resource accounts and grammars as (relatively) simple mechanisms for understanding the component systems, and for analysis and integration, with the accounts having the additional benefit of demanding that each value represented in the account is backed by further data in the form of additional tables, the values being linked by simple arithmetic functions and congruence rules;
3 the inclusion of a wide set of topical areas (food, energy, water, human population, land use and environmental systems as natural capital, economy and wealth) into a coherent, single and holistic analytical framework in which their interaction and co-dependencies can be described (diagnostic mode) and explored (simulation mode); and
4 the synergies within the flow-fund accounts, taken as an integrated, multi-scale whole, that describe the viability, feasibility and desirability of both the whole system and its parts.

15.3 Resource accounting for sustainability assessment with the MuSIASEM approach

The MuSIASEM approach has been developed by taking the specific characteristics of sustainability science seriously.

The procedures and processes of MuSIASEM clearly acknowledge that scientists are part of the observed system. To do this, MuSIASEM acknowledges the unavoidable existence of a bias in the series of choices of:

1 issue definition (the relevance of the narrative, or story, to the existence of goals and problems);

2 narratives about the problem (what the system is about and what it does); and
3 what to observe and how to observe it.

Thus, we acknowledge that the MuSIASEM toolkit does not generate the 'right' perception and representation of a given situation, nor does it generate the 'best possible' perception, and not even necessarily a good perception. What we claim is that the MuSIASEM toolkit generates one of many possible perceptions and representations of a given situation.

- *MuSIASEM is semantically open and provides a toolkit for handling many non-equivalent perceptions and representations of the observed system, and allows them to be integrated and compared.* MuSIASEM thus gives insight into the operation of the whole system, however the system is defined. It is important to emphasize that the categories of accounting, and the identities of the compartments to be used in MuSIASEM, are to be defined based on the interests and perceptions of those using the toolkit. The only condition is that categories have to create closure in the accounting scheme. Therefore, even when dealing with the same case study, it is possible to define the identity of the observed system (the compartments made up of fund and flow elements) in non-equivalent ways, depending on the different aspects of interest, and different narratives to be considered in the use of MuSIASEM.

  The MuSIASEM accounting method's semantic openness also allows use of different dimensions of analysis (socio-economic and biophysical) linked to different logics of observation (external and internal views) and different measurement schemes (flows per hour and flows per hectare), and a combination of different methods of quantitative accounting (bottom-up aggregation, top-down disaggregation) to search for meaningful results. In the process of using MuSIASEM it becomes likely that some of the characteristics of the observed systems will end up affecting the choices made by the analyst about what to observe and how, and the choices may need to be revisited. For example, in the case study of Punjab (Chapter 13), comparison of the metabolic characteristics of Punjab with the characteristics of other countries and other Indian states allowed rapid detection of an anomaly in the metabolic pattern of monetary flows. This uncovered the important role of foreign remittances in keeping the income of rural Punjab within acceptable levels. However, remittances were not considered as a relevant attribute for observation and measurement in the first run of the analysis. On the contrary, when imposing an observed system using a fixed, given and semantically closed observation protocol, based on an associated given choice of identities (and scales of observation), the most probable result is that it is the closed set of pre-analytical choices that will most affect what is observed. The analysis will then show only what the closed protocol allows to be seen.

  Finally, in the case of legitimate contrasting opinions about issue definition and the narrative to be used for analysis, the transparency of the MuSIASEM method makes explicit any existing power relations affecting decisions about how the study will be carried out. As noted earlier, since the case studies presented in Chapters 12–14 were theoretical exercises, we did not have this experience. However, the implementation of the MuSIASEM approach can be easily integrated with participatory processes.

- *The procedure clearly acknowledges that the quality criterion for quantitative analysis is its usefulness in helping an informed deliberation.* The diagnostic–simulation toolkit can be used to generate information helping to support informed discussion on the current performance of both the system studied and policy options. When used in diagnostic mode MuSIASEM provides the possibility of generating indicators 'à la carte' referring to different dimensions of analysis using a combination of intensive and extensive variables. This makes it possible to compare systems of different size (when looking at values per hour or per hectare) or to assess the feasibility of the overall metabolic pattern. When used in the simulation mode, an analysis of the Sudoku effect makes it possible to identify three different typologies of constraints determining feasibility and viability:

  i constraints that are given and very unlikely to change in the future, such as the laws of thermodynamics, and characteristics of fund elements that are difficult to change, such as the biophysical characteristics of human beings and some characteristics of biogeochemical cycles;
  ii constraints that are given but that may change in the future, such as technical coefficients describing the performance of technology (e.g. yield per hectare for crops), or characteristics of fund elements that can change, albeit at a slow speed (e.g. demographic changes, structural changes of the economy); and
  iii constraints that are given but that can be changed relatively easily and quickly, such as laws and regulations, prices, and preferences for specific goods and services.

  The integration of quantitative information in grammars and multi-level tables also makes MuSIASEM useful for application in governance, since it embeds the numbers in a rich context of relations and meanings.
- *The MuSIASEM toolkit makes management of the challenges of multiple scales and non-linearity possible.* In this book we have shown, in theoretical and practical terms, that it is possible to establish a link between the perception and representation of events across different dimensions and different scales. Moreover, by adopting the theoretical concept of metabolic pattern, it is also possible to address the implications of the unavoidable existence of a dual perception of these events – the view from inside and the view from the outside – and the resulting non-linearity of the relation between inputs and outputs implied by the existence of internal autocatalytic loops. The complexity of the information space generated with the MuSIASEM toolkit makes it possible to obtain a robust set of relations over quantities even if they refer to quantities defined at different scales. Additionally, within MuSIASEM,

quantitative assessments are not just single numbers coming from a measurement done at a given scale. Rather they are determined by a given set of expected relations between varieties of different observable attributes of the systems investigated, which can be observed and represented at different scales and in relation to different dimensions and narratives. These quantitative assessments have to provide results that are consistent with each other across domains, dimensions and scales. The ability to establish a coherent relation between relevant characteristics of different socio-economic processes (prices, subsidies, remittances), which have to be observed at different scales (crop/field level, agricultural sector level, state level, national level, international level) in order to be able to determine the viability and the feasibility of the metabolic pattern at different scales (the level of the household, the level of the aquifers, the level of the whole state), is illustrated in the Punjab case study.

- *The MuSIASEM toolkit makes handling the unavoidable mismatch between semantic, accounting categories and available data possible.* As illustrated in the different case studies, the quantification of funds and flows in the metabolic pattern is obtained by handling impredicative relations. For example, the size of the metabolic pattern of a society can be measured in terms of either fund sizes, for example the number of people (total human activity) or hectares of managed land, or flow sizes, for example the GDP or the total energy throughput. Moreover, a given metabolic pattern implies an expected relation between the size of the different fund and flow elements described at different levels and scales. However, the given typology of a metabolic pattern is always realized by a specific instance. This implies that we can study metabolic types only by looking at individual instances, which, by default, are all special. For this reason, when applying the MuSIASEM toolkit it is necessary to accept a certain degree of arbitrariness when defining accounting categories and the resulting data to be used. The analysis of the case studies illustrates this issue clearly. As a consequence of this, the analysis we present cannot be effectively done from the desk or an office. It requires the active involvement of local social actors, from decisions about the semantics of the grammars, to evaluating the robustness of the data to be used in their formalization. As we have stated, we did not use participatory processes in our analysis, and for this reason we attach a disclaimer about the meanings of the material presented in Chapters 12, 13 and 14. However, the process to be followed to apply the MuSIASEM toolkit to generate quantitative assessments (defined by the grammars) is transparent and portable. It would be straightforward to involve social actors through asking for explicit feedback about the series of choices to be made in the process of developing and applying MuSIASEM. In conclusion, we recommend that the MuSIASEM toolkit should be used with participatory processes, especially to check the quality of: 1) the pre-analytical choices about the semantics of the grammars (relevant narratives); 2) the analytical choices about the formalization of the grammars (data and models); and 3) the plausibility and relevance of scenarios.

15.4 A step in the right direction for resource accounting and sustainability assessment?

In his seminal book *The Postmodern Condition*, Lyotard predicted a crisis for a model of science that legitimates itself by making reference to some grand meta-narrative about the external world (Lyotard 1984). Since then other authors have stressed the need for the development of a new science to be used for governance. In particular, Funtowicz and Ravetz (1990, 1993) have proposed the concept of *post-normal science*, focusing on the ineptitude of conventional science, 'normal science' according to the definition given by Kuhn (1962), to generate useful input to the process of decision making when "facts are uncertain, values are in dispute, stakes high and decisions urgent" (Funtowicz and Ravetz 1993). Similarly, the concept of *civic epistemologies* has been introduced (Jasanoff 2005), to indicate the need for establishing societal institutions guaranteeing a quality control on knowledge claims, originating in science, to be used for governance. Certainly, the effective establishment of a post-normal science to be used for the governance of sustainability will have to address these key aspects.

The contribution of this book is the development of innovative analytical tools that can be applied to issues of the food, energy and water nexus and that address the distinctive characteristics of sustainability problems. The tools are also compatible with a post-Cartesian philosophy. We hope that the material presented in this book, even representing an exploratory attempt, may open a new direction of research in quantitative analysis in relation to the future development of a new type of science for governance.

Glossary

Autocatalytic loops: Processes generating an output that is partially used as input. They are associated with the existence of autopoietic and self-organizing systems.

Autopoietic systems: A class of systems that are capable of producing themselves (*auto* means 'self', and *poiesis* means 'production').

Benchmark: An indicator that serves as a standard or as point of reference by which other quantitative values may be measured or judged. In MuSIASEM a benchmark is an expected value describing one of the metabolic characteristics of a known type of socio-ecological system.

Bioeconomic pressure (BEP): An indicator of the material standard of living and hence of the *desirability* of the metabolic pattern. The stronger the BEP in a society, the larger the share of production factors that ought to be allocated to the dissipative macro-compartment. It is formalized as the ratio of the total amount of production factors (fund and flow elements) of the society over the amount of production factors (fund and flow elements) allocated to hypercyclic compartments (the larger the share in the dissipative compartment, the smaller the share in the hypercyclic compartment).

Desirability: Compatibility of the perceived performance of society with human expectations. It is one of the conditions for sustainability to be checked with the MuSIASEM approach (together with feasibility and viability).

Dissipative compartment: The part of the society consuming the surplus of food or energy generated by the hypercyclic part. Using economic jargon we can say that it includes the compartments dealing with transaction activities (service and government) and final consumption activities (household sector).

Economic energy intensity: An indicator measuring the energy consumption per unit of value added at the level of the whole economy (GDP). It is measured in MJ/USD and calculated as $EI_{AS} = TET/GDP$.

Economic labour productivity (ELP): It measures value added per hour of paid work in sector *i*. Calculated as $ELP_i = GDP_i/HA_i$.

Endosomatic metabolism: Metabolic processes taking place inside the human body determining the conversion of different types of food energy inputs, i.e. food items, into end uses, i.e. physiological processes.

Energy carrier (relates to 'secondary energy' in energy statistics): Various forms of energy inputs required by the different sectors of a society to perform their functions. The characteristics of the energy carriers are defined by the characteristics of the energy converters (exosomatic devices) using them. Energy carriers are produced by the energy sector of a society by using *primary energy sources*. Energy carriers include liquid fuels, electricity and process heat.

Energy efficiency of production (ELP/EMR) for an economic sector: Analogous to the economic energy efficiency, but it is calculated at the level of individual sectors. It measures the value added generated per unit of energy consumption in sector *i*. It is measured in 'USD/hour'/'MJ/hour' and calculated as ELP_i/EMR_i.

Energy end uses: Useful tasks or work performed by the various sectors of society when converting energy carriers into applied power. Examples of end uses include moving goods, smelting iron, building a road and air-conditioning a room. The concept of end use implies the simultaneous presence of a given mix of production factors: both flow elements, for example energy inputs, wastes and materials, and fund elements, for example power capacity and human activity.

Energy return on investment (EROI): In semantic terms it indicates the ratio between the amount of energy output obtained by society in a process of exploitation of primary energy sources and the amount of energy input required for such an exploitation. However, it is impossible to implement the accounting of this indicator using a simple ratio among two numbers. In formal terms this assessment can only be obtained using data arrays and multi-level tables (to deal with the different quality of different energy carriers and existence of non-equivalent categories of accounting for energy flows).

Exosomatic metabolic rate (EMR): Measure of the exosomatic energy consumption per hour of human activity (measured in joules per hour). It can be calculated, across different hierarchical levels, for the various compartments making up a socio-economic system ($EMR_i = ET_i/HA_i$) (in MJ/h). It can be measured in joules of energy carriers (then it is specific for the category of accounting, e.g. electricity, fuel, process heat), or it can be measured in joules of gross energy requirement (primary energy equivalent).

Exosomatic metabolism: Technical conversions of different types of energy inputs (energy carriers) into end uses that take place outside the human body, but under direct human control.

Exosomatic power level (EPL): The quantity of power capacity available per capita, measured in kW p.c. in a specific year.

External constraints: They are determined by the existing favourable boundary conditions (availability of required inputs on the supply side and required sink capacity on the waste side), which are generated by processes beyond human control. Lack of favourable boundary conditions limits the possible forms of interaction of the metabolic system with its context and as a consequence limits the possibility of expressing functions inside the system. An external constraint is present when the limits to the expansion of the activity of the system are not determined by shortage of technical capital but by shortage of natural resources (supply of inputs or sink capacity for the dumping of wastes).

Feasibility: Compatibility with external constraints. It is one of the conditions for sustainability to be checked with the MuSIASEM approach (together with desirability and viability).

Flow elements: Those elements which are either produced (appear) or consumed (disappear) during the analytical representation. They reflect the choice made by the analyst when deciding *what the system does* and *how it interacts with its context*. Examples of relevant flow elements are food, energy, income and materials.

Fund elements: Structural elements whose identity remains 'the same' during the analytical representation. They reflect the choice made by the analyst when deciding *what the system is* and *what the system is made of*. Examples include humans associated with human activity, power capacity and land.

Fund-flow (renewable) primary energy sources: Energy systems exploiting natural processes that can be considered stable in time, for example solar, hydro, wind and biomass, to generate energy carriers.

Grammar: A set of expected relations between a given set of semantic categories and a given set of formal categories. The definition of a grammar requires a pre-analytical choice of: 1) a lexicon – the typology of categories associated with the chosen narratives; 2) a vocabulary – the list of semantic and formal categories used in the representation; 3) a list of expected relations over the various semantic categories; and 4) a set of production rules determining a given formal representation of these relations – how to calculate names from the values of tokens. The grammar has to be implemented through a set of semantic decisions about the choice and use of data.

Gross domestic product (GDP): A flow defined as the added value generated by an economy (or economic sector) in one year, generally measured in US dollars (USD). GDP is taken from statistical sources.

Gross domestic state product (GDSP): Quantities of GDP produced at a subnational level by a political entity called a state or province in different countries.

Gross energy requirement (GER): A virtual quantity of thermal energy that is calculated using the partial substitution method (see Chapter 8) to assess the total energy throughput of a society. This assessment is based on five different pieces of information: 1) the mix of energy carriers required as net supply by the 'end uses' of the various compartments; 2) the choice of accounting rules used to convert assessment referring to joules of electricity into assessments referring to joules of thermal energy; 3) the mix of primary energy sources; 4) the characteristics of the various processes of conversions; and 5) distribution losses in the energy sector.

Gross food consumption: All the food consumed in society (in the sense of disappearance) for the endosomatic metabolism. This quantity includes: 1) final domestic consumption; 2) food used in the operation of the food system itself (animal feed, eggs and seeds used in the hypercycle); and 3) losses and waste in processing, distribution and storage.

Gross food supply: Total food supply entering the domestic food supply chain. It can be calculated from the FAO Food Balance Sheets by summing the following categories: local production, imports and changes of stocks.

Gross supply of energy carriers (GSEC): Corresponds to the supply of energy carriers actually made available to the society by the energy sector and by imports. This supply consists in a mix of energy carriers belonging to the categories of thermal energy (heat and fuels) and mechanical energy (electricity).

Gross value added (GVA): A measure of the economic value of goods and services produced in an area, industry or sector of an economy. It equals production minus intermediate consumption.

Gross water use (GWU): A flow of water that is managed by the society, including the water extracted from ecological funds that is actually reaching the end users, plus the quantitative losses of the distribution system and the reused water.

Human activity (HA): The fund element required for controlling the generation and the effective delivery of the applied power generated by exosomatic devices. Human activity (a proxy of the presence of humans in the functional compartment), at the local scale, is measured in hours (per year) and when accounted for within the compartments belonging to the paid work sector is also referred to as human labour.

Hypercyclic compartment of the societal metabolic pattern: The macro-compartment including the sectors responsible for generating the required flows (food, energy, mineral, water), technology and infrastructures for the whole society. Since the hypercyclic compartment uses part of these flows, technology and infrastructure for its own use, it must generate much more than it consumes (hypercycle) in order to produce an abundant supply of these production factors to the rest of society.

Intensity of power capacity (IPC) of a compartment: The ratio of energy carriers (per year) consumed in the compartment and the power capacity in the compartment. It can be calculated in relation to: 1) the aggregate flow of energy carriers (expressed in gross energy requirement equivalent) and the overall power capacity (electric and thermal); or 2) a specific type of energy carrier (e.g. electricity) and its corresponding power capacity. It depends on the utilization factor of the power capacity, which is the product of operation load (the hours of use in a year) and the capacity load (the fraction of the maximum power capacity used during operation, averaged over the year).

Internal constraints: They are determined by combining information referring to different levels: 1) local-scale metabolic characteristics – the technical coefficients of a given converter to convert an energy input into useful work at a given rate or the rate of evapotranspiration of a given crop per hectare, or the conversion of grain fed to animals into meat; and 2) medium-scale metabolic characteristics determining the congruence between the total amount of production factors and their requirement in each of the functional compartments (the so-called Sudoku effect) of MuSIASEM determined by the organization of data in multi-level tables. Lack of viable operating conditions limits the possibility of expressing functions inside the system and as a consequence limits the possibility of interaction that the metabolic system has with its context. An internal constraint is present when the limits to the expansion of the activity of the system are not determined by shortage of natural resources (supply of inputs or sink capacity for the dumping of wastes) but by the impossibility of taking advantage of them.

Land use (LU): Hectares of land included in one of the categories used for the accounting of managed land. It represents the social and economic functions and purposes of land.

Managed land (ML): The part of terrestrial ecosystems that is being used primarily for human activities. Managed land is characterized by the fact that its metabolic characteristics (quantity and quality of standing biomass, density of flows per hectare) are not determined solely by natural processes but are also determined by human management.

Metabolic system: Any system using energy, materials and other natural resources to maintain, reproduce and improve its own existing structures and functions.

Net food supply (NFS): The quantity of food products and nutrient carriers utilized at the level of the household.

Net supply of energy carriers (NSEC): The amount of the energy carriers of different types required by the set of functional compartments of the society (including exports) in a given mix.

Net water use (NWU): Flows of water, assessed at the local and the global scale, that effectively reach the end users and provide them with a service.

Non-equivalent descriptive domain: Two descriptive domains are non-equivalent when they use representations of metrical relations (perception of space) and temporal relations (perception of time) not reducible to each other, for example the observation of a face obtained using a microscope and a telescope, or the analysis of temporal variation through geological eras and in a 110m hurdle race at the Olympic Games. Two descriptive domains are non-equivalent if it is impossible to: 1) establish a logical relation between the definitions of boundaries for the same system across the two representations; 2) find a measuring scheme providing a common set of data valid for the two representations; 3) identify a combination of resolution (grain) and extent compatible with the two representations. As a consequence, the internal relations of a given system when represented using non-equivalent descriptive domains are based on a set of observable attributes, variables and parameters that are logically incoherent: they cannot be reduced to a single model.

Power capacity (PC): The fund element associated with exosomatic devices operating in the functional compartments of society. It is defined as the ability to convert a flow of an energy carrier input into a flow of applied power at the local scale in order to express a defined task (function). Power capacity is measured in kilowatts (kW).

Primary energy source (relates to 'primary energy' in energy statistics): An energy system capable of taking advantage of physical gradients expressed in biophysical units (not in energy units!) – e.g. tons of coal, cubic metres of gas, tons of uranium, mass and speed of either blowing wind or falling water, intensity of sun radiation, tons of biomass – to make available an amount of 'energy input' usable to generate energy carriers. The accounting of primary energy sources is problematic, since they are defined across two logical bifurcations for the accounting: 1) in relation to the nature of energy forms: mechanical versus thermal energy; 2) in relation to the perspective used in the perception: external versus internal view of the metabolic process.

Production factor(s): The mix of fund elements (human activity, power capacity and land use) and flow elements (energy, water, materials) required to guarantee the expression of a given function by a compartment or sub-compartment. The combination of production factors required by a given compartment is described by the data array of 'end uses'.

Societal appropriation of soil (SAS): A semantic category referring to the quantitative and qualitative damage inflicted by human use (e.g. erosion, depletion, degradation) over the soil funds. SAS is the semantic category that connects the soil use by *societal* funds with the state of the *ecological* soil funds.

Societal appropriation of water (SAW): A semantic category referring to the quantitative and qualitative damage inflicted by society on water funds (e.g. water withdrawal, nitrification or bacterial contamination). SAW is the semantic category that connects the water use by *societal* funds with the state of the *ecological* water funds.

Societal metabolism: A notion used to characterize the set of conversions of energy and material flows occurring within a society that are necessary for its continued existence. This set of conversions can be analysed assuming that the society is composed of functional compartments made up of structural elements. The structural elements are the fund elements (people – associated with human activity; exosomatic devices – associated with power capacity; land – associated with land uses and ecological processes), which can be measured using extensive variables (their size). These structural elements are accounted for within functional compartments of the society, expressing specific metabolic characteristics (flow/fund ratios – intensive variables). Then the various flows associated with the functions of the various compartments can be obtained by multiplying the size of the funds by their specific flow/fund ratio: $flow_i = fund_i \times (flow/fund)_i$. The forced relation of congruence of flows across compartments defined at different levels implies that we can expect the emergence of metabolic patterns associated with different structures or functions of a socio-economic system.

Socio-ecological system: The combination of a set of processes of self-organization under human control (determining the viability of the pattern in relation to internal constraints), associated with the concept of society, coupled to a set of natural processes of self-organization beyond human control (determining the stability of boundary conditions for society and therefore the feasibility in relation to external constraints), associated with the concept of ecosystems. In socio-ecological systems societal processes determine the viability of the metabolic pattern and ecological processes determine the feasibility; however, the analysis of these two sets of processes requires the simultaneous adoption of different scales. This means that they cannot be described in a single descriptive domain (and thus they cannot be described in a single quantitative model).

Stock-flow (non-renewable) primary energy sources: Energy systems exploiting favourable physical gradients associated with stocks of material (potential chemical energy in fossil material, and potential nuclear fission energy in uranium).

Strength of the exosomatic hypercycle (SEH): An indicator of the vigour of the hypercyclic compartment determined by the quality of the natural resources exploited and the quality of the technology and the know-how used in their exploitation. The stronger is the SEH in society, the smaller the share of production factors that must be allocated to the hypercyclic macro-compartment (leaving them for the dissipative compartment). It is formalized as a data array, including the ratios of the total amounts of production factors (fund and flow elements) of the society over the amounts of production factors (fund and flow elements) allocated to the hypercyclic compartment.

Sudoku effect: An integrated set of forced relations of congruence across the characteristics determining the dynamic budgets over data arrays describing end uses included in a multi-level table. The data belonging to the MuSIASEM multi-level tables have to be consistent in relation to vertical constraints, horizontal constraints and block constraints.

Total energy throughput (TET): In general terms, the total amount of 'energy' gathered from the context of the metabolic systems and dissipated inside the metabolic system. Therefore TET can be perceived as a supply/requirement of primary energy sources (external view – 'energy' gathered from the context) and/or a supply/requirement of energy carriers (internal view – 'energy' dissipated inside). These two perceptions require the adoption of different accounting categories. In relation to the external view TET is measured in energy statistics as either gross energy requirement or total supply of primary energy sources.

Total food throughput (TFT): The quantity of food products and nutrient carriers disappearing at the level of the whole society for the nutrition of the local population. This quantity is determined by the sum of net food consumption at the household level, the food that is consumed inside the food system for the production of food products (e.g. seeds, feed and eggs) and food losses. This set of assessments refers only to the endosomatic metabolism of the local population. To calculate the total flow of food products in a society one has to add exports to TFT.

Total human activity (THA): The key fund element of human society, representing the total amount of human time available for conducting different activities. It is measured in hours (h) and calculated as THA = population size × 8,760 hours. HA_i represents the human activity allocated to activity or sector *i* per year: HA_i = hours of human activity in sector *i* per year.

Total managed land (TML): The fund element representing the total amount of land managed by the society. This amount of TML is divided into different categories of land use, such as agriculture, forestry and urban uses, which can be divided again into subcategories, for example different types of crops within agriculture.

Total power capacity (TPC): The fund element representing the total amount of power capacity controlled by society. This amount of TPC is divided into different categories, reflecting the allocation of this power capacity to the different metabolic compartments.

Total primary energy supply (energy statistics): A virtual quantity of energy that is calculated using the physical energy content method (see Chapter 8) to assess the total energy throughput of a society. It estimates a total supply of joules of 'energy commodities' to assess the contribution provided by primary energy sources. It is obtained by summing joules of thermal energy (calculated in relation to fossil energy and nuclear energy) to joules of mechanical energy (calculated in relation to hydro and wind energy). However, this sum is not admissible according to what is known in thermodynamics.

Viability: Compatibility with internal constraints. It is one of the conditions for sustainability to be checked with the MuSIASEM approach (together with desirability and feasibility).

Water appropriation (WA): See *Societal appropriation of water (SAW)*.

Water metabolic rate (WMR): A measure of the water consumption per hour of human activity within a societal compartment. It can be calculated, across different hierarchical levels, for the various compartments making up a socio-economic system ($WMR_i = WT_i/HA_i$), in m^3/h.

Water supply (WS): Quantity and quality of water provided by the water cycle to the water funds of the system. It mainly comes from precipitation or inflow from other systems.

Water throughput (WT): Total water required for the maintenance of the societal metabolism for the complete system (total) or for a given compartment (*i*). It can be given in any of the semantic categories of accounting.

References

Ahl, V. and Allen, T.F.H. (1996) *Hierarchy Theory*, New York: Columbia University Press.

Allan, J.A. (1998) Virtual water: A strategic resource. Global solutions to regional deficits. *Groundwater* 36 (4): 545–546.

Allen, T.F.H. and Hoekstra, T.W. (1992) *Toward a Unified Ecology*, New York: Columbia University Press.

Allen, T.F.H. and Starr, T. (1982) *Hierarchy: Perspectives for Ecological Complexity*, Chicago: University of Chicago Press.

Allen, T.F.H., Tainter, J.A. and Hoekstra, T.W. (2003) *Supply Side Sustainability*, New York: Columbia University Press.

Amthor, J.S. (1989) *Respiration and Crop Productivity*, New York: Springer-Verlag.

Amthor, J.S. and Baldocchi, D.D. (2001) Terrestrial higher plant respiration and net primary production, in J. Roy, B. Saugier and H. Mooney (eds), *Terrestrial Global Productivity* (pp. 33–59), London: Academic Press.

Anderson, J.R., Hardy, E.E., Roach, J.T. and Witmer, R.E. (1976) *A Land Use and Land Cover Classification System for Use with Remote Sensor Data*, Geological Survey Professional Paper 964, Washington, DC: US Geological Survey.

Andreasen, J.K., O'Neill, R.V., Noss, R. and Slosser, N.C. (2001) Considerations for the development of a terrestrial index of ecological integrity. *Ecological Indicators* 1: 21–35.

Arctur, D.K. and Zeiler, M. (2004) *Designing Geodatabases: Case Studies in GIS Data Modeling*, Redlands, CA: ESRI Press.

Arizpe-Ramos, N., Giampietro, M. and Ramos-Martin, J. (2011) Food security and fossil energy dependence: An international comparison of the use of fossil energy in agriculture (1991–2003). *Critical Reviews in Plant Sciences* 30 (1–2): 45–63.

Arrojo, P. (2006) *El reto ético de la nueva cultura del agua: Funciones, valores y derechos en juego*. Barcelona: Editorial Paidós.

Aspinall, R.J. (2002) A land-cover data infrastructure for measurement, modeling, and analysis of land-cover change dynamics. *Photogrammetric Engineering and Remote Sensing* 68: 1101–1105.

Aspinall, R.J. (2004) Modelling land use change with generalized linear models: A multi-model analysis of change between 1860 and 2000 in Gallatin Valley, Montana. *Journal of Environmental Management* 72: 91–103.

Aspinall, R.J. (2006) Editorial. *Journal of Land Use Science* 1: 1–4.

Beddington, J. (2010) Food security: Contributions from science to a new and greener revolution. *Philosophical Transactions of the Royal Society B – Biological Sciences* 365: 61–71.

Bettencourt, L.M.A. and Kaur, J. (2011) Evolution and structure of sustainability science. *Proceedings of the National Academy of Sciences of the United States of America* 108: 19540–19545.

Bhullar, A. and Sidhu, R. (2007) Integrated land and water use: A case study of Punjab. *Economic and Political Weekly* 41 (52): 5353–5357.

Bibby, J.S. and Mackney, D. (1969) *Land Use Capability Classification*, Harpenden: Rothamsted Experimental Station.

Bibby, J.S., Douglas, H.A., Thomasson, A.J. and Robertson, J.S. (1982) *Land Capability for Agriculture*, Soil Survey of Scotland Monograph, Aberdeen: Macaulay Institute for Soil Research.

Bibby, J.S., Heslop, R.E.F. and Hartnup, R. (1988) *Land Capability Classification for Forestry in Britain*, Soil Survey Monograph, Aberdeen: Macaulay Land Use Research Institute.

Blottnitz, H. von (2006) *Alternative Biofuel Crops in South Africa: What to Look For from a Life Cycle Perspective?*, Cape Town: University of Cape Town. Available at: url:http://www.corpoica.org.co/sitioweb/Documento/JatrophaContrataciones/ALTERNATIVEBIOFUELSCROPSINSOUTHAFRICA-LCA.pdf (accessed 19 March 2013).

Boulding, K.E. (1966) The economics of the coming spaceship earth, in H. Jarrett (ed.), *Environmental Quality in a Growing Economy* (pp. 3–14), Baltimore, MD: Resources for the Future/Johns Hopkins University Press.

Brown, I., Towers, W., Rivington, M. and Black, H.I.J. (2008) Influence of climate change on agricultural land-use potential: Adapting and updating the land capability system for Scotland. *Climate Research* 37: 43–57.

Brown, I., Poggio, L. and Gimona, A. (2011) Climate change, drought risk and land capability for agriculture: Implications for land use in Scotland. *Regional Environmental Change* 11: 503–518.

Brown, L.R. (2006) *Plan B 2.0: Rescuing a Planet under Stress and a Civilization in Trouble* (data in Chapter 9), Washington, DC: Earth Policy Institute. Available at: http://www.earth-policy.org/books/pb2/pb2ch9_ss4 (accessed 31 July 2013).

Burrough, P.A. and McDonnell, R.A. (1998) *Principles of Geographical Information Systems*, 2nd edn, Oxford: Oxford University Press.

Carpenter, S.R. and Kitchell, J.F. (1987) The temporal scale of variance in limnetic primary production. *American Naturalist* 129: 417–433.

Carpenter, S.R., Mooney, H.A., Agard, J., Capistrano, D., DeFries, R.S. *et al.* (2009) Science for managing ecosystem services: Beyond the Millennium Ecosystem Assessment. *Proceedings of the National Academy of Sciences of the United States of America* 106: 1305–1312.

Castán Broto, V., Allen, A. and Rapoport, E. (2012) Interdisciplinary perspectives on urban metabolism. *Journal of Industrial Ecology* 16 (6): 851–861.

Central Water Authority of the Republic of Mauritius (2012) *Annual Report July 2009 – December 2010*. Available at: http://cwa.gov.mu/English/Documents/Home%20page%20docs/CWA%20Annual%20Web.pdf (accessed 31 October 2013).

Certain, G., Skarpaas, O., Bjerke, J.W., Framstad, E., Lindholm, M. *et al.* (2011) The nature index: A general framework for synthesizing knowledge on the state of biodiversity. *PLoS ONE* 6 (4): 12.

Chave, J. and Levin, S. (2003) Scale and scaling in ecological and economic systems. *Environmental and Resource Economics* 26: 527–557.

Chung Tze Cheong, M., Ramasamy, S. and Adelaide, S. (2011) *The 2010 Land Use Map of Mauritius*, MSIRI Occasional Paper No. 41, Reduit: Mauritius Sugar Industry Research Institute (MSIRI).

CIA (2012) South Africa, in *The World Factbook*, Washington, DC: Central Intelligence Agency of the United States. Available at: https://www.cia.gov/library/publications/the-world-factbook/geos/sf.html (accessed 19 March 2013).

Cilliers, P. (1998) *Complexity and Postmodernism: Understanding Complex Systems*, London: Routledge.

Clayton, A.M.H. and Radcliffe, N.J. (1996) *Sustainability: A Systems Approach*, London: Earthscan.

Costantini, E.A.C. (ed.) (2009) *Manual of Methods for Soil and Land Evaluation*, Enfield: Science Publishers.

Cottrell, W.F. (1955) *Energy and Society: The Relation between Energy, Social Change, and Economic Development*, New York: McGraw-Hill.

CRSES (2013) Renewable energy research and education at Stellenbosch University. Presentation by W. van Niekerk and A. Brent, Centre for Renewable and Sustainable Energy Studies, Stellenbosch University, 20 February.

Daily, G.C. (ed.) (1997) *Nature's Services: Societal Dependence on Natural Ecosystems*, Washington, DC: Island Press.

Daily, G.C. and Matson, P.A. (2008) Ecosystem services: From theory to implementation. *Proceedings of the National Academy of Sciences of the United States of America* 105: 9455–9456.

Daly, H.E. (ed. and contributor) (1973) *Toward A Steady-State Economy*, San Francisco: W.H. Freeman and Co.

Daly, H.E. (1994) Operationalizing sustainable development by investing in natural capital, in A.M. Jansson, M. Hammer, C. Folke and R. Costanza (eds), *Investing in Natural Capital* (pp. 22–37), Washington, DC: Island Press.

Dhawan, B.D. (1993) Ground water depletion in Punjab. *Economic and Political Weekly* 28: 2397–2401.

Diaz-Maurin, F. (2013) *The Viability and Desirability of Alternative Energy Sources: Exploring the Controversy over Nuclear Power*. Ph.D. dissertation presented at the Universitat Autònoma de Barcelona, October. Available at: http://iaste-researchgroup.org/wp-content/uploads/PHDTHESIS_FRANCOISDIAZMAURIN.pdf.

Diaz-Maurin, F. and Giampietro, M. (2013) A 'grammar' for assessing the performance of power-supply systems: Comparing nuclear energy to fossil energy. *Energy* 49: 162–177.

Directorate of Overseas Surveys (1957) Soil map of Mauritius. D.O.S. (Misc) 317. Base map prepared from Series Y682 published by D. Survey, War Office and Air Ministry.

Directorate of Overseas Surveys (1967) Agro-climatic map of Mauritius. D.O.S. (Misc) 446. Base map prepared from Series Y682 published by D. Survey, War Office and Air Ministry.

Doing, H. (1997) The landscape as an ecosystem. *Agriculture Ecosystems and Environment* 63: 221–225.

EAGP (Economic Adviser to Government of Punjab) (2011a) *Disaggregated Estimates of Gross State Domestic Product Handbook Punjab*, Publication No. 935. Available at: http://pbplanning.gov.in/pdf/Disaggregated%20Estimates%20of%20Gross%20State%20Domestic%20Product%20-%20Punjab.pdf (accessed 29 March 2013).

EAGP (Economic Adviser to Government of Punjab) (2011b). *State Domestic Product of Punjab 2004–05 to 2009–10*, Publication No. 931. Available at: http://pbplanning.gov.in/pdf/State%20income%20punjab%20pub_GSDP.pdf (accessed 29 March 2013).

Easterling, W. and Apps, M. (2005) Assessing the consequences of climate change for food and forest resources: A view from the IPCC. *Climatic Change* 70, 165–189.

EEA (2010) Proposal for a common international classification of ecosystem goods and services (CICES) for integrated environmental and economic accounting. Paper prepared for the EEA by Centre for Environmental Management, University of Nottingham, United Kingdom, Background document ESA/STAT/AC.217, UNCEEA/5/7/Bk, Fifth Meeting of the UN Committee of Experts on Environmental-Economic Accounting, New York, 23–25 June.

Eldredge, N. and Gould, J.S. (1972) Punctuated equilibria: An alternative to phyletic gradualism, in T.J.M. Schopf (ed.), *Models in Paleobiology*, San Francisco: Freeman, Cooper and Co.

Falkenmark, M. (1995) Land–water linkages: A synopsis, in *Land and Water Integration and River Basin Management* (pp. 15–16), Rome: Food and Agriculture Organization of the United Nations.

FAO (2001) *Food Balance Sheets: A Handbook*, Rome: Food and Agriculture Organization of the United Nations. Available at: http://www.fao.org/docrep/003/x9892e/x9892e00.htm (accessed 10 December 2012).

FAO (2003) *Food Energy: Methods of Analysis and Conversion Factors*, FAO Food and Nutrition Paper 77, Rome: Food and Agriculture Organization of the United Nations. Available at: ftp://ftp.fao.org/docrep/fao/006/y5022e/y5022e00.pdf (accessed 16 December 2012).

FAO (2007) *Land Evaluation: Towards a Revised Framework*, Land and Water Discussion Paper 6, Rome: Food and Agriculture Organization of the United Nations.

FAO (2012a) Cropwat for Windows 8.0. Available at: http://www.fao.org/nr/water/infores_databases_cropwat.html (accessed November 2012).

FAO (2012b) Climwat database. Available at: http://www.fao.org/nr/water/infores_databases_climwat.html (accessed November 2012).

FAO (2013a) FAOSTAT: Food Balance Sheets. Available at: http://faostat3.fao.org/faostat-gateway/go/to/download/FB/FB/E (accessed 30 June 2013).

FAO (2013b) *Food Wastage Footprint: Impacts on Natural Resources – Summary Report*, Rome: Food and Agriculture Organization of the United Nations. Available at: http://www.fao.org/docrep/018/i3347e/i3347e.pdf (accessed 31 July 2013).

Fischer-Kowalski, M. (1997) Society's metabolism: On the childhood and adolescence of a rising conceptual star, in M. Redclift and G. Woodgate (eds), *The International Handbook of Environmental Sociology* (pp. 119–137), Cheltenham: Edward Elgar.

Fischer-Kowalski, M. and Haberl, H. (2007) *Socioecological Transitions and Global Change*, Cheltenham: Edward Elgar.

Fluri, T.P. (2009) The potential of concentrating solar power in South Africa. *Energy Policy* 37: 5075–5080.

Foley, J.A., DeFries, R., Asner, G.P., Barford, C., Bonan, G. *et al.* (2005) Global consequences of land use. *Science* 309: 570–574.

Foley, J.A., Ramankutty, N., Brauman, K.A., Cassidy, E.S., Gerber, J.S. et al. (2011) Solutions for a cultivated planet. *Nature* 478: 337–342.

Foresight (2011) *The Future of Food and Farming: Executive Summary*, London: Government Office for Science.

Foresight Land Use Futures Project (2010) *Land Use Futures: Making the Most of Land in the 21st Century: Final Project Report*, London: Government Office for Science.

FSA (2010) *The South African Forestry and Forest Products Industry 2009*, Johannesburg: Forestry South Africa. Available at: http://www.forestry.co.za/uploads/File/home/facts/SA_Forestry_Industry_2010_colour.ppt (accessed 19 March 2013).

Funtowicz, S.O. and Ravetz, J.R. (1990) *Uncertainty and Quality in Science Policy*, Dordrecht: Kluwer Academic Publishers.

Funtowicz, S.O. and Ravetz, J.R. (1993) Science for the post-normal age. *Futures* 25: 735–755.

GADM database of Global Administrative Areas (2012) Administrative boundaries map. Available at: http://www.gadm.org/ (accessed 20 November 2012).

Geist, H.J. and Lambin, E.F. (2004) Dynamic causal patterns of desertification. *Bioscience* 54: 817–829.

Georgescu-Roegen, N. (1971) *The Entropy Law and the Economic Process*, Cambridge, MA: Harvard University Press.

Georgescu-Roegen, N. (1975) Energy and economic myths. *Southern Economic Journal* 41: 347–381.

Giampietro, M. (1997a) Socioeconomic constraints to farming with biodiversity. *Agriculture, Ecosystems and Environment* 62: 145–167.

Giampietro, M. (1997b) Socioeconomic pressure, demographic pressure, environmental loading and technological changes in agriculture. *Agriculture, Ecosystems and Environment* 65 (3): 201–229.

Giampietro, M. (2002) Energy use in agriculture, in *Encyclopedia of Life Sciences*, Chichester: John Wiley & Sons. Available at: http://www.els.net/ (accessed 15 August 2013).

Giampietro, M. (2004) *Multi-Scale Integrated Analysis of Agro-Ecosystems*, Boca Raton, FL: CRC Press.

Giampietro, M. (2008) The future of agriculture: GMOs and the agonizing paradigm of industrial agriculture, in A. Guimaraes Pereira and S. Funtowicz (eds), *Science for Policy: Challenges and Opportunities*, New Delhi: Oxford University Press.

Giampietro, M. and Mayumi, K. (2000a) Multiple-scale integrated assessment of societal metabolism: Introducing the approach. *Population and Environment* 22 (2): 109–153.

Giampietro, M. and Mayumi, K. (2000b) Multiple-scale integrated assessments of societal metabolism: Integrating biophysical and economic representations across scales. *Population and Environment* 22 (2): 155–210.

Giampietro, M. and Mayumi, K. (2009) *The Biofuel Delusion: The Fallacy of Large-Scale Agro-Biofuel Production*, London: Earthscan.

Giampietro, M. and Pastore, G. (1999) Multidimensional reading of the dynamics of rural intensification in China: The AMOEBA approach. *Critical Reviews in Plant Sciences* 18 (3): 299–330.

Giampietro, M. and Pimentel, D. (1991) Model of energy analysis to study the biophysical limits for human exploitation of natural processes, in C. Rossi and E. Tiezzi (eds), *Ecological Physical Chemistry* (pp. 139–184), Amsterdam: Elsevier.

Giampietro, M. and Sorman, A.H. (2012) Are energy statistics useful for making energy scenarios? *Energy* 37 (1): 5–17.

Giampietro, M., Pimentel, D. and Cerretelli, G. (1992) Energy analysis of agricultural ecosystem management: Human return and sustainability. *Agriculture, Ecosystems and Environment* 38: 219–244.

Giampietro, M., Allen, T.F.H. and Mayumi, K. (2006) The epistemological predicament associated with purposive quantitative analysis. *Ecological Complexity* 3 (4): 307–327.

Giampietro, M., Allen, T.F.H. and Mayumi, K. (2007) Science for governance: The implications of the complexity revolution, in A. Guimaraes Pereira, S. Guedes-Vaz and S. Tognetti (eds), *Interfaces between Science and Society* (pp. 82–99), Sheffield: Greenleaf Publishing.

Giampietro, M., Mayumi, K. and Ramos-Martin, J. (2009) Multi-scale integrated analysis of societal and ecosystem metabolism (MuSIASEM): Theoretical concepts and basic rationale. *Energy* 34: 313–322.

Giampietro, M., Mayumi, K. and Sorman, A.H. (2012) *The Metabolic Pattern of Societies: Where Economists Fall Short*, Abingdon: Routledge.

Giampietro, M., Mayumi, K. and Sorman, A.H. (2013) *Energy Analysis for a Sustainable Future: Multi-Scale Integrated Analysis of Societal and Ecosystem Metabolism*, Abingdon: Routledge.

Gibson, C.C., Ostrom, E. and Ahn, T.K. (2000) The concept of scale and the human dimensions of global change: A survey. *Ecological Economics* 32: 217–239.

Glansdorff, P. and Prigogine, I. (1971) *Thermodynamics Theory of Structure, Stability and Fluctuations*, New York: Wiley.

Global Land Project (2005) *Science Plan and Implementation Strategy*, IGBP Report No. 53/IHDP Report No. 19, Stockholm: IGBP Secretariat.

Godfray, H.C.J., Beddington, J.R., Crute, I.R., Haddad, L., Lawrence, D. *et al.* (2010) Food security: The challenge of feeding 9 billion people. *Science* 327: 812–818.

Goel, V. and Bhaskaran, S. (2006) Marketing practices and distribution system of rice in Punjab, India. *Journal of International Food and Agribusiness Marketing*, 19 (1): 103–135.

GoI (Government of India) (2006) *Integrated Energy Policy: Report of the Expert Committee, Planning Division*, New Delhi: GoI. Available at: http://planningcommission.nic.in/reports/genrep/rep_intengy.pdf (accessed 31 March 2013).

GoI (Government of India) (2011a) *Annual Report 2010–11*, New Delhi: Ministry of Consumer Affairs, Food and Public Distribution – Department of Food and Public Distribution. Available at http://dfpd.nic.in/fcamin/sites/default/files/userfiles/annual201011.pdf (accessed 10 December 2012).

GoI (Government of India) (2011b) *Report on Employment and Unemployment 2011–12*, Vol. I, New Delhi: Ministry of Labour and Employment. Available at: http://pbplanning.gov.in/pdf/Second%20Annual%20EUS%20Report-Volume-I.pdf (accessed 14 December 2012).

GoI (Government of India) (2011c) *Report on Employment and Unemployment 2011–12*, Vol. II, New Delhi: Ministry of Labour and Employment. Available at: http://pbplanning.gov.in/pdf/Second%20Annual%20EUS%20Report-Volume-II.pdf (accessed 14 December 2012).

GoI (Government of India) (2011d) *Key Indicators of Household Consumer Expenditure in India 2009–2010*, New Delhi: National Statistics Organisation. Available at: http://mospi.nic.in/Mospi_New/upload/Key_Indicators-HCE_66th_Rd-Report.pdf (accessed 21 January 2013).

GoI (Government of India) (2012a) *Household Consumption of Various Goods and Services in India*, NSS 66th Round, July 2009 – June 2010, New Delhi: Ministry of Statistics and Programme Implementation.

GoI (Government of India) (2012b) *Energy Statistics 2010*. Available at: http://mospi.nic.in/mospi_new/upload/Energy_Statistics_2012_28mar.pdf?status=1&menu_id=201 (accessed 11 January 2013).

GoI (Government of India) (2013a) *Indian Petroleum and Natural Gas Statistics 2010–11*, New Delhi: Ministry of Petroleum and Natural Gas of India. Available at: http://petroleum.nic.in/pngstat.pdf (accessed 11 January 2013).

GoI (Government of India) (2013b) *State Domestic Product and Other Aggregates, 2004–05 series*, New Delhi: Ministry of Statistics and Programme Implementation.

GoK (Government of Kerala) (2013) *Gross Domestic Product of Kerala and India from 2004–05 to 2011–12*, Department of Economics and Statistics, Thiruvananthapuram: GoK.

Golubiewski, N. (2012) Is there a metabolism of an urban ecosystem? An ecological critique. *Ambio* 41 (7): 751–764.

GoP (Government of Punjab) (2011a) *Statistical Abstract of Punjab 2011*, Publication No. 930, Chandigarh: Economic and Statistical Organisation. Available at: http://punjab.gov.in/General/Abstract/default1.asp (accessed 15 January 2013).

GoP (Government of Punjab) (2011b) *Economic Survey 2011–2012*, Chandigarh: Economic and Statistical Organisation. Available at: http://pbplanning.gov.in/pdf/economicsurvey%202011-12.pdf (accessed 29 March 2013).

GoP (Government of Punjab) (2012a) *Punjab State Action Plan on Climate Change*, December, Chandigarh: Department of Science, Technology and Environment and Non-Conventional Energy. Available at: http://www.indiaenvironmentportal.org.in/files/file/Punjab_action_plan_on_Climate_change.pdf (accessed 11 October 2013).

GoP (Government of Punjab) (2012b) *Statistical Abstract of Punjab 2012*, Publication No. 938, Chandigarh: Economic and Statistical Organisation.

GoP (Government of Punjab) (2012c) *Family Budgets of Selected Cultivators in Punjab 2008–09*, Publication No. 929, Chandigarh: Economic and Statistical Organisation.

GoU (Government of Uttarakhand) (2013) Gross state domestic product at factor cost by industry, 2004–05 to 2012–13, at current prices, Directorate of Economics and Statistics. Available at: http://des.uk.gov.in/files/GSDP-NSDP_%282004-05_to_2012-13%29_-Report_as_on_15_June_2013.pdf (accessed 30 October 2013).

Goudriaan, J., Rob Groot, J.J. and Uithol, P.W.J. (2001) Productivity of agro-ecosystems, in J. Roy, B. Saugier and H. Mooney (eds), *Terrestrial Global Productivity* (pp. 301–313), London: Academic Press.

Gould, S.J. (1992) Life in punctuation. *Natural History* 101: 10–21.

Gould, S.J. and Eldredge, N. (1977) Punctuated equilibria: The tempo and mode of evolution reconsidered. *Paleobiology* 3 (2): 115–151.

Grünbühel, C.M. and Schandl, H. (2005) Using land-time-budgets to analyse farming systems and poverty alleviation policies in the Lao PDR. *International Journal of Global Environmental Issues*, 5 (3): 142–180.

Gustavsson, J., Cederberg, C., Sonesson, U., Otterdijk, R. and Meybeck, A. (2011) *Global Food Losses and Food Waste: Extent, Causes and Prevention*, Study conducted for the International Congress SAVE FOOD! at Interpack 2011, Düsseldorf, Germany, Rome: Food and Agriculture Organization of the United Nations. Available at: http://www.fao.org/docrep/014/mb060e/mb060e00.pdf (accessed 29 November 2012).

Gutman, G., Janetos, A.C., Justice, C.O., Moran, E.F., Mustard, J.F. et al. (eds) (2004) *Land Change Science: Observing, Monitoring and Understanding Trajectories of Change on the Earth's Surface*, Dordrecht: Kluwer Academic Publishers.

Hall, C.A.S., Cleveland, C.J. and Kaufman, R. (1986) *Energy and Resource Quality: The Ecology of the Economic Process*, Boulder: University Press of Colorado.

Hall, C.A.S., Balogh, S. and Murphy, D.J.R. (2009) What is the minimum EROI that a sustainable society must have? *Energies* 2 (1), 25–47. Available at: www.mdpi.com/journal/energies (accessed 30 September 2013).

Hanjra, M.A. and Qureshi, M.E. (2010) Global water crisis and future food security in an era of climate change. *Food Policy* 35: 365–377.

Hansen, D. and Hall, C.A.S. (eds) (2011) New Studies in EROI (Energy Return on Investment), special issue of *Sustainability* 3: 1773–2499. Available at: www.mdpi.com/journal/sustainability (accessed 30 September 2013).

Hoekstra, A.Y. and Chapagain, A.K. (2008) *Globalization of Water: Sharing the Planet's Freshwater Resources*, Malden, MA: Blackwell.

Holland, J.H. (1995) *Hidden Order: How Adaptation Builds Complexity*, New York: Perseus Books.

Holland, J.H. (2006) Studying complex adaptive systems. *Journal of System Science and Complexity* 19 (1): 1–8.

Holling, C.S. (1973) Resilience and stability of ecological systems. *Annual Review of Ecology and Systematics* 4: 1–23.

IAMR (Institute of Applied Manpower Research) (2011) *India Human Development Report 2011: Towards Social Inclusion*, New Delhi: Oxford University Press. Available at: http://www.pratirodh.com/pdf/human_development_report2011.pdf (accessed 23 January 2013).

IEA (International Energy Agency) (2005) *Energy Statistics Manual*. Available at: http://www.iea.org/stats/docs/statistics_manual.pdf (accessed 19 March 2013).

IFPRI (International Food Policy Research Institute) (2007) *Withering Punjab Agriculture: Can It Regain Its Leadership?* New Delhi: IFPRI.

IISS (Indian Institute of Soil Science) (2010) *GIS Based Phosphorus and Nitrogen Status of Punjab Soils*, Bhopal: IISS.

ILO (International Labour Organization) (2007) *Working Time around the World: Trends in Working Hours, Laws and Policies in a Global Comparative Perspective*, Abingdon: Routledge.

ILO (International Labour Organization) (2013) *Hours of Work, by Economic Activity*. Available at: http://laborsta.ilo.org/STP/guest (accessed 18 December 2012).

Ingram, J., Ericksen, P. and Liverman, D. (eds) (2010) *Food Security and Global Environmental Change*, Oxford: Routledge.

IRENA (International Renewable Energy Agency) (2013) *Concentrating Solar Power: Technology Brief*. Available at: http://www.irena.org/DocumentDownloads/Publications/IRENA-ETSAP%20Tech%20Brief%20E10%20Concentrating%20Solar%20Power.pdf (accessed 19 March 2013).

Jasanoff, S. (2005) *Designs on Nature: Science and Democracy in Europe and in the United States*, Princeton, NJ: Princeton University Press.

Jevons, W.S. ([1865] 1906). *The Coal Question: An Inquiry Concerning the Progress of the Nation, and the Probable Exhaustion of Our Coal Mines*, reprint of 3rd edn, New York: Augustus M. Kelley.

Kapp, K.W. (2011) *The Foundations of Institutional Economics*, Abingdon: Routledge.

Karr, J. (1999) Ecological integrity and ecological health are not the same, in P.C. Schulze (ed.), *Engineering within Ecological Constraints* (pp. 97–109), Washington, DC: National Academy Press.

Kates, R.W. (2011) What kind of a science is sustainability science? *Proceedings of the National Academy of Sciences of the United States of America* 108, 19449–19450.

Kates, R.W., Clark, W.C., Corell, R.W., Hall, J.M., Jaeger, C.C. *et al.* (2001) Sustainability science. *Science* 292: 641–642.

Kauffman, S.A. (1993) *Origins of Order: Self-Organization and Selection in Evolution*, Oxford: Oxford University Press.

Kay, J.J. (2000), Ecosystems as self-organizing holarchic open systems: Narratives and the second law of thermodynamics, in S.E. Jorgensen and F. Muller (eds), *Handbook of Ecosystems Theories and Management* (pp. 135–160), London: Lewis Publishers.

Kay, J.J. and Regier, H. (2000) Uncertainty, complexity, and ecological integrity: Insights from an ecosystem approach, in P. Crabbé, A. Holland, L. Ryszkowski and L. Westra (eds), *Implementing Ecological Integrity: Restoring Regional and Global Environmental and Human Health* (pp. 121–156), NATO Science Series, Environmental Security, Dordrecht: Kluwer Academic Publishers.

Kay, J.J. and Schneider, E.D. (1992) Thermodynamics and measures of ecosystem integrity, in D.H. McKenzie, D.E. Hyatt and V.J. McDonald (eds), *Ecological Indicators*, Vol. 1 (pp. 159–182), Proceedings of the International Symposium on Ecological Indicators, Fort Lauderdale, FL: Elsevier.

Kay, J.J., Regier, H., Boyle, M. and Francis, G. (1999) An ecosystem approach for sustainability: Addressing the challenge of complexity. *Futures* 31: 721–742.

Klingebiel, A.A. and Montgomery, P.H. (1961) *Land Capability Classification*, Washington, DC: USDA Soil Conservation Service.

Koestler, A. (1969) Beyond atomism and holism: The concept of the holon, in A. Koestler and J.R. Smythies (eds), *Beyond Reductionism* (pp. 192–232), London: Hutchinson.

Kuhn, T. (1962) *The Structure of Scientific Revolutions*, Chicago: University of Chicago Press.

Kumar, M.D., Scott, C.A. and Singh, O.P. (2013) Can India raise agricultural productivity while reducing groundwater and energy use? *International Journal of Water Resources Development*, iFirst article: 1–17. Available at: http://www.tandfonline.com/eprint/BWD2sAaiTFkIG4kmxUwr/full#.UnevmhD-p6Y (accessed 4 November 2013).

Lambin, E.F. and Geist, H. (eds) (2006) *Land-Use and Land-Cover Change: Local Processes and Global Impacts*, Berlin: Springer-Verlag.

Lambin, E.F., Turner, B.L., Geist, H.J., Agbola, S.B., Angelsen, A. *et al.* (2001) The causes of land-use and land-cover change: Moving beyond the myths. *Global Environmental Change: Human and Policy Dimensions* 11: 261–269.

Larrain, T. and Escobar, R. (2012) Net energy analysis for concentrated solar power plants in northern Chile. *Renewable Energy* 41: 123–133.

Levin, S.A. (1992) The problem of pattern and scale in ecology. *Ecology* 73: 1943–1967.

Lide, D.R. (2009) *CRC Handbook of Chemistry and Physics*, 90th edn, Boca Raton, FL: CRC Press.

Lifset, R. (2004) Probing metabolism. *Journal of Industrial Ecology* 8 (3): 1–3.

Longley, P.A., Goodchild, M.F., Maguire, D.J. and Rhind, D.W. (2010) *Geographic Information Systems and Science*, Chichester: Wiley.

Lotka, A.J. (1922) Contribution to the energetics of evolution. *Proceedings of the National Academy of Sciences* 8: 147–151.

Lotka, A.J. (1956) *Elements of Mathematical Biology*, New York: Dover Publications.

Lyotard, J.-F. (1984) *The Postmodern Condition: A Report on Knowledge*, Manchester: Manchester University Press.

Maddox, K.P. (1978) Energy analysis and resource substitution, in F.S. Roberts (ed.), *Symposium Papers: Energy Modeling and Net Energy Analysis* (Colorado Springs, CO, 21–25 August) (pp. 133–144), Chicago: Institute of Gas Technology.

Madrid, C., Cabello, V. and Giampietro, M. (2013) Water-use sustainability in socioecological systems: A multiscale integrated approach. *BioScience* 63 (1): 14–24.

Margalef, R. (1968) *Perspectives in Ecological Theory*, Chicago: University of Chicago Press.

Martens, P. (2006) Sustainability: Science or fiction? *Sustainability: Science, Practice, and Policy* 2: 36–41.

Martinez-Alier, J. (1987) *Ecological Economics: Economics, Environment and Society*, Oxford: Basil Blackwell.

Maturana, H.R. and Varela, F.J. (1980) *Autopoiesis and Cognition: The Realization of the Living*, Dordrecht: D. Reidel Publishing.

Maturana, H.R. and Varela, F.J. (1998) *The Tree of Knowledge: The Biological Roots of Human Understanding*, rev. edn, Boston, MA: Shambhala Publications.

Mayumi, K. (1991) Temporary emancipation from land: From the industrial revolution to the present time. *Ecological Economics* 4: 35–56.

Mayumi, K. (2001) *The Origins of Ecological Economics: The Bioeconomics of Georgescu-Roegen*, London: Routledge.

Mayumi, K. and Giampietro, M. 2004. Entropy in ecological economics, in J. Proops and P. Safonov (eds), *Modelling in Ecological Economics* (pp. 80–101), Cheltenham: Edward Elgar.

Mekonnen, M.M. and Hoekstra, A.Y. (2010) A global and high-resolution assessment of the green, blue and grey water footprint of wheat. *Hydrology and Earth System Sciences* 14 (7): 1259–1276.

Millennium Ecosystem Assessment (2005) *Ecosystems and Human Well-Being: Synthesis*, Washington, DC: Island Press.

Ministry of Finance and Economic Development of the Republic of Mauritius (2010) Labour force employment and unemployment based on the results of the Continuous Multi Purpose Household Survey – year 2010. *Economic and Social Indicators*. Available at: http://www.gov.mu/portal/goc/cso/ei896/cmphs.pdf (accessed 29 March 2013).

Ministry of Finance and Economic Development of the Republic of Mauritius (2012a) *Digest of Agricultural Statistics 2011*. Available at: http://www.gov.mu/portal/goc/cso/file/DigestAgric2011.pdf (accessed 21 January 2013).

Ministry of Finance and Economic Development of the Republic of Mauritius (2012b) *Digest of Statistics on Rodrigues 2011*. Available at: http://www.gov.mu/portal/goc/cso/file/DigestStatisticsRod2011.pdf (accessed 21 January 2013).

Ministry of Finance and Economic Development of the Republic of Mauritius (2012c) *Digest of Labour Statistics 2011*. Available at: http://www.gov.mu/portal/goc/cso/file/DigestLabour2011.pdf (accessed 14 December 2012).

Ministry of Finance and Economic Development of the Republic of Mauritius (2012d) *Digest of International Travel and Tourism Statistics 2011*. Available at: http://www.gov.mu/portal/goc/cso/file/DigestTravel2011.pdf (accessed 14 December 2012).

Ministry of Finance and Economic Development of the Republic of Mauritius (2012e) *Housing and Population Census 2011*, Vol. V: *Economic Characteristics*. Available at: http://www.gov.mu/portal/goc/cso/report2013/2011PCVOLV.pdf (accessed 14 December 2012).

Ministry of Finance and Economic Development of the Republic of Mauritius (2012f) *National Accounts of Mauritius 2011*. Available at: http://www.gov.mu/portal/goc/cso/file/nationalaccts.pdf (accessed 14 December 2012).

Ministry of Housing and Lands of Mauritius (2003) Settlement structure map, 2003. Available at: http://housing.gov.mu/English/Documents/Maps/map1Settlement.pdf (accessed 14 January 2013).

Moss, T. and Newig, J. (2010) Multilevel water governance and problems of scale: Setting the stage for a broader debate. *Environmental Management* 46 (1): 1–6.

MREPU (Ministry of Renewable Energy and Public Utilities of Mauritius) (2010) *Digest of Energy and Water Statistics 2010*. Available at: http://www.gov.mu/portal/goc/cso/report/natacc/energy10/energy.pdf (accessed 15 November 2012).

Nicolis, G. and Prigogine, I. (1977) *Self-Organization in Non-Equilibrium Systems*, New York: Wiley.

North, D.C. (1990) *Institutions, Institutional Change and Economic Performance*, Cambridge: Cambridge University Press.

Odum, E.P. (1968) Energy flow in ecosystems: A historical review. *American Zoologist* 8: 11–18.

Odum, E.P. (1969) The strategy of ecosystem development. *Science* 164: 262–270.
Odum, E.P. (1971) *Fundamentals of Ecology*, 3rd edn, Philadelphia: Saunders.
Odum, H.T. (1971) *Environment, Power, and Society*, New York: Wiley-Interscience.
Odum, H.T. (1983) *Systems Ecology: An Introduction*, New York: Wiley-Interscience.
Odum, H.T. (1996) *Environmental Accounting: Energy and Environmental Decision Making*, New York: John Wiley.
OECD (2013) *OECD National Accounts: Gross Domestic Product*. Available at: http://stats.oecd.org/Index.aspx?DatasetCode=SNA_TABLE1 (accessed 23 September 2013).
OECD/IEA (2011) *2009 Energy Balance for South Africa*, Paris: International Energy Agency. Available at: http://www.iea.org/stats/balancetable.asp?COUNTRY_CODE=ZA (accessed 19 March 2013).
OECD/IEA/EUROSTAT (2004) *Energy Statistics Manual*. Available at: http://epp.eurostat.ec.europa.eu/cache/ITY_PUBLIC/NRG-2004/EN/NRG-2004-EN.PDF (accessed 31 August 2013).
Ostwald, W. (1907) The modern theory of energetics. *Monist* 17: 481–515.
Ostwald, W. (1911) Efficiency. *The Independent* 71: 867–871.
Padovan, D. (2000) The concept of social metabolism in classical sociology. *Theomai Journal* 2. Available at: http://www.redalyc.org/articulo.oa?id=12400203 (accessed 7 September 2013).
Pastore, G., Giampietro, M. and Li Ji (1999) Conventional and land–time budget analysis of rural villages in Hubei province, China. *Critical Reviews in Plant Sciences* 18 (3): 331–358.
Pastore, G., Giampietro, M. and Mayumi, K. (2000) Societal metabolism and multiple-scales integrated assessment: Empirical validation and examples of application. *Population and Environment* 22 (2): 211–254.
Pimentel, D. and Pimentel, M. (1996) Energy use in grain and legume production, in D. Pimentel and M. Pimentel (eds), *Food, Energy, and Society* (pp. 107–130), Niwot: University Press of Colorado.
Pimentel, D., Herz, M., Glickstein, M., Zimmerman, M., Allen, R. *et al.* (2002) Renewable energy: Current and potential issues. *Bioscience* 52 (12): 1111–1120.
Pretty, J., Sutherland, W.J., Ashby, J., Auburn, J., Baulcombe, D. *et al.* (2010) The top 100 questions of importance to the future of global agriculture. *International Journal of Agricultural Sustainability* 8: 219–236.
Prigogine, I. (1961) *Introduction to Thermodynamics of Irreversible Processes*, 2nd edn, New York: Wiley.
Prigogine, I. (1978) *From Being to Becoming*, San Francisco: W.H. Freeman and Co.
Prigogine, I. and Stengers, I. (1984) *Order Out of Chaos*, New York: Bantam Books.
Protermosolar (2011) Macroeconomic impact of STE sector in Spain in 2011. Available at: http://www.protermosolar.com/saladeprensa/sites/default/files/comunicados/Macroeconomic%20Impact%20STE%20sector%202011.pdf (accessed 19 March 2013).
PSTC (Punjab State Transmission Corporation), State Load Dispatch Center (SLDC) (reporting year 2010–11). Available at: http://www.punjabsldc.org (accessed 11 January 2013).
Pyke, G.H. (1984) Optimal foraging theory: A critical overview. *Annual Review of Ecology and Systematics* 15: 523–575.
Quental, N., Lourenço, J.M. and Silva, F.N. da (2011) Sustainability: Characteristics and scientific roots. *Environment, Development and Sustainability* 13: 257–276.
Ramos-Martin, J., Canellas-Bolta, S., Giampietro, M. and Gamboa, G. (2009) Catalonia's energy metabolism: Using the MuSIASEM approach at different scales. *Energy Policy* 37: 4658–4671.

Raquez, P. and Lambin, E.F. (2006) Conditions for a sustainable land use: Case study evidence. *Journal of Land Use Science* 1, 109–125.

RBI (Reserve Bank of India) (2013) Appendix III: Capital receipts of states and union territories with legislature. Available at: http://rbidocs.rbi.org.in/rdocs/Publications/PDFs/03_A3SF280311.pdf (accessed 21 January 2013).

Reza, M.I.H. and Abdullah, S.A. (2011) Regional Index of Ecological Integrity: A need for sustainable management of natural resources. *Ecological Indicators* 11 (2): 220–229.

Rosen, R. (1985) *Anticipatory Systems: Philosophical, Mathematical and Methodological Foundations*, New York: Pergamon Press.

Rosen, R. (2000) *Essays on Life Itself*, New York: Columbia University Press.

SARB (South African Reserve Bank) (2010) *Annual Economic Report 2010*. Available at: http://www.resbank.co.za/Lists/News%20and%20Publications/Attachments/3614/aer2010.pdf (accessed 19 March 2013).

Saugier, B., Roy, J. and Mooney, H.A. (2001) Estimations of global terrestrial productivity: Converging toward a single number?, in J. Roy, B. Saugier and H. Mooney (eds), *Terrestrial Global Productivity* (pp. 543–557), London: Academic Press.

Scheidel, A. and Sorman, A.H. (2012) Energy transitions and the global land rush: Ultimate drivers and persistent consequences. *Global Environmental Change: Human and Policy Dimensions* 22: 588–595.

Scheidel, A., Giampietro, M. and Ramos-Martin, J. (2013) Self-sufficiency or surplus: Conflicting local and national rural development goals in Cambodia. *Land Use Policy* 34: 342–352.

Schneider, E.D. and Kay J.J. (1994) Life as manifestation of the second law of thermodynamics. *Mathematical and Computer Modelling* 19 (6–8): 25–48.

Schrödinger, E. (1967) *What Is Life?* and *Mind and Matter*, Cambridge: Cambridge University Press.

Schumpeter, J.A. (1942) *Capitalism, Socialism and Democracy*, New York: Harper.

Serrano-Tovar, T. and Giampietro, M. (2014) Multi-scale integrated analysis of rural Laos: Studying metabolic patterns of land uses across different levels and scales. *Land Use Policy* 36: 155–170.

Shuttle Radar Topographic Mapping Mission (2000) Available at: NASA Earth Explorer, http://earthexplorer.usgs.gov/ (accessed 12 January 2013).

Sidhu, M.S. and Singh, G. (2010) A study on staggered public procurement of wheat in Punjab. *Agricultural Economics Research Review* 23: 325–334.

Simon, H.A. (1962) The architecture of complexity. *Proceedings of the American Philosophical Society* 106: 467–482.

Singh, S. and Mittal, J.P. (1992) *Energy in Production Agriculture*, New Delhi: Mittal Publications.

Soddy, F. (1926) *Wealth, Virtual Wealth and Debt*, London: George Allen & Unwin.

Solow, R.M. (1974) The economics of resources or the resources of economics. *American Economic Review* 64 (2): 1–14.

Sorman, A.H. (2011) The energetic metabolism of societies. Ph.D. dissertation, Institute of Environmental Science and Technology (ICTA), Universitat Autònoma de Barcelona, Bellaterra, Spain.

SSA (Statistics South Africa) (2001) *A Survey of Time Use*. Available at: http://unstats.un.org/unsd/demographic/sconcerns/tuse/Country/SouthAfrica/sourcezaf00c.pdf (accessed 19 March 2013).

SSA (Statistics South Africa) (2009a) *Labour Force Survey, Historical Revision, September Series – September 2001 to September 2007*. Available at: http://www.statssa.gov.za/

Publications/P0210/P0210September2000,2001,2002,2003,2004,2005,2006,2007.pdf (accessed 19 March 2013).

SSA (Statistics South Africa) (2009b) *Mining Industry 2009*, Report No. 20-01-02. Available at: http://www.statssa.gov.za/publications/Report-20-01-02/Report-20-01-022009.pdf (accessed 19 March 2013).

SSA (Statistics South Africa) (2012a) *Census 2011*, Statistical release P0301.4. Available at: http://www.statssa.gov.za/publications/P03014/P030142011.pdf (accessed 19 March 2013).

SSA (Statistics South Africa) (2012b) *Labour Market Dynamics in South Africa, 2011.* Available at: http://www.statssa.gov.za/Publications/Report-02-11-02/Report-02-11-022011.pdf (accessed 19 March 2013).

SSA (Statistics South Africa) (2012c) *Electricity, Gas and Water Supply 2010*, Report No. 41-01-02. Available at: http://www.statssa.gov.za/publications/Report-41-01-02/Report-41-01-022010.pdf (accessed 19 March 2013).

SSA (Statistics South Africa) (2012d) *Gross Domestic Product: Annual Estimates 2002–2011, Regional Estimates 2002–2011, Third Quarter 2012.* Available at: http://www.statssa.gov.za/publications/P0441/P04413rdQuarter2012.pdf (accessed 19 March 2013).

SSA (Statistics South Africa) (2012e) *Tourism Satellite Account for South Africa: Provisional 2010*, Report No. 04-05-07. Available at: http://www.statssa.gov.za/publications/Report-04-05-07/Report-04-05-072010.pdf (accessed 19 March 2013).

SSA (Statistics South Africa) (2012f) *Transport and Storage Industry 2010*, Report No. 71-02-01. Available at: http://www.statssa.gov.za/publications/Report-71-02-01/Report-71-02-012010.pdf (accessed 19 March 2013).

Statistics Mauritius, Government of the Republic of Mauritius (2011) *Energy and Water Statistics 2010–2011.* Available at: http://statsmauritius.gov.mu/English/Pages/Energy-and-Water-Statistics---2011--.aspx (accessed 4 November 2013).

Tainter, J.A. (1988) *The Collapse of Complex Societies*, Cambridge: Cambridge University Press.

Tainter, J.A. (2003) A framework for sustainability. *World Futures* 59: 213–223.

Torresol Energy (2011) *Gemasolar Power Plant.* Available at: http://www.torresolenergy.com/TORRESOL/gemasolar-plant/en (accessed 22 March 2013).

Tsuchida, A. and Murota, T. (1987) Fundamentals in the entropy theory of ecocycle and human economy, in G. Pillet and T. Murota (eds), *Environmental Economics: The Analysis of a Major Interface* (pp. 11–35), Geneva: Roland Leimgruber.

Turner, B.L., Lambin, E.F. and Reenberg, A. (2007) The emergence of land change science for global environmental change and sustainability. *Proceedings of the National Academy of Sciences of the United States of America* 104: 20666–20671.

Turner, M.G. (2005) Landscape ecology in North America: Past, present, and future. *Ecology* 86: 1967–1974.

UK National Ecosystem Assessment (2011) *The UK National Ecosystem Assessment Technical Report*, Cambridge: UNEP-WCMC.

Ulanowicz, R.E. (1979) Complexity, stability and self-organization in natural communities. *Oecologia* (Berlin) 43: 295–298.

Ulanowicz, R.E. (1986) *Growth and Development: Ecosystem Phenomenology*, New York: Springer-Verlag.

Ulanowicz, R.E. (1995) Ecosystem integrity: A causal necessity, in L. Westra and J. Lemons (eds), *Perspectives on Ecological Integrity* (pp. 77–87), Dordrecht: Kluwer Academic Publishers.

Ulanowicz, R.E. (1997) *Ecology: The Ascendent Perspective*, New York: Columbia University Press.

Ulanowicz, R.E. (2004) On the nature of ecodynamics. *Ecological Complexity* 1: 341–354.

UNDP (2013) *Human Development Index (HDI)*. Available at: http://hdr.undp.org/en/statistics/hdi/ (accessed July 2013).

UNFCCC (United Nations Framework Convention on Climate Change) (2012) *Project 7841: Bokpoort CSP (Concentrating Solar Power) Project, South Africa*. Available at: http://cdm.unfccc.int/Projects/DB/CarbonCheck_Cert1350990641.93/view (accessed 22 March 2013).

Vogelmann, J.E., Howard, S.M., Yang, L., Larson, C.R., Wylie, B.K. *et al.* (2001) Completion of the 1990s National Land Cover Dataset for the conterminous United States from Landsat Thematic Mapper data and ancillary data sources. *Photogrammetric Engineering and Remote Sensing* 67: 650–662.

Walker, D.A. and Walker, M.D. (1991) History and pattern of disturbance in Alaskan Arctic terrestrial ecosystems: A hierarchical approach to analyzing landscape change. *Journal of Applied Ecology* 28: 244–276.

Waltner-Toews, D., Kay, J.J. and Lister, N.M.E. (2008) *The Ecosystem Approach: Complexity, Uncertainty, and Managing for Sustainability*, New York: Columbia University Press.

WB (World Bank) (reporting year 2009) *Statistics on Electric Power Consumption (kWh) in South Africa*. Available at: http://data.worldbank.org/indicator/EG.USE.ELEC.KH (accessed 19 March 2013).

WB (World Bank) (2013) *World Data Bank: Development Indicators*. Available at: http://databank.worldbank.org/data/home.aspx (accessed 29 March 2013).

White, L.A. (1943) Energy and evolution of culture. *American Anthropologist* 14: 335–356.

White, L.A. (1949) *The Science of Culture: A Study of Man and Civilization*, New York: Farrar, Straus and Company.

Whyte, L.L., Wilson, A.G. and Wilson, D. (eds) (1969) *Hierarchical Structures*, New York: Elsevier.

Young, O.R., Berkhout, F., Gallopin, G.C., Janssen, M.A., Ostrom, E. *et al.* (2006) The globalization of socio-ecological systems: An agenda for scientific research. *Global Environmental Change* 16 (3): 304–316.

Zampella, R.A., Brunnell, J.F., Laidig, K.J. and Procopio, N.A. (2006) Using multiple indicators to evaluate the ecological integrity of a coastal plain stream system. *Ecological Indicators* 6: 644–663.

Zipf, G.K. (1941) *National Unity and Disunity: The Nation as a Biosocial Organism*, Bloomington, IN: Principia Press.

Zipf, G.K. (1949) *Human Behaviour and the Principle of Least Effort: An Introduction to Human Ecology*, Cambridge, MA: Addison-Wesley.

Index